AF576987

New Hampshire Notables

New Hampshire Notables

Presenting Biographical Sketches of Men and Women who have helped shape the Character of the Granite State

By Charles Brereton

Published for the
New Hampshire Historical Society
by
Peter E. Randall Publisher

Portsmouth

1986

Printed in the United States of America

New Hampshire Historical Society
30 Park Street, Concord, NH 03301

Peter E. Randall Publisher
Box 4726, Portsmouth, NH 03801

Library of Congress Cataloging-in-Publication Data

New Hampshire notables.

Includes index.
1. New Hampshire--Biography. I. Brereton, Charles.
CT248.N48 1986 920' .0742 86-24854
ISBN 0-914339-11-7

Introduction

THE 1986 EDITION of *New Hampshire Notables* is part of a rich, cultural tradition. Since the American Revolution, Americans have been obsessed with recording, not just the history of the various states, but biographical information about the people who gave shape to those states. New Hampshire has not been remiss in this endeavor. It seems each generation of New Hampshire historians has taken at least one stab at compiling, recording and publishing biographical information pertaining to its "notables."

Since incorporation in 1823, the New Hampshire Historical Society has been a willing partner in this effort. The Historical Society is a non-profit, membership organization dedicated to "investigating, collecting, preserving and interpreting whatever may relate to New Hampshire and its people." Our sponsorship of the 1986 edition of *New Hampshire Notables* gives us the unique opportunity to both record and preserve a significant piece of New Hampshire history. It was a pleasure for us at the Historical Society to have worked with Charles Brereton, Peter Randall and the New Hampshire Charitable Fund in keeping a noble historical tradition alive.

New Hampshire Notables is designed as a reference book; it contains a great deal of information in readily-accessible form. Businessmen, civic leaders, professionals, the media and others will find this to be a very handy book. Yet future generations will enjoy it as well. Like its predecessors, the 1986 edition of *New Hampshire Notables* will have a long life--to be mined time and again for rare and useful information.

And like its predecessors, this latest edition of "notables" may also be regarded as a tribute. Most of the people featured in this volume have given time, money and expertise to a wide range of community-based and statewide organizations. In so doing, they have made New Hampshire a much better place. We hope that future generations will "catch" the public spirit of our Granite State notables.

R. Stuart Wallace
Director, New Hampshire
Historical Society

Foreword

HENRY H. METCALF, A CONCORD JOURNALIST, was the first intrepid New Hampshire editor to assemble biographical sketches of fellow Granite Staters who he then called "notable." He cast a large net in 1919, listing 1,000 worthies. That act of sagacity increased the size of the market for his book, reduced the volume of angry letters after publication and enabled him to include himself among the noteworthy.

Metcalf disclaimed any intentions of publishing a Who's Who of New Hampshire. He said persons included were merely representative of New Hampshire men and women, native or resident. However, he did compare the organization of the book to a recent Who's Who, and his subtitle said it was about persons "prominent in public, professional, business, educational, fraternal or benevolent work."

Whether Metcalf or his emulators who published similar compilations in 1932 and 1955 succeeded in dispelling a hint of elitism, the books make for fascinating glimpses into the history and values of the periods. The persons chosen for listing, the happenings and associations they were encouraged to list--even their names--all enrich our understanding of the times in which they lived.

Take the names. In the 1919 book, *One Thousand New Hampshire Notables*, there are names that conjure images of an agrarian, God-fearing era when our nation was in its infancy. Consider Jabez Stevens, Amasa Saltus, Solon I. Bailey, Zoheth Sparrow Freeman, Andoniram Hopkins, Orison Sargent, Irad Keeler, Dillwyn Rollins, Lucia True Ames Mead.

Connections with the nation's founding were important, and Metcalf's notables invoked that heritage.

Zoheth Sparrow Freeman, born in Hyannis, Mass., and educated in Concord public schools, went on to become a banker in New York City after learning the business in Concord. His biography explains that he was "tenth generation from Edmund Freeman...chief founder of Sandwich, Mass., the first town on Cape Cod; and eighth in descent from Major and Judge John Freeman of Sandwich, who married Mercy, dau. of Gov. Thomas Prence and granddaughter of William Brewster of the Mayflower."

William Spooner Huntington identified himself as "seventh in descent from Christopher Huntington, the first male child b. in Norwich, Conn. (1660), who was grandson of Simon Huntington, the Puritan immigrant." Similar references to seventeenth century forebears abound in the book. They don't strike a contemporary reader as posturing. Within one's family, oral anecdotes could easily reach back into the 18th century. Vestiges of 17th and 18th century New England abounded in the state's buildings, boats, roads, furniture and religions. A land of farms, travel by coach, and hand-made goods was not remote to those in Metcalf's book.

It must be said that the 1919 notables tended to be lawyers, educators, bankers, public office holders, physicians and male. Concord and Manchester residents were disproportionately represented. And, journalist Metcalf was generous to his fellow journalists. Women listed usually were married to prominent husbands, and the description of preference in that era was "clubwoman."

Descriptions recall Victorian propriety. One worthy was a "statesman." Another characterized himself as a "banker, traveler, author, lecturer." Though one notable was a "traveling salesman," another was a more proper "commercial traveler." Marilla Ricker of Dover, the first woman admitted to the N.H. Bar (in 1882), was a "lawyer, author, humanitarian."

But there also was the notable who was director of the Corset Manufacturers Association of the U.S. and one who listed among his memberships the N.E. Fat Men's Club. Clubs and fraternal organizations were important, and 1919's men belonged to many. Throughout the book are references to the A.F. & A.M., Wonolancet Club, Derryfield Club, I.O.O.F., Knights of Columbus, Greek societies and fraternities, local Granges and historical societies. Women did social work.

Strong political convictions burst through the dry descriptions of allegiances. Harlan Pearson "attends the Universalist church; votes the Republican ticket." George Amos Parker was a "Congregationalist; Republican ('born and bred')." "Dr. Frederick Wallace Abbott was a "Freethinker; Democrat."

The 1919 book has one iron founder; one musical comedian; but one liveryman; one Medal of Honor winner (Maj. Gen. Leonard Wood, "for distinguished conduct in the campaign against the Apaches"); and numerous biographies that evoke admiration for the accomplishments of native or adopted sons and daughters.

Lucy Nettie Fletcher died of meningitis the year before and was buried in France with full military honors. She was the first nurse in Gen. Pershing's Army to die. She was interred in the officer's cemetery. Solon Bailey sited Harvard's observatory in Peru and ran it for 11 years. William Clough invented the GEM paperclip and the wire corkscrew. New Hampshire produced men who were editors and publishers of many out-of-state newspapers, including the *Providence Journal* and the *Boston Traveler*, and two who became vice presidents of the Associated Press. John Runnells became president of the Pullman Company, which employed more than 20,000 people; he was the great-grandson of Ralph Farnham, the last survivor of the battle of Bunker Hill, who died at age 105 in 1860.

And then there was a brief entry for a Franconia resident, Robert Frost. He said he had taught at Pinkerton Academy in Derry and the N.H. State Normal School in Plymouth. Prior to that, he had "engaged in agriculture" in Derry.

The 1932 *New Hampshire Notables* was published by The Concord Press and edited by its president, George William Conway. He assembled biographies of 474 notables ("noteworthy for excellence, quality, merit or high rank or standing--distinguished, prominent," according to one dictionary definition; also: "capable of being noted"). Having cut the ranks in half since Metcalf's volume, Conway discretely omitted the editor's identity.

Conway standardized and shortened the biographies and restricted comment to occupations, affiliations, awards and vital statistics. Concord and Manchester residents appear to have been favored. The volume has a more serious tone about it and there is a monochromatic nature to its contents. Gone are most of the farmers, all of the traveling salesmen. The aim of the book, according to Conway, was to continue the enterprise begun by Henry Metcalf, featuring active and prominent New Hampshire men and women who were living.

What were the standards for selection? Conway is silent on the matter, but a reading of the book suggests it helped to be in public service or in business. However, unlike the earlier book, legislative service alone did not qualify one for inclusion. It was important to be male, Republican, a Christian, a Mason and to have attended Phillips Exeter, Phillips Andover, Dartmouth or Harvard. School ties counted; education was valued. Teachers, preachers and lawyers seem to predominate along with business leaders. Stiff collars and Anglo Saxon and Celtic names abound. The book is solid with accounts of outstanding accomplishment.

We learn that Arthur Lowe, president of the Amoskeag Manufacturing Company, held important posts, belonged to numerous social clubs and planted 500,000 trees in Rindge. Anne Skinner Worthern, her maiden surname, became for 22 years a prominent dentist in Massachusetts after attending Tufts. When she was 43, she married John Randall Worthern who died five weeks later. Fifteen years later she moved to Concord and married John H. Worthern, an equally prominent N.H. dentist active in the same regional dental societies.

Ancestry still counted. Thomas Varick, a Manchester merchant, detailed his links to a Revolutionary Army captain, Richard Varick, in greater detail than his own accomplishments, which included membership in the Society of Cincinnati and two years as catcher of the Phillips Exeter baseball team.

Dr. Charlotte Stewartson Smith of Manchester was a descendant of Thomas Besbedge, who sailed from Sandwich, England and landed at Scituate, Mass., harbor in 1634.

And, one was not forgotten if one moved away. Dartmouth graduate Frank Pierce Hill, Concord born, left the state to serve as a librarian in Lowell, Mass., New Jersey, Salem, Mass., Newark, N.J., and Brooklyn, N.Y., married a Lowell woman and was residing in Winchester, Mass., in 1932. He was still remembered 51 years after leaving the state.

Alice Whittemore Upton Pearmain, born in East Jaffrey and graduated from Wellesley, had married and lived an active life in Massachusetts for 46 years. The inclusion of their biographies and others who had left the state many years before suggests that New Englanders had become more mobile. Wide-ranging networks of acquaintances, based on hometown and school friendships, changed a New Hampshire that in 1919 still had a parochial character.

In the 1932 *Notables* women were not called "clubwomen." They were doctors, dentists, businesswomen and educators. They seem to have attended Wellesley College, Vassar and Smith.

Another feature of the 1932 book is that, in contrast to the 1919 group, many prominent people were born outside New Hampshire and came to this state to make their mark. Among them were Gov. John Winant; United States Senator Styles Bridges; former Gov. Robert P. Bass; and physician and mental health specialist Charles H. Dolloff.

Whether sensing that the Metcalf formula was highly personal and idosyncratic or responding to a post-war spirit of egalitarianism, the editors of the 1955 edition of *New Hampshire Notables* introduced a diversity of people not present in the two earlier editions.

Co-editors George Conway, of Concord Press, and journalist Stephen Winship enlisted five knowledgable, long-time residents of the state to select entries from nominations that came from all segments of the state and society. Selectors' identities were concealed and a conscious effort was made to expand the scope of the book. These sketches were not just of friends and close acquaintances who were prominent statewide. The 1955 editors sought to include "men and women who have helped shape the character of New Hampshire and their communities."

The editors likened the book to "a yearbook--a book of this period...(people) representative of the many elements of life in modern New Hampshire. All are residents."

They placed sketches of the chief elective officeholders at the beginning, thereby getting them in the book but leaving to history a determination of their notability.

"Clubwoman" yielded to "housewife." Narrative accounts of ancestral glory were excised, but free reign was permitted for the listing of club memberships, directorships, awards, associations and affiliations. One notable, a vigorous joiner, included membership in the National Geographic Society and the Old Guard State Fencibles. One notable belonged to the Ineffable Lodge of Perfection.

Artists, writers, sculptors and musicians pepper the ranks of the 553 notables in this edition. The locus of attention shifted away from the businessmen and club officers of Concord and Manchester and embraced Berlin and Lebanon. There were fewer Masons. Jews appear. And women populate the book on their own merits, not simply as wives of husbands with longer citations. They present a formidable array of accomplishments in medicine, business, education and in the arts.

There are war heroes, Frank D. Merrill and Edward H. Brooks; sports greats, Red Rolfe, Doug Everett, Walter Prager and Sel Hanna; outdoorsmen like Joseph Brooks Dodge; accomplished artists like Paul Sample, Nora Unwin, Tasha Tudor and Maxfield Parrish. There were photographic great Winston H. Pote, writers Elizabeth Yates McGreal and Carolyn Sherwin Bailey Hill and editor Robb Sagendorph.

There are heavyweight businessmen, educators, diplomats and attorneys too, at a time when New Hampshire was moving with confidence far away from its rural and agrarian roots.

What lingers from a reading of this 30-year-old list of notables is a sense of vitality, diversity and confidence. The interlocking directorships and shared educational backgrounds persist. Education counts and so do shared interests. Dartmouth, Harvard,

Phillips Exeter, St. Paul's appear commonly, especially in the backgrounds of financial, legal and business leaders.

One is intrigued at the directorships and club memberships shared by the super prominent--the Brown Company, B&M Railroad, Newcomen Society, the Union and Algonquin Clubs in Boston, Harvard Clubs in Boston and New York, the Golden Rule Farm in Tilton, the Tobique Salmon Club in New Brunswick. The book is a study of changing circles of shared associations, different from and slightly less circumscribed than in earlier *Notables*.

One also becomes aware of a nucleus of wealthy, well-schooled and accomplished people in the Monadnock region of New Hampshire who have begun to shift their attention and residences from Boston and elsewhere to the Granite State. A longtime Boston orientation in Southern New Hampshire is especially apparent in this book.

There are a few farmers and a lawyer who is a poet, but one senses that 1955 was a serious time, a time when people tended to business and educational institutions served their needs. People in the book were capable and sober. They were perhaps more multi-dimensional than those in previous compilations and we see recognition of more varied pursuits.

As with the two previous *Notables*, things both laudable and odd come into clearer focus with the passage of the years. The books capture the moment and that is their great value, a value that grows with time.

The present edition of *New Hampshire Notables* sketches the lives of 422 individuals selected by a nominating committee formulated by author Charles Brereton. Brereton, a resident of the state for almost 20 years, writes about politics and public affairs.

This edition contains a far higher percentage of women (20 percent) than the previous books and the large number of photographs is noteworthy as well. They add a dimension to this publication others lacked. Also different, and useful to social archeologists, is the extensive dating of people's involvement in various activities.

The readers and researchers who seek clues to the nature of the Granite State in the mid-1980s have in this permanent record a guide to the era, the fourth such guide in this century.

George Wilson
Publisher, Concord Monitor

Preface

DURING THE PREPARATION of this edition of *New Hampshire Notables* the question was frequently asked as to what procedure was being utilized to select individuals for inclusion in this publication.

An extensive list of people involved in the arts, banking, business, communications, education, environmental protection, government, law, manufacturing, medicine, religion, social services and other professions and occupations was compiled.

These names were then submitted to a nominating committee which was comprised of five individuals.

In order to be selected as a Notable it was necessary to receive the endorsement of at least three members of the nominating committee. Five different files of names were provided to the nominating committee and almost 4,000 names were evaluated. In order to ensure a range of input from various regions of the state and a variety of professions, the nominating committee's composition was changed at each stage and only one person served during the entire five phases of selection.

The biographies are based on information the Notables submitted after receiving a questionnaire and they are organized in a somewhat standard fashion. Following the listing of the Notable's primary profession, business or occupation is his or her place and date of birth and first and last names of parents, with the mother's maiden name in parentheses.

After this information are the name, location and year of high school or preparatory school graduation, and the name of college or university with degree and year received. If no degree was granted, the years of college or university attendance are listed.

Military service includes the branch of military, year of entry and discharge, and rank at time of discharge. With only a few exceptions this does not include reserve duty, just active service.

The positions held in one's profession, business or occupation follows and the next section includes business associations, political service, and community service, all with emphasis on longterm and current activities.

In the questionnaire the people nominated were asked to provide information concerning any literary works of note, artistic endeavors or awards, as well as any honors, awards or noteworthy accomplishments.

If just a small portion of such information submitted had been included, the length of this book would have been much greater, so it was decided to include in this section just the number of honorary degrees and number of books published, with an occasional reference to the title and year of publication of one or two books in most cases.

In the section concerning marriage, the first and last name of the Notable's spouse is listed with wife's maiden name in parentheses, along with the date of marriage. Next follows the first names of any children and their dates of birth. There are also some cases when a Notable did not wish to include information on a marriage, and there is an infrequent use of St. ch. for stepchildren and M. for marriage if it was determined this was necessary for clarity.

Each biography concludes with religious preference and then home address, which does not necessarily coincide with the business or mailing address, although there are cases when this information is provided rather than home address.

In expressing my appreciation to those who helped make this book possible, I would like to list the names of those who served on the nominating committee. Since this group must remain anonymous, that is not possible, but these individuals must know of my gratitude for their many hours of work reviewing the files of names they received.

This book was conceived in early 1980 and had as my initial collaborator Harlan Logan of Meriden. Mr. Logan had to withdraw from this enterprise in late 1980 due to health and family considerations, but I am most thankful for his initial support of this undertaking.

The assistance of Richard Upton, George Wilson and Sally Helms, all of Concord; Ralph McIninch of Manchester; and Stephen Winship of Hopkinton was invaluable, as was the assistance of the three people who labored to fashion the publishing plan: William Hart Jr., former president of the New Hampshire Charitable Fund; R. Stuart Wallace, director of the New Hampshire Historical Society; and Peter Randall, the publisher.

This book's publication could have been realized only with the cooperation of the Notables and they should feel some satisfaction that their presence in the fourth edition of *New Hampshire Notables* this century is a confirmation by others that their accomplishments and contributions to New Hampshire's unique way of life have been noticed by others.

I would also like to express my deep appreciation to David Putnam of Keene, for without the assistance of the Putnam Revolving Loan Fund this book probably would never have reached fruition.

Charles Brereton
Concord, New Hampshire
June 9, 1986

Joseph John Acorace

Finance director, Manchester. Lynn, Mass., Nov. 29, 1935, Dominic and Anna (Calabro) Acorace. Bishop Bradley High School, Manchester, 1953, Univ. of N.H., B.A., 1960, Boston College, M.B.A., 1970. U.S. Naval Reserve, 1955-57, hospitalman 1st cl. Medical technician, Elliot Hospital, Manchester, 1957-58, production manager, purchasing agent, Jodi Shoe Co., Derry, 1960-69, city auditor, Manchester, 1969-72, finance director, Manchester, 1972--. Trustee, Catholic Medical Center, 1975--, chairman, 1980-83; chairman, N.H. Retirement System, 1977-80, trustee, Notre Dame Hospital, 1972-76, N.H. Right to Life Committee, 1970-80, alderman, Manchester, 1966-70, N.H. Executive Council, 1969-71, chairman, Youth Development Center, 1969-70, director, St. Mary's Bank, 1983--, president, N.H. Government Finance Officers Association, 1985--, president, N.E. States Government Finance Officers Association, 1985--, director, Greater Manchester Development Corp., 1983--, treasurer, 1985--. Carol (Savoy), Feb. 16, 1957. Anthony, Sept. 11, 1965, Elena, Dec. 7, 1966. Catholic. 410 Bremer St., Manchester.

Shirley Gray Adamovich

Commissioner, Department of Libraries, Arts and Historical Resources. Pepperill, Mass., May 8, 1927, Willard and Carrie (Shattuck) Gray. Winthrop (Mass.) High School, 1945, Univ. of N.H., B.A., 1954, Simmons College, M.L.S., 1955. U.S. Air Force, 1949-53, staff sgt. Coordinator, North Country Libraries Film Cooperative, 1966-70, coordinator, N.H. Public Library Techniques Program, 1969-71, director, Manchester Interlibrary Cooperative, 1970-72, director, Library Technology Program, Merrimack Valley branch, Univ. System of N.H., 1972-75, library director, Merrimack Valley, 1973-75, assistant state librarian, N.H. State Library, 1979-81, state librarian, 1981-85, commissioner, Department of Libraries, Arts and Historical Resources, 1985--. Instructor, Merrimack Valley branch, Univ. System of N.H., 1969-79, Nathaniel Hawthorne College, 1963-66, director, N.E. Library Board, 1981-82, chairman, N.H. Automated Information Systems Board, 1982--, chairman, Advisory Committee to the Law Library, 1982--. Author, *A Reader in Library Technology*, 1975. Frank Adamovich, Aug. 31, 1960. Carrie, Jan. 17, 1963, Elizabeth, Sept. 21, 1967. Unitarian. 14 Thompson Ln., Durham.

Benjamin Clark Adams

Commissioner, Department of Employment Security, retired. Manchester, N.H., July 14, 1915, Benjamin F. and Josephine (Clark) Adams. Pinkerton Academy, Derry, 1931, Tabor Academy, 1931-32, Bowdoin College, 1932-33, U.S. Naval Academy, B.S., 1938. U.S. Navy, 1938-40, ensign. Vice president, general manager, Builders Lumber and Supply Corp., Londonderry, 1941-60, commissioner, Department of Employment Security, 1960-84. N.H. Senate, 1953-60, selectman, Derry, 1968-71, Derry Planning Board, 1972-81. Betty (Iler), Feb. 25, 1939. Judith, Dec. 14, 1941, Jean, Feb. 14, 1943, Janice, April 28, 1944, John, July 5, 1947, Jill, Dec. 29, 1948. Ferne (Nickerson), Nov. 20, 1959. Protestant. Floyd Rd., Derry.

Sherman Adams

Sherman Adams

Former governor of New Hampshire. East Dover, Vt., Jan. 8, 1899, Clyde and Winnie (Sherman) Adams. Hope High School, Providence, R.I., 1916, Dartmouth College, A.B., 1920. U.S. Marine Corps, 1918, pvt.. Treasurer, Black River Lumber Co., Healdville, Vt., 1921-23, assistant timberland manager, Parker Young Co., Lincoln, 1923-28, manager, 1928-45; U.S. Congress, Second District, 1945-47, governor, N.H., 1949-53, chief of staff, Eisenhower presidential campaign, 1952, assistant, President Dwight D. Eisenhower, 1953-58, president, Loon Mountain Recreation Corp., 1966-79, chairman, 1980--. N.H. House of Rep., 1941-45, speaker, 1943-45; president, White Mountain Center for Music and Arts, 1962-67, chairman, Mount Washington Commission, 1971--, trustee, Linwood Medical Center, 1971--, president, Loon Realty Corp., 1968--, Lincoln Planning Board, 1960-64. Author, *First Hand Report* , 1961. Nine honorary degrees. Rachel (White), July 28, 1923 (dec. Dec. 16, 1979). Marion, March 24, 1924, Jean, May 17, 1925, Sarah, Jan. 4, 1928, Samuel, Jan. 26, 1937. Episcopal. Pollard Rd., Lincoln.

Lea Hutchinson Aeschliman

Commissioner, Public Utilities Commission. Lynn, Mass., May 15, 1943, Albert and Eleanor (Newhall) Hutchinson. Lynnfield (Mass.) High School, 1960, Smith College, B.A., 1964, Univ. of N.H., M.P.A., 1981. Investment administrator, Bankers Trust Co., N.Y.C., 1964-65, research analyst, Joint Economic Committee, U.S. Congress, 1965-68, N.H. House of Rep., 1976-82, commissioner, Public Utilities Commission, 1982--. Trustee, Portsmouth Public Library, 1969-75, president, Portsmouth League of Women Voters, 1971-72, Seacoast United Way, Seacoast YWCA, corporator, Portsmouth Hospital, member, N.H. Advisory Council on Libraries, 1978-80, National Association of Regulatory Utility Commissioners, 1982--, N.E. Conference of Public Utilities Commissioners, 1982--. Nicholas Aeschliman, 1965. Christopher, 1966, Matthew, 1972. Unitarian-Universalist. 24 Kensington Rd., Portsmouth.

Lea Hutchinson Aeschliman

Bradford Fullerton Alden

Bradford Fullerton Alden

Banker. Plymouth, Mass., Oct. 22, 1928, Frederick and Bertha (Bradford) Alden. Governor Dummer Academy, South Byfield, Mass., 1945, Boston Univ., B.S., 1950. U.S. Army, 1950-53, 1st lt. General clerical, First National Bank, Concord, 1953-57, assistant cashier, First National Bank, Portsmouth, 1957-62, vice president, Kingston (Pa.) National Bank, 1962-64, assistant to the president, National Bank, Lebanon, 1964-68, president, 1968-74; president, Indian Head Bank, Exeter, 1974-80, senior vice president, Indian Head Banks Inc., 1976--, executive vice president, Indian Head National Bank, 1982-86, chairman, chief executive officer, Indian Head Bank and Trust Co., Portsmouth, 1980-86. President, N.H. Bankers Association, 1975, director, N.H. Business Development Corp., 1974-80, Havenwood Retirement Community, 1984--. Sylvia (Jacobs), Dec. 23, 1950. Dianne, Aug. 8, 1952, Janet, Oct. 4, 1954, Judith, Oct. 4, 1954, Peter, Dec. 5, 1959. Congregational. 35 Harborview Dr., Rye.

Kenneth David Andler

Attorney, bank president, retired. Newport, N.H., March 24, 1904, Louis and Emma (Byars) Andler. Newport High School, 1921, Dartmouth College, A.B., 1926. Attorney, Newport, 1932-71. Trustee, Newport Savings Bank, 1944-70, director, First National Bank of Newport, 1947-75, president, 1960-68, chairman, 1968-70; director, First Citizens National Bank, 1975-77, trustee, Richards Free Library, former trustee, president, Newport Charitable Association. Author of three books, contributor to a number of periodicals, landscape painter. Dolores (McGown), Aug. 15, 1931. Caroline, Feb. 9, 1938. United Methodist. 8 Whitney Ave., Newport.

Kenneth David Andler

Neal Davis Andrew Jr.

Neal Davis Andrew Jr.

Deputy commissioner, Department of Education, retired. Canaan, N.H., Sept. 11, 1925, Neal and Blanche (Dustin) Andrew. Canaan High School, 1943, Univ. of N.H., B.S., 1951, M.Agr.Ed., 1959, Ohio State Univ., Ph.D., 1974. U.S. Army, 1943-46, cpl. Teacher, New Boston High School, 1950-55, principal, New Boston, 1952-55, Department of Education, state director, agricultural education, 1955-66, acting director, distributive education, 1955-60, assistant chief, vocational education, 1966, chief, division of vocational-technical education, 1966-76, deputy commissioner, 1976-85. Director, National Association Future Farmers of America, 1962-65, N.H. Council on Economic Education, 1985, trustee, National Future Farmers of America Foundation, 1962-65, school board, Canterbury, 1959-64. Elizabeth (Williams), Sept. 11, 1948. Wallace, March 30, 1951, Serena, May 19, 1953, Warren, May 12, 1957, Abbie, July 9, 1960. Protestant. 108 Hopkinton Rd., Concord.

John Boardman Andrews

Executive director, New Hampshire Municipal Association. Bridgton, Maine, July 14, 1946, Harold and Thelma (Embich) Andrews. Yarmouth (Maine) High School, 1964, Univ. of So. Maine, B.A., 1968, Univ. of Maine School of Law, J.D., 1971. Assistant to city manager, Portland, 1966-68, assistant executive director, Maine Municipal Association, 1971-75, executive director, N.H. Municipal Association, 1975--. Member, Governor's Advisory Council on Growth, 1979-81, International City Management Association, 1975--, American Society of Association Executives, 1975--, national panel of construction arbitrators, American Arbitration Association, 1975--, director, N.E. Muncipal Center, 1975-83, National League of Cities, 1982-84, member, Public Employee Labor Relations Board, 1986--. Sharon (Bagley), Aug. 16, 1969. Elizabeth, Nov. 17, 1972, John, Dec. 30, 1974, Matthew, Sept. 27, 1978. Catholic. 122 South St., Concord.

John Boardman Andrews

Maurice Louis Arel

Maurice Louis Arel

Former mayor of Nashua. Nashua, N.H., May 21, 1937, Maurice and Dolores (Hogue) Arel. Nashua High School, 1955, St. Anselm College, B.A., 1959, St. John's Univ., M.S., 1961. Sprague Electric Co., 1961-67, Sanders Associates, 1967-77, mayor, Nashua, 1977-84, president, Pennichuck Water Works Inc., 1984--. Alderman, Nashua, 1964-73, president, 1968-71; advisory commission, N.H. Department of Resources and Economic Development, 1965-73, trustee, St. Anselm College, 1977--, advisory board, Rivier College, 1973--, chairman, Nashua chapter, American Red Cross, 1977-78, president, Nashua Boys Club, 1976-78, treasurer, Nashua Chamber of Commerce, 1968-78, president 1972-74; executive committee, N.H. Municipal Association, 1978-84, president, 1982-83; director, Blue Cross and Blue Shield, 1985--, Indian Head National Bank, 1985--, N.H. Association of Commerce and Industry, 1984--. Joyce (Latvis), June 25, 1960. Jocelyn, June 26, 1963, Matthew, March 24, 1965, Timothy, March 29, 1967. Catholic. 10 Virginia Dr., Nashua.

Mary Molitor Atchison

Director, Division of Public Health, retired. Dubuque, Iowa, Dec. 11, 1905, Hugh and Julia (Molitor) Atchison. Dubuque High School, 1922, Univ. of Dubuque, B.A., 1928, Univ. of Iowa Medical School, M.D., 1931, Harvard Univ. School of Public Health, M.P.H., 1938. Director, Maternal and Child Health and Crippled Children's Services, 1938-42, deputy state health officer, 1942-57, acting state health officer, 1944-46, state health officer, 1957-58, deputy state health officer, 1958-62, director, Division of Public Health, 1962-72. Former consultant, Division of Public Health, Glencliff Home for the Elderly, Havenwood Retirement Community, member, Board of Registry in Medicine, 1939-72, State Council on Aging, 1962-72, Commission on the Status of Women, 1960-62. Methodist. 13 Carter St., Concord.

Mary Molitor Atchison

Paul Flagg Avery Jr.

Paul Flagg Avery Jr.

Management consultant. Boston, Mass., May 7, 1929, Paul and Roberta (Shailer) Avery. Belmont (Mass.) Hill School, 1947, Williams College, B.S., 1951. Drafting, estimating, engineering, sales, vice president of operations, Avery and Saul Co., Cambridge, Mass., 1953-63, president, P.F. Avery Co., Billerica, Mass., president, treasurer, C-E Avery, Newington, 1967-74, president, chief executive officer, CE-KSB Pump Co., Newington, 1974-82, management consultant, 1982--. General partner, Mine Falls hydro project, Nashua, 1985--, director, Seaward Construction, 1983--, board member, Strawbery Banke, 1974-78, sub chairman, Master Plan Committee, Kensington, 1979-80. Mary (Caskey), June 6, 1953. Fred, Jan. 23, 1955, Paul III, July 31, 1957, Christopher, Jan. 27, 1960. Protestant. Drinkwater Rd., Kensington.

Robert Allison Backus

Attorney. Goffstown, N.H., May 26, 1939, Richard and Harriet (Wright) Backus. Holderness School, 1957, Wesleyan Univ., B.A., 1961, Harvard Law School, J.D., 1964. Law clerk to U.S. Circuit Court Judge Peter Woodbury, 1964-65, MIT fellow, Africa, 1965-66, attorney, Manchester, 1966--. Publicity chairman, United Way of Greater Manchester, 1969-70, chairman, Continuing Legal Education Committee, N.H. Bar Association, 1974-75, executive committee, Manchester regional office, Child and Family Services, 1978-79, founder, board member, N.H. Energy Coalition, 1979-83, trustee, Holderness School, 1979--, director, advisory committee, Campaign for Ratepayers' Rights, 1983--, vice president, Hillsborough County, Society for the Protection of N.H. Forests, 1973--. Ann (Newell), June 28, 1964. Gillian, July 20, 1969, Bradford, Dec. 26, 1972. Unitarian. Back Mountain Rd., RFD 5, Goffstown.

Merwyn Bagan

Merwyn Bagan

Neurosurgeon. Philadelphia, Pa., Jan. 25, 1936, Frank and Shirley (Lindenbaum) Bagan. The Hill School, Pottstown, Pa., 1953, Dartmouth College, A.B., 1957, Boston Univ. School of Medicine, M.D., 1962, intern, Boston City Hospital, 1962-63. U.S. Public Health Service, 1963-65, lt. comdr. Clinical associate, National Institutes of Health, 1963-65, residency, neurological surgery, The Johns Hopkins Hospital, 1965-70, neurosurgeon, Concord Hospital, 1970--, president, medical staff, 1986--; neurosurgeon, Elliot Hospital, 1973--, Catholic Medical Center, 1977--. Adjunct assistant professor of clinical surgery, Dartmouth Medical School, 1981--, trustee, N.E. Neurosurgical Society, 1977-83, president, N.H. Medical Society, 1983, director, N.H. Joint Underwriting Association, 1977--, chairman, Healthsource Inc., 1985--, president, Healthsource N.H. Inc., 1985--, member, Medical Liabilities Commission, 1985--. Carol (Joseph), Nov. 14, 1964. Eric, Seth, Karin. 173 School St., Concord.

George Michael Bald

Economic development director, Rochester. Biddeford, Maine, Aug. 16, 1950, Joseph and Theresa (Sansoucy) Bald. Somersworth High School, 1968, Univ. of N.H., 1973-76. U.S. Navy, 1969-72, E-4. Machinist, Portsmouth Naval Shipyard, 1976-78, mayor, Somersworth, 1978-84, economic development director, Rochester, 1984--. Councilman, Somersworth, 1974-76, commissioner, N.H. Housing Commission, 1982, state chairman, Great American Smokeout, 1982--, director, Great Falls Development Corp., 1984--, United Way of Strafford County, 1985--, Franco-American Cultural Exchange Commission, 1983--, American Cancer Society, N.H. division, 1983--, Somersworth Children's Festival, 1981--. Candace (Small), Jan. 14, 1977. Casey, July 14, 1980. 2 Otis Rd., Somersworth.

Henry Ives Baldwin

Retired forester. Saranac Lake, N.Y., Aug. 23, 1896, Edward and Mary (Ives) Baldwin. Hotchkiss School, 1915, Yale Univ., B.A., 1919, M.F., 1922, Ph.D., 1931. U.S. Army Signal Corps, 1918-19, 2nd lt., U.S. Army Air Force, 1942-46, lt. col. Instructor, Saranac Lake High School, 1919-20, assistant to the dean, Yale Univ., 1922, chief, forest investigations, Brown Co., Berlin, 1924-32, research forester, N.H. Forestry Commission, 1933-62, consultant, State Planning Project, 1962-65, professor of botany, Franklin Pierce College, 1965-72, consulting forester, land surveyor, 1972-81. Trustee, Society for the Protection of N.H. Forests, 1966-72, consultant, Federal Reserve Bank, Boston, 1950, fellow, American Academy of Arts and Sciences, Society of American Foresters, American Association for the Advancement of Science, founder, Adirondack Mountain Club, 1916. Author of a number of books on forestry. Birgit (Sverdrup), Sept. 4, 1924. Barbara, March 7, 1927, Harriet, July 21, 1931, Edward, April 30, 1935, Gunnar, May 3, 1937. Protestant. Center Rd., Hillsboro.

Marilyn Austin Baldwin

Vice provost, Dartmouth College. Richmond, Ind., Nov. 10, 1935, Alfred and Esther (Stockinger) Austin. Richmond High School, 1953, Ind. Univ., B.S., 1957, Univ. of Mich., 1958-59, Rutgers Univ., M.A., 1960, Ph.D., 1963. Teacher, Bloomington (Ind.) High School, 1957-58, instructor, English, Augusta (Ga.) College, 1961-63, lecturer, English, Dartmouth College, 1967-71, adjunct professor, English, Dartmouth, 1972--, assistant, acting provost, 1971-72, assistant vice president of student affairs, 1972-77, associate dean, 1982-84, vice provost, 1984--. Coordinator, Women's Program, 1972-78, trustee, Colby-Sawyer College, 1974-80, Univ. System of N.H., 1980-84, member, Committee for the Concerns of Women in N.E. Colleges and Universities, 1973--, trustee, United Development Services, 1984--, panelist, N.H. Women in Higher Education Association, 1986--. David Baldwin, Aug. 10, 1957. Sarah, March 24, 1960, Rebecca, Aug. 29, 1965, Emily, July 27, 1968. Society of Friends. 2 Ridge Rd., Hanover.

John Joseph Ballentine

Book publisher. Didsbury, England, April 2, 1927, Joseph and Winifred (Knight) Ballentine. Brewster Academy, Wolfeboro, 1946, Syracuse Univ., A.B., 1950, Univ. of Minn., M.A., 1951. Executive director, building and development program, Brewster Academy, 1951-53, editorial page director, *Laconia Evening Citizen*, 1953-55, editor, *Somersworth Free Press*, 1955-67, owner, publisher, 1956-67; owner, N.H. Publishing Co., Somersworth, 1967--. Incorporator, Somersworth Savings Bank, 1969-72, Seacoast Savings Bank, 1974--, N.H. Charitable Fund, 1977-82, trustee, Brewster Academy, 1970-72, president, N.E. Weekly Press Association, 1965-66, co-founder, chairman, Somersworth Conservation Commission, 1969-73, president, Somersworth Historical Society, 1983-84, co-founder, Greater Somersworth Chamber of Commerce, 1958, president, 1959-60; N.H. House of Rep., Laconia, 1955-56. Pat (Morse), July 10, 1965. Episcopal. 14 Oak Ridge Dr., Somersworth.

Marilyn Austin Baldwin

James Sherman Barker

Banker, retired. Dorchester, Mass., June 9, 1911, Williston and Gertrude (Sherman) Barker. Roxbury Latin School, West Roxbury, Mass., 1928, Harvard Univ., A.B., 1932, Harvard Business School, M.B.A., 1934. Indian Head National Bank, 1935-52, assistant trust officer, 1938-45, trust officer, 1946-52; vice president, trust officer, Mechanicks National Bank, Concord, 1952-57, president, 1957-69; vice chairman, Bank of N.H., N.A., 1969-72, chairman, 1972; chairman, Indian Head National Bank, Concord, 1972-81, honorary director, 1982. Trustee, Merrimack County Savings Bank, 1953-69, Concord Hospital, 1961-78, president, N.H. Bankers Association, 1967-68, director, president, N.H. Charitable Fund, 1962-69, director, N.E. Telephone, 1965-80, Concord General Mutual Insurance Co., 1964--, John Swenson Granite Co., 1969-83, Richard D. Brew and Co., 1958-64. Barbara (Willard), April 27, 1940. James Jr., May 22, 1942, Alison, Oct. 6, 1944, Stephen, Feb. 28, 1948. Episcopal. 106 Hilltop Pl., New London.

Everett Raymond Barrows

Minister, retired. Haverhill, Mass., July 24, 1904, Theodore and Lillian (Currier) Barrows. Bucksport (Maine) Preparatory School, 1927, Boston Univ., B.S., 1931, Boston Univ. School of Theology, S.T.B., 1934. Ordained, April 9, 1933. Pastor, Methodist churches, Mass., 1931-48, associate minister, treasurer, N.H. Congregational-Christian Conference, 1948-61, conference minister, N.H. Conference of the United Church of Christ, 1962-74, minister emeritus, 1974--. Trustee, Bangor Theological Seminary, 1962-74, emeritus, 1974--; United Church of Christ Council on Mission Priorities, 1962-74, South Congregational Church, Concord, 1975-81, board of governors, Boston Seaman's Friend Society, 1968--, director, United Church of Christ Retirement Communities, Concord, 1975-81, life member, 1981--. Two honorary degrees. Anne (Fessenden), Aug. 27, 1929. Robert, Nov. 9, 1931, Richard, Jan. 11, 1937, Ruth, March 1, 1942. United Church of Christ. 28 Auburn St., Concord.

Everett Raymond Barrows

Charles Everett Barry

Charles Everett Barry

Former executive director, New Hampshire Fish and Game Department. Warren, N.H., Feb. 25, 1937, Everett and Sadie (Griffin) Barry. Dow Academy, Franconia, 1955, Plymouth Teachers College, B.Ed., 1959. N.H. Fish and Game Department, 1954-86, conservation officer trainee, officer, sergeant, executive director, 1978-86, investigator, Matson Associates, Ossipee, 1986--. Chairman, policy committee, Conn. River Atlantic Salmon Restoration Committee, 1981-86, member, law enforcement committee, International Association of Fish and Wildlife Agencies, 1981--, chairman, 1981-86; member, Water Supply and Pollution Control Commission, 1978-86, Merrimack River Policy Committee, 1978-86, Pesticides Control Board, 1978-86, Bulk Power Supply Site Evaluation Committee, 1981-86. Robert, Sept. 13, 1963, Amy, Sept. 16, 1968. Rebecca (Barnes), Dec. 29, 1983. Methodist. RR 1, Box 219, Benton Rd., North Haverhill.

Everhard Hendrik Bartelink

Engineer and physicist. Zutphen, Netherlands, June 13, 1904, Frederik and Anna (Wisselink) Bartelink. The Hague, 1923, Delft Univ., M.S., 1928, Munich Univ., Ph.D., 1936. Netherlands Telephone operations, The Hague and Amsterdam, 1929-36, General Electric Co., Schenectady, N.Y., 1937-43, Radiation Laboratory, MIT, 1943-46, chief radio engineer, General Telephone Corp., N.Y.C., 1946-49, assistant director of research, General Precision Laboratory, Pleasantville, N.Y., 1949-52, founder, president, Northeast Electronics Corp., Concord, 1953-74, telecommunications consulting, 1974--, president, Bartelink Enterprises Corp., 1974--. Member, White Mountain Environment Committee, 1968--, chairman, Appalachian Mountain Club, N.H. chapter, 1973-74, incorporator, N.H. Charitable Fund, 1976-85, trustee, Society for the Protection of N.H. Forests, 1978-84, chairman, 1984. Author, *Telephone Transmission Theory*, 1969, holder of 45 U.S. patents. Henriette (Bijnen), Nov. 10, 1933. Anna, Aug. 27, 1935, Johanna, Feb. 5, 1939, Elizabeth, Oct. 3, 1945. Protestant. 15 Ridge Rd., Concord.

Everhard Hendrik Bartelink

Carl Palmeter Barton

New Hampshire Liquor Commission. Haverhill, Mass., Dec. 31, 1916, Clifford and Bertha (Palmeter) Barton. Manchester Central High School, 1935, Hesser College, 1935-36. Ga. National Guard, 1943-45, pfc. N.H. Insurance Co., Manchester, 1936-82, assistant secretary, 1953-56, secretary, 1956-63, comptroller, 1960-63, vice president, comptroller, then executive vice president, 1963-73, president, 1973-77, chief executive officer, 1977-82, chairman, N.H. Insurance Group, 1979-82, executive vice president, director, American International Group, N.Y.C., 1977-82, commissioner, N.H. Liquor Commission, 1985--. Director, N.H. Insurance Co., 1963-85, Merchants National Bank, 1971-75, Amoskeag Industries, 1973-81, trustee, Notre Dame College, 1974-77, Governor's Management Review, 1981-82, former member, Tramway Safety Board. One honorary degree. Lance, Jan. 11, 1940. Ada (Brown), Jan. 15, 1954. Jon, June 4, 1955, Jill, Jan. 9, 1960. Protestant. Mountain Rd., Goffstown.

Perkins Bass

Former United States congressman, attorney. Walpole, Mass., Oct. 6, 1912, Robert and Edith (Bird) Bass. Milton (Mass.) Academy, 1930, Dartmouth College, A.B., 1934, Harvard Law School, LL.B., 1938. U.S. Army Air Force, 1942-45, maj. Attorney, Manchester, 1938-41, law clerk to U.S. First Circuit Court Judge Peter Woodbury, 1941-42, attorney, Manchester, 1945-55, U.S. Congress, Second District, 1955-63, attorney, Peterborough, 1963--. N.H. House of Rep., 1939-41, 47-49, N.H. Senate, 1949-51, president, 1949-51; Republican National Committeeman, 1964-68, selectman, Peterborough, 1972-75, National Advisory Committee on Oceans and Atmosphere, 1973-76, director, Bird Inc., 1946-83, trustee, N.H. Savings Bank, 1950-80. Two honorary degrees. Katharine (Jackson), June 7, 1941 (dec. Feb. 9, 1972). Alexander, Feb. 28, 1942, Katharine, Dec. 7, 1943, William, Dec. 20, 1949, Charles, Jan. 8, 1952, Roberta, Jan. 18, 1954. Rosaly (Riley), Sept. 30, 1973. Episcopal. Orchard Hill Farm, Peterborough.

Perkins Bass

Robert Perkins Bass Jr.

Robert Perkins Bass Jr.

Attorney. Peterborough, N.H., Sept. 23, 1923, Robert and Edith (Bird) Bass. Deerfield (Mass.) Academy, 1942, Harvard Univ., B.A., 1948, LL.B., 1951. U.S. Army, 1942-46, 1st lt. Central Intelligence Agency, 1951-54, attorney, Concord, 1955--. Chairman, Republican State Committee, 1968-71, Republican National Committeeman, 1972-80, director, Bird Inc., 1962--, Bank of N.H., 1981--, N.H. Charitable Fund, 1971-81, chairman, 1979-81; trustee, Franklin Pierce College, 1968-74, Society for the Protection of N.H. Forests, 1970-76, N.H. Symphony, 1981--, Currier Gallery, 1983--, member, American College of Probate Counsel, 1978--, board of overseers, Franklin Pierce Law Center, 1977--, trustee, N.E. Natural Resources Center, 1985--, member, N.H. Commission on the Arts, 1972-76, president, N.H. Council on World Affairs, 1958-62. Patricia (May), Sept. 10, 1955 (div. Jan. 23, 1986). Timothy, Jan. 28, 1958, Patricia, Aug. 10, 1960. Protestant. 125 North State St., Concord.

William Foster Batchelder

Associate justice, New Hampshire Supreme Court. Plymouth, N.H., Oct. 15, 1926, Lyman and Ella (Fleming) Batchelder. Plymouth High School, 1944, Univ. of N.H., B.A., 1949, Boston Univ. School of Law, J.D., 1952. Attorney, Plymouth, 1952-70, county attorney, Grafton County, 1959-65, associate justice, N.H. Superior Court, 1970-81, associate justice, N.H. Supreme Court, 1981--. Faculty, Franklin Pierce Law Center, 1979--, trustee, Squam Lakes Science Center, 1968-76, president, 1968-69; director, American Judicature Society, 1984--, fellow, American Bar Foundation, 1986--. Elizabeth (Hayward), July 9, 1955. Stephen, Sept. 23, 1956, Anne, May 26, 1958, Mary, April 25, 1960, Susan, July 11, 1961, Robert, March 16, 1963, David, Oct. 4, 1967. Fairgrounds Rd., Plymouth.

William Foster Batchelder

Joseph Andrew Baute

Joseph Andrew Baute

Chairman, chief executive officer, Markem Corporation. East Greenwich, R.I., Jan. 30, 1928, Joseph and Helen (Brueckner) Baute. Lockwood High School, Warwick, R.I., 1946, Dartmouth College, A.B., 1952, M.S., 1954. U.S. Marine Corps, 1946-48,50-51, platoon sgt. Markem Corp., manufacturing engineer, 1954, printing elements manager, 1956, new product development manager, 1958, manager of sales, 1961, manager of operations, 1966, vice president, chief operating officer, 1968, president, director, 1973, chief operating officer, 1977, chairman, chief executive officer, 1979--. Director, board chairman, N.E. Council for Economic Development, 1974-82, member, chairman, overseers, Thayer School of Engineering, Dartmouth, 1972-82, director, Federal Reserve Bank of Boston, 1981--, chairman, 1986--; Keene Clinic, 1982--, Houghton Mifflin Co., 1982--, Governor's Management Review, 1981-82, Keene Board of Education, 1958-71, chairman, 1967-68,71; N.H. Constitutional Convention, 1974. Susan, May 10, 1954, Alison, Dec. 24, 1955, Sarah, March 18, 1961, Deborah, Dec. 27, 1962, Joseph III, Nov. 21, 1963. Stephanie (Heselton), April 15, 1972. Tamarack, East Surry Rd., Keene.

Arthur Edward Bean Jr.

Associate justice, New Hampshire Superior Court. Concord, N.H., Nov. 11, 1918, Arthur and Beulah (Sargent) Bean. Concord High School, 1935, Univ. of N.H., class of 1940, Boston Univ. School of Law, LL.B., 1951. U.S. Army Air Force, 1940-47, lt. col. Assistant attorney general, N.H., 1951-57, attorney, Manchester, 1957-77, associate justice, N.H. Superior Court, 1977--. Member, chairman, N.H. Eminent Domain Commission, 1973-77, chairman, N.H. Personnel Commission, 1970-75, director, Londonderry Bank, 1972-77. Alice (Whipple), June 29, 1941. David, Dec. 13, 1942. Dorothy (Batchelder), Dec. 27, 1971. Protestant. 38 Juniper Dr., Bedford.

Emile Dorilas Beaulieu

Emile Dorilas Beaulieu

Former mayor, Manchester. Nashua, N.H., April 2, 1930, Emile J. and Albina (Claveau) Beaulieu. High school general education development, 1961. U.S. Air Force, 1951-52,60-61, sen. master sgt. Owner, president, Beaulieu's Floor Covering, Manchester, 1958-84, welfare commissioner, Manchester, 1974-81, mayor, Manchester, 1982-84, business administrator, settlement officer, N.H. Division of Welfare, 1984-85, vice president of development, Woodmaster Inc., Hooksett, 1985--. N.H. House of Rep., 1973-75, N.H. Constitutional Convention, 1974, president, Big Brother/Big Sister of Greater Manchester, 1963-73, former president, director, Easter Seal/Goodwill Industries of N.H., 1968-82, incorporator, director, Manchester Emergency Housing, 1979-81, trustee, Elliot Hospital, 1982-83, N.H. Symphony Orchestra, 1982-83, incorporator, Catholic Medical Center, 1982-85, executive committee, N.H. Municipal Association, 1982-83. Pauline (Leclerc), May 10, 1952. Diane, May 30, 1953, Jane, Oct. 23, 1954, Leonard, April 19, 1957, Susan, Sept. 16, 1959, Paul, July 21, 1963 (dec. Sept. 1984), Brenda, Sept. 8, 1969. Christian. 65 Hubbard St., Manchester.

John Angus Beckett

Professor, retired. Portland, Oreg., April 27, 1916, John and Agnes (Scott) Beckett. U.S. Grant High School, Portland, 1934, Univ. of Oreg., B.S., 1939, Harvard Business School, M.B.A., 1945. U.S. Army, 1942-45, 1st lt. Assistant professor, MIT, 1946-52, senior consultant, McKinsey and Co., San Francisco, 1952-54, treasurer, Spreckels Sugar Co., San Francisco, 1954-56, director, management services, Arthur Young and Co., Chicago, 1956-58, assistant director, U.S. Bureau of the Budget, 1958-60, administrative manager, Smith, Barney and Co., N.Y.C., 1960-62, Forbes professor of management, Univ. of N.H., 1962-81. N.H. House of Rep., 1971-75, chairman, Durham Budget Committee, 1974-76. Author of three books. One honorary degree. Elizabeth (De Busk), June 15, 1940. Ann, Jan. 2, 1944, Kathleen, March 17, 1948, J. Thomas, March 8, 1955. 55 Mill Pond Rd., Durham.

John Angus Beckett

Ernest Lorne Bell III

Ernest Lorne Bell III

Attorney. Boston, Mass., June 12, 1926, Ernest Jr. and Ellamay (Currier) Bell. Vermont Academy, Saxtons River, 1944, Harvard Univ., A.B., 1949, Univ. of Mich. Law School, LL.B., 1952. Attorney, Keene, 1952--. City solicitor, Keene, 1955-60, director, Connecticut River Bank, 1969--, Connecticut River Bancorp., 1975--, N.H. Aeronautics Commission, 1979--, N.H. Constitutional Convention, 1964,74, trustee, Keene Public Library, 1979-86, president, board of advisors, Horatio Colony Museum, 1980--, president, N.H. Bar Association, 1978-79. Margaret (Depue), April 14, 1951. David, March 30, 1952, Robin, May 29, 1958, Roseanne, April 18, 1964. Protestant. 54 School St., Keene.

Gail Alicia Bigglestone

Director, women's athletics, University of New Hampshire. Melrose, Mass., Sept. 26, 1938, William and Norah (Comber) Bigglestone. Montpelier (Vt.) High School, 1956, Univ. of N.H., B.S., 1960, Univ. of Mass., M.S., 1966. Instructor, Colby Junior College, 1960-63, Killington ski area, 1963-64, North Andover High School, 1964-65, graduate assistant, Univ. of Mass., 1965-66, instructor, 1966-69; instructor, Mount Holyoke College, 1969-70, assistant professor, Univ. of N.H., 1970--, director, women's athletics, 1976--. Skiing committee, U.S. Collegiate Sport Council, 1969-72, team official, World Univ. Games, 1972, executive board, Women's Eastern Intercollegiate Ski Association, 1972-77, advisor, Women's Intercollegiate Ski Conference, 1964-73, executive committee, UNH Pro-Am Classic, 1980--, committee on committees, NCAA, 1981-82, ski committee, NCAA, 1985--, UNH Wildcat Winners Circle, 1983--. Protestant. Colony Cove, Durham.

Gail Alicia Bigglestone

Clesson Joseph Blaisdell

State senator. Keene, N.H., Sept. 18, 1926, Clesson and Mary (Sweeney) Blaisdell. Keene High School, 1944. U.S. Navy, 1944-46, seaman 1st cl. President, treasurer, Junie Blaisdell's Sport-A-Rama, Keene, 1969--. N.H. Senate, 1973--, State Athletic Commission, 1960-71, corporator, Keene Savings Bank, 1978--, Cheshire Hospital, 1979--, Savings Bank of Walpole, 1978--, advisory board, Keene Co-op Bank, 1982--, president, N.H. Basketball Officials Association, 1967--, trustee, Cedarcrest Handicapped Childrens Home, 1978--, baseball scout, Los Angeles Dodgers, 1971--, sports official, basketball, baseball and football, 1951--, consultant, Northeast Alcohol and Drug Services Inc., 1985--. One honorary degree. Beverly (Palmer), Jan. 6, 1948. Peter, Jan. 28, 1950, Michael, Oct. 4, 1957, Lucinda, Aug. 30, 1960. Catholic. Clarksdale Rd., Spofford.

Jane Blalock

Professional golfer. Concord, N.H., Sept. 19, 1945, Richard and Barbara (Madden) Blalock. Portsmouth High School, 1963, Rollins College, B.A., 1967. Substitute high school teacher, Portsmouth, 1967-68, professional golfer, 1969--, winner of 29 Ladies Professional Golf Association titles. Creator, co-owner, Women's Professional Softball League, president, Jane Blalock Associates, professional athlete management company, 1979-80, consultant, Descente Ltd., clothing company, Japan, 1979-85, Ping Golf Clubs, 1985--, Bogner of America, clothing company, 1986--. Author, *Guts to Win*, 1975. Catholic. 148 Brackett Rd., Portsmouth.

Jane Blalock

Horace Shepard Blood

Horace Shepard Blood

Physician. Concord, N.H., Jan. 5, 1923, Robert and Pauline (Shepard) Blood. Concord High School, 1940, Dartmouth College, A.B., 1944, N.Y.U. Medical School, M.D., 1947. U.S. Army Medical Corps, 1952-54, capt. Staff, Manhattan Eye and Ear Hospital, 1948-51, staff, Concord Hospital, 1951--, Associated Doctors, Concord, 1951-64, Concord Ear, Nose and Throat, P.A., 1966--. Owner, Crystal Spring Farm, East Concord, 1975-86, Concord Planning Board, 1968-80, chairman, 1975-80; director, Weeks Dairy, 1977--, Concord National Bank, 1980--, Concord YMCA, 1959-70, chairman, Concord Hospital Capital Fund Drive, 1979-80, chairman, city manager form of government campaign, Concord, 1970, member, N.H. Medical Society, Merrimack County Medical Society, 1948--. Gene (Pierce), June 25, 1949. Deborah, Feb. 17, 1954, Robert, May 26, 1956. Congregational. 248 Mountain Rd., Concord.

Paul Otto Bofinger

President, forester, Society for the Protection of New Hampshire Forests. Passaic, N.J., Sept. 23, 1934. Otto and Gertrude (Hollstein) Bofinger. Hempstead (N.Y.) High School, 1951, Cornell Univ., 1951-53, Univ. of Mich., B.S., 1955. Forester, Kimberly-Clark Corp., 1955-56, forester, lumber sales, N.E. Forest Industries, 1956-60, lumber sales, Johnson Lumber Co., 1960-61, assistant forester, Society for the Protection of N.H. Forests, 1961-65, forester, executive director, 1965-73, president, forester, 1973--. Chairman, White Mountain Environment Committee, 1967-85, director, American Forestry Association, 1981--, incorporator, N.H. Savings Bank, 1974-82, Franconia Notch Citizens Advisory Committee, 1966-69, chairman, treasurer, Wood Energy Institute, 1975-79, chairman, White Mountain National Forest Advisory Committee, 1977-85. Lenita (Deming), Aug. 28, 1956. Lise, Aug. 13, 1959, Paul, Feb. 11, 1961. 86 Mountain Rd., Concord.

Paul Otto Bofinger

Varujan Yegan Boghosian

Sculptor, professor. New Britain, Conn., June 26, 1926, Mesrop and Badjar (Sylandjian) Boghosian. New Britain Senior High School, 1944, Conn. Teachers College, 1946-48, Vesper George School of Art, 1948-50, Yale Univ., B.F.A., 1957, M.F.A., 1959. U.S. Navy, 1944-46, petty officer, 3rd cl. Art instructor, Univ. of Fla., 1958-59, Pratt Institute, Brooklyn, 1961, Cooper Union, N.Y.C., 1959-61, assistant professor, 1961-64; Yale Univ., 1962--64, associate professor, Brown Univ., 1964-68, artist in residence, professor, Dartmouth College, 1968--, sculptor, 1962--. Board co-chairman, MacDowell Colony, 1983--, sculptor in residence, American Academy in Rome, 1966-67,75, Guggenheim fellow, 1985-86, Fulbright grantee, 1953. Two honorary degrees. Marilyn (Cummins), Sept. 1, 1953. Heidi, April 3, 1955. 1 Read Rd., Hanover.

Maurice Paul Bois

Associate justice, New Hampshire Supreme Court, retired. Manchester, N.H. Aug. 14, 1917, Thomas and Hattie (Wurtele) Bois. Manchester Central High School, 1935, St. Anselm College, A.B., 1939, Fordham Univ. Law School, 1939-40, Boston Univ. School of Law., LL.B., 1946. U.S. Army, 1940-45, 1st lt. Attorney, Manchester, 1946-55,61-73, auditor, Hillsborough County, 1948-52, U.S. attorney, District of N.H., 1955-61, associate justice, N.H. Superior Court, 1973-76, associate justice, N.H. Supreme Court, 1976-83. Yeteve (Vezina), Nov. 11, 1942. Maurice Jr., Sept. 21, 1944, Judith, Sept. 8, 1947, Pamela, Sept. 19, 1950, Richard, July 21, 1956. Catholic. 1434 Union St., Manchester.

Maurice Paul Bois

James Dougan Bolle

James Dougan Bolle

Music director, New Hampshire Symphony Orchestra. Evanston, Ill., July 26, 1931, Theodore and Dorothy (Dougan) Bolle. New Trier Township High School, Winnetka, Ill., 1949, Harvard Univ., 1949-51, Antioch College, 1951-55, B.A., 1957, Northwestern Univ., M.M., 1968. U.S. Army, 1955-57, spec. 2nd cl. Instructor, Univ. of Saskatchewan, 1957-59, assistant director, North Shore Community Music Center, Winnetka, 1959-61, director, Chicago Community Music Foundation, 1961-68, director, Living Music, Chicago, 1960-62, music director, South Suburban Symphony Orchestra, Park Forest, Ill., 1963-68, director, Monadnock Music, 1966--, faculty, Keene State College, 1969-73, music director, N.H. Symphony Orchestra, 1974--. Director, Grand Monadnock Arts Council, 1975-79. One honorary degree. Jocelyn (Faulkner), March 21, 1953. Christopher, May 28, 1957, Edward, July 15, 1960, Susanna, Aug. 6, 1968. Main St., Francestown.

Earl Murphy Bourdon

Labor union leader, retired. Claremont, N.H., Dec. 16, 1917, Eli and Agnes (Murray) Bourdon. Stevens High School, Claremont, 1935, Suffolk Law School, 1935-37. Heat treater, Joy Manufacturing, Claremont, 1943-57, assistant legislative agent, N.H. Labor Council, 1956-57, staff representative, U.S. Steelworkers of America, AFL-CIO, 1957-78. President, N.H. Association for the Elderly, 1981--, member, officer, N.H. Industrial Union Council, 1943-56, Sullivan County Labor Council, 1943--, member, N.H. advisory council, Federal Civil Rights Commission, 1977--, board member, National Council of Senior Citizens, 1980--, president, Senior Citizens Housing Development Corp., Claremont, 1979--, president, Twin State Area Ministry, Unitarian-Universalist Association, 1968-69, director, Southwestern Community Services, 1965--, former chairman; chairman, N.H. Employment and Training Council, 1981-82, member, State Council on Aging, 1981-82, president, Congress of Senior Citizens, Claremont, 1975--. One honorary degree. Honorine (Hadley), April 5, 1967. St. ch., Rhoda, Sept. 22, 1951, Christopher, June 1, 1953, Valerie, Jan. 21, 1957. Unitarian. Juniper Hill, Claremont.

Earl Murphy Bourdon

Bernard Louis Boutin

Bernard Louis Boutin

Retired banker, college president. Belmont, N.H., July 2, 1923, Joseph and Annie (LaFlam) Boutin. Belmont High School, 1942, Catholic Univ. of America, 1942-43, St. Michael's College, Ph.B., 1945. Partner, Boutin Real Estate, Laconia, 1945-63, president, treasurer, Boutin Insurance Agency, 1945-63, partner, Busy Corner Store, 1956-59, mayor, Laconia, 1955-59, deputy administrator, General Services Administration, 1961, administrator, 1961-64; executive vice president, National Association of Home Builders, 1964-65, deputy director, Office of Economic Opportunity, 1965-66, administrator, Small Business Administration, 1966-67, director, corporate information services, Sanders Associates, Nashua, 1967-69, president, St. Michael's College, Winooski, Vt., 1969-74, executive vice president, Burlington (Vt.) Savings Bank, 1975-76, president, 1976-80. Democratic National Committeeman, 1956-60. Three honorary degrees. Alice (Boucher), April 2, 1945. Edmund, Jan. 16, 1946, Joseph, Aug. 29, 1947, Bernadette, July 26, 1948, Michelle, April 10, 1950, Marie, April 29, 1951, Louis, June 15, 1954, Elizabeth, June 25, 1955, John, June 16, 1956, Paul, March 8, 1958, Suzanne, June 24, 1959, Bernard II, Sept. 30, 1967. Catholic. 26 Wildwood Village, Laconia.

Jack Lawton Bowers

Chairman, chief executive officer, Sanders Associates. Colorado Springs, Colo., Aug. 25, 1920, Ernest and Margaret (Lawton) Bowers. Weatherwax High School, Aberdeen, Wash., 1938, Carnegie Institute of Technology, B.S.E.E., 1942. U.S. Army Air Force, 1943-46, capt. General Dynamics Corp., Calif., 1946-60, Avco Corp., Cincinnati, 1960-64, General Dynamics, N.Y. and Calif., 1964-73, assistant secretary of the Navy, installations and logistics, 1973-76, president, chief operating officer, Sanders Associates, 1976-78, president, chief executive officer, 1978-82, chairman, chief executive officer, 1982--. Member, American Business Conference, 1981--, Navy League of the U.S., 1965--, Association of the U.S. Army, 1977--, American Defense Preparedness Association, 1977--, trustee, N.H. Symphony, 1982--, Carnegie-Mellon Univ., 1967-73, director, Sanders Associates, 1976--, Federated Arts of Manchester, 1982--, incorporator, N.H. Charitable Fund, 1983--. One honorary degree. Mildred (Neel), July 25, 1942. Bruce, June 8, 1946, Steven, Feb. 9, 1948, Ann, Oct. 21, 1950, Robin, Aug. 15, 1956. 31 Nathan Lord Rd., Amherst.

Jack Lawton Bowers

Raimond Bowles

Raimond Bowles

Former state representative. Littleton, N.H., July 10, 1923, A. Raimond and Ella (Shannon) Bowles. Manchester Central High School, 1940, Univ. of N.H., B.A., 1947. U.S. Army, 1943-46, 1st lt. Assistant clerk, chief clerk, U.S. Senate Banking and Currency Committee, 1948-52, insurance, government contract administration, advertising and sales, Manchester, 1953-57, president, general manager, owner, Batchelder Oil Co., Newington, 1957-66, director of finance and business management, N.E. School Development Council and N.E. Education Data Systems, Newton, Mass., 1966-71, staff, Law Enforcement Assistance Administration, U.S. Department of Justice, 1971-77, committee research coordinator, N.H. House of Rep., 1977-79, chief planner and program coordinator, N.H. Crime Commission, 1979-80, office manager, Sanders Lobster Co., Portsmouth, 1980--. N.H. House of Rep., 1961-63,69-70,71, Portsmouth School Board, 1964-71,79, chairman, Portsmouth-Kittery Armed Services Committee, 1965. Ruth (Abbott), Sept. 2, 1945. Pamela, June 24, 1946, Paul, Jan. 9, 1949, Mary-Ella, Feb. 16, 1951, James, July 22, 1960. Protestant. 43 Pray St., Portsmouth.

Hugh Henry Bownes

Judge, United States First Circuit Court of Appeals. New York, N.Y., March 10, 1920, Hugh and Margaret (Henry) Bownes. Horace Mann School for Boys, N.Y., N.Y., 1937, Columbia Univ., B.A., 1941, Columbia Law School, LL.B., 1948. U.S. Marine Corps, 1941-46, maj. Attorney, Laconia, 1948-66, associate justice, N.H. Superior Court, 1966-68, judge, U.S. District Court, 1968-77, judge, U.S. First Circuit Court of Appeals, 1977--. City council, Laconia, 1953-57, mayor, Laconia, 1963-65, president, Belknap County Bar Association, 1965, board president, Laconia Hospital Association, 1963-64, Democratic National Committeeman, 1963-66, president, Laconia Chamber of Commerce, 1961-62. Irja (Martikainen), Dec. 30, 1944. Barbara, June 2, 1946, David, April 12, 1949, Ernest, April 12, 1949. Protestant. 4 Poor Richards Dr., Bow.

Richard Edward Boyer

Richard Edward Boyer

State senator, attorney. Pawtucket, R.I., Sept. 3, 1944, Matthew and Jeanie (Young) Lefebvre. Los Altos High School, Hacienda Heights, Calif., 1963, Fitchburg State College, 1965-67, Univ. of Nebr., B.S., 1969, Univ. of Maine, J.D., 1972. U.S. Army, 1963-67, capt. Attorney, Nashua, 1972--. N.H. House of Rep., 1978-80, N.H. Senate, 1980--, chairman, N.H. Democratic Party, 1981-83, member, Democratic National Committee, 1981-83, trustee, Daniel Webster College, 1982--, director, So. N.H. Association of Commerce and Industry, 1980-81, director, Boys Club of Nashua, 1974-81, president, 1981; N.H. Constitutional Convention, 1984. Karen (Johnson), Jan. 21, 1967. Holly, March 18, 1971, Matthew, Nov. 20, 1972. Methodist. 19 Wellesley Rd., Nashua.

Wyman Pender Boynton

Attorney, retired. Portsmouth, N.H., Oct. 8, 1908, Harry and Helen (Pender) Boynton. Portsmouth High School, 1926, MIT, B.S., 1931, Univ. of Mich. Law School, LL.B., 1936. U.S. Army Reserve, 1940-45, bat. comdr. Attorney, Portsmouth, 1936-86. Rockingham County attorney, 1947-50, N.H. House of Rep., 1933-34, Portsmouth City Council, 1937-38, Portsmouth School Board, 1954-58,62-70, N.H. Constitutional Convention, 1974, trustee, Portsmouth Public Library, 1955-70, N.H. Industrial School, 1956-66, chairman, 1958-66; Portsmouth Cooperative Bank, 1946-81, vice president, 1973-76, chairman, 1976-81; Portsmouth Historical Society, 1940--, vice president, 1946--; Mark H. Wentworth Home for Chronic Invalids, 1948-81, president, 1950-81; trustee, Chase Home for Children, 1946--, president, 1950-77; president, Portsmouth Athenaeum, 1977-80, registered professional engineer. Mildred (Ballard), Feb. 1, 1935. Elizabeth, April 19, 1936. Congregational. 668 Middle St., Portsmouth.

David Hammond Bradley

David Hammond Bradley

Attorney. Keene, N.H., May 8, 1936, Homer and Alice (Proctor) Bradley. Keene High School, 1954, Dartmouth College, A.B., 1958, Amos Tuck School, 1957-58, Harvard Law School, J.D., 1965. U.S. Navy, 1958-61, lt. jg. Assistant to the director of admissions, Dartmouth College, 1961-62, attorney, Hanover, 1965--. N.H. House of Rep., 1971-73, N.H. Senate, 1973-78, Hanover School Board, 1966-69, chairman, 1967-68; Dresden School Board, 1966-69, chairman, 1968-69; trustee, Cardigan Mountain School, 1974--, member of corporation, Mary Hitchcock Memorial Hospital, 1975--, trustee, 1985--; member of corporation, Hanover Improvement Society, 1979--. Ann (DeRoma), June 18, 1960. David Jr., Oct. 31, 1962, Jeffrey, Aug. 14, 1965, Christopher, May 1, 1970. Congregational. 5 Fox Field Ln., Hanover.

David John Bradley

Writer, lecturer. Chicago, Ill., Feb. 22, 1915, Harold and Josephine (Crane) Bradley. Wisconsin High School, Madison, 1933, Dartmouth College, B.A., 1938, St. John's College, Cambridge, England, 1938-39, Harvard Medical School, M.D., 1944. U.S. Army Medical Corps, 1943-47, capt. Senior lecturer, Amos Tuck School, Dartmouth, 1965-81, lecturer, policy studies, Dartmouth, 1981--. N.H. House of Rep., 1955-61,71-75, selectman, Hanover, 1965-68, National Ski Hall of Fame, 1985, member, Physicians for Social Responsibility, 1981--, Union of Concerned Scientists, 1980--. Author of five books, including *No Place to Hide*, 1948. Elisabeth (McLane), April 26, 1941. Kim, Jan. 29, 1944, Darby, April 2, 1945, Wendy, Dec. 9, 1948, Ben, Oct. 18, 1952, Bronwen, June 19, 1954, Steven, Dec. 11, 1959. 30 Occom Ridge, Hanover.

Arthur Frederick Brady Jr.

Arthur Frederick Brady Jr.

President, Brady Ford Sales. Quincy, Mass., March 30, 1928, Arthur and Anna (Murphy) Brady. Boston College High School, 1945, Univ. of Notre Dame, B.A., 1948. U.S. Marine Corps, 1950-54, 1st lt. Vice president, Stilphen Motor, Dorchester, Mass., 1954-66, president, Brady Ford Sales, Portsmouth, 1966--. Mayor, Portsmouth, 1972-74, Portsmouth Police Commission, 1981-82, trustee, Piscataqua Savings Bank, 1974--, Portsmouth Hospital, 1974-81, chairman, 1978-79; executive board, Forum on N.H.'s Future, 1978-82, president, Strawbery Banke, 1974-78, chairman, N.H. Odyssey House, 1970-74,77-84, Portsmouth Economic Commission, 1969-71, Prescott Park Arts Festival, 1981-82, Governor's Committee for Youth and Child Services, 1971. Mary Jane (Willard), Nov. 25, 1953. St. ch., Thomas, Aug. 19, 1952. Mary Jane, Oct. 2, 1954, Elizabeth, Dec. 13, 1955, Arthur III, July 25, 1957, George, Jan. 14, 1959, Matthew, June 15, 1960, Adam, April 5, 1963. Catholic. 18 Cherry Rd., North Hampton.

Raymond Arthur Brighton

Newspaper editor, retired, author. Boston, Mass., Aug. 6, 1914, Albert and Prudence (Butler) Brighton. Peterborough High School, 1932, Antioch College, 1932-35, Ohio State Univ., B.S., 1938. U.S. Army, 1941-46, 1st lt. Teacher, State Industrial School, Manchester, 1938-41, reporter, *Portsmouth Herald*, 1946-51, news editor, 1951-60, managing editor, 1960-69, editor, 1969-79. Director, Herald Publishing Co., 1963-68, trustee, Portsmouth Trust Funds, 1981-86, member, former president, Portsmouth Historical Society, member, former president, Portsmouth Athenaeum, member, Old Newbury Historical Society, Hampton Historical Society, Peterborough Historical Society, N.H. Historical Society, Old Berwick Historical Society, Exeter Historical Society. Author, *They Came to Fish*, 1973, plus four books since. Mary (Pridham), July 24, 1942. Prudence, Sept. 24, 1948, Mark, June 23, 1952. 169 Essex Ave., Portsmouth.

David Allen Brock

David Allen Brock

Associate justice, New Hampshire Supreme Court. Stoneham, Mass., July 6, 1936, Herbert and Margaret (Morris) Brock. Manchester Central High School, 1953, Holderness School, 1954, Dartmouth College, B.A., 1958, Univ. of Mich. Law School, LL.B., 1963. U.S. Marine Corps, 1958-61, lieut. Attorney, Manchester, 1963-69, U.S. attorney, District of N.H., 1969-72, attorney, Concord, 1972-76, associate justice, N.H. Superior Court, 1976-78, associate justice, N.H. Supreme Court, 1978--. Chairman, N.H. Supreme Court Committee on Judicial Conduct, member, N.H. Judicial Council, Education and Appellate Advocacy Committees of the Appellate Judges Conference of the American Bar Association, chairman, N.H. Supreme Court Rules Advisory Committee. Sandra (Ford), Sept. 3, 1960. Kimberly, Deborah, Tammy, Margaret Ann, Frederick, William. Sugar Hill, Hopkinton.

Arthur Furber Brown Jr.

Banker. Dover, N.H., July 26, 1918, Arthur and Marion (Wallace) Brown. Portsmouth High School, 1937, Plymouth Business School, Portsmouth, 1938. U.S. Army, 1941-45, m.sgt. Teller, N.H. National Bank, Portsmouth, 1938-41, cashier, 1945-62; president, director, Carroll County Trust Co., Conway, 1962-81, chairman, Indian Head Bank North, 1981--. President, White Mountains Region Association, 1966-68, N.H. Bankers Association, 1969-70, president, advisory board, 1972-82; treasurer, N.H./Vt. Development Corp., 1969-73, assistant moderator, Conway, 1971-76, moderator, Conway School District, 1978-81, moderator, Conway Village Fire District, 1978-81, vice president, treasurer, Conway Area Business Development Corp., 1964-85, chairman, Conway Recreation Commission, 1968-75, treasurer, Route 16 East/West Highway Commission, 1969-73, president, trustees, Memorial Hospital, North Conway, 1971-82. Ruth (Hersey), Sept. 8, 1946. Janet, Oct. 21, 1947, Marion, April 26, 1951, Joyce, Dec. 10, 1955, Nancy, Sept. 4, 1959. Protestant. 46 Washington St., Conway.

Arthur Furber Brown Jr.

Douglas C. Brown

President, Dartmouth Woolen Mills. Keene, N.H., May 30, 1937, Gordon and Persis (Goodnow) Brown. Phillips Academy, Andover, Mass., 1955, Harvard Univ., B.A., 1959. U.S. Navy, 1959-62, lt. jg. Assistant general manager, Dartmouth Woolen Mills, 1962-67, general manager, Homestead Woolen Mills, 1967-71, president, 1973-85; president, Dartmouth Woolen Mills, 1971--. Director, Woods Woolen Co., 1967-72, Indian Head National Bank, Keene, 1972--, Indian Head Banks Inc., 1976-77, J.A. Wright Co., 1975--, Northern Textile Association, 1972-84, president, 1979-82; American Textile Manufacturers Association, 1979-82, Business and Industry Association of N.H., 1980--, Cheshire County YMCA, 1967-80, trustee, 1980-82; Monadnock United Way, 1969-75, president, 1975; trustee, Cheshire Hospital, 1971-81, chairman, 1977-78. Sarah (Gilda), June 18, 1960. Douglas M., May 29, 1961, Dixon, Feb. 6, 1963, Daniel, May 15, 1964. Protestant. Red Fox Run, Keene.

J. Willcox Brown

Natural resources consultant. Wilmington, Del., Jan. 29, 1915, J. Thompson and Yolande (deVignier) Brown. Tower Hill School, Wilmington, 1933, Dartmouth College, A.B., 1937, Yale Univ., M.F., 1941, Univ. of Mich., M.S., 1953. Supervisor, Rhododendron State Park, Fitzwilliam, 1947-51, forestry employment, N.Y., Calif., Penn., Mich., 1941-55, assistant professor, Forestry and Conservation Department, Univ. of Mich., 1953-55, assistant forestor, Society for the Protection of N.H. Forests, 1955-59, natural resources consultant, 1959--. N.H. Water Resources Board, 1965-76, vice chairman, Water Supply and Pollution Control Commission, 1979-81, chairman, 1981-84; chairman, N.H. Coordinating Committee on Acid Rain, 1980-82, co-chairman, N.H. Committee for the Canal Treaties, 1977-78, selectman, Dunbarton, 1967-73, moderator, 1976-82, school moderator, 1977-82, N.H. Constitutional Convention, 1964,74, Democratic National Committeeman, 1976-84, director, Merrimack River Watershed Council, 1984--, N.H. Council on World Affairs, 1966--, trustee, Science Center of N.H., 1985--, Audubon Society of N.H., 1973-79, member, N.E. Interstate Water Pollution Control Commission, 1980-84, chairman, 1982-83. Natale (Linton), July 25, 1941. J. Thompson, Nov. 22, 1942, Nancy, Nov. 5, 1943, Susan, April 6, 1946, Stephen, Jan. 25, 1951. Episcopal. Burnham Ln. and Grapevine Rd., Dunbarton.

J. Willcox Brown

Mary Pillsbury Brown

Commissioner, New Hampshire Department of Postsecondary Vocational-Technical Education. Manchester, N.H., March 4, 1923, Hobart and O. Augusta (Weller) Pillsbury. Manchester Central High School, 1941, Smith College, A.B., 1945, Harvard Graduate School of Education, M.Ed., 1963. Research assistant, U.S. State Department, 1945-46, English teacher, Goffstown High School, 1947-51,62-64, English teacher, drama coach, Central High School, 1951-62, humanities faculty, N.H. College, 1964-84, commissioner, N.H. Department of Postsecondary Vocational-Technical Education, 1984--. Manchester School Board, 1965--, chairman, N.H. Developmental Disabilities Council, 1983--, chairman, Manchester Historic District Commission, 1976--, former director, Manchester Red Cross, Manchester Association of Retarded Citizens. Div. Congregational. 184 Linden St., Manchester.

Robert Leo Brunelle

Executive director, Excellence in Education Project. Somersworth, N.H., Sept. 19, 1924, Lorenzo and Laomie (Carter) Brunelle. Somersworth High School, 1942, Maine Maritime Academy, 1944, Univ. of N.H., B.A., 1949, M.Ed., 1958, Boston Univ., Ed.D., 1972. U.S. Navy, 1944-46, ensign. Teacher, principal, elementary and junior high schools, 1950-55, supervising principal, elementary schools, 1955-58, superintendent of schools, Oyster River School District, 1958-68, deputy commissioner of education, Department of Education, 1968-76, commissioner, 1976-86; executive director, Excellence in Education Project, 1985--. Trustee, Univ. System of N.H., 1976-86, director, Philbrook Foundation, 1974--, board of governors, Great Bay School and Training Center, 1966--, Concord United Way, 1972-80. Diane (Gagnon), June 14, 1947. Roberta, May 7, 1955, Marc, July 20, 1960. Catholic. 83 Rockingham St., Concord.

Robert Leo Brunelle

Nancy Head Bryant

Civic leader. Laconia, N.H., Aug. 14, 1926, George and Georgia (Fecteau) Head. Laconia High School, 1944, Univ. of N.H., B.A., 1949, M.A., 1962. Laconia School District, director of adult education, 1962-77, director of adult basic education, 1965-77. Laconia School Board, 1976-79, chairman, 1978; trustee of trust funds, Laconia, 1974--, advisory committee, Putnam Free Lecture Fund, 1970--, president, 1980--; City Charter Revision Commission, 1975, trustee, New Hampton School, 1979, chairman, 1981-85; vice president, R.H. Smith Co., 1967-82, director, vice president, Head's Electric Inc., 1960--, incorporator, Lakes Region General Hospital, 1965--, director, vice president, Lakes Region Chamber of Commerce, 1974-77, director, Lakes Region Family Service, 1963-66, former president, Lakes Region Hospital Auxiliary. Harry Bryant Jr., Dec. 27, 1947. Anne, July 8, 1952, Ellen, Sept. 13, 1953, Susan, Oct. 4, 1954. Catholic. 8 Wildwood Rd., Laconia.

Creeley Shepard Buchanan

Federal government official, retired. Watertown, Mass., Oct. 4, 1917, Alexander and Gertrude (Shepard) Buchanan. Arlington (Mass.) High School, 1935, Tilton School, 1936, Univ. of N.H., B.A., 1940. U.S. Army, 1941-45, capt. Agent, Phoenix Mutual Life Insurance Co., 1946-48, manager, Phoenix Mutual, Manchester agency, 1949-69, director, Federal Housing Administration, Manchester, 1969-70, area director, U.S. Department of Housing and Urban Development, Manchester office, 1970-79. Moderator, Amherst School District, 1955-80, commissioner, Amherst Village District, 1958-70, N.H. Senate, 1965-69, president, Univ. of N.H. Alumni Association, 1969-71, director, N.H. Heart Association, 1965-70, trustee, Tilton School, 1959-64, Univ. System of N.H., 1983--, board of governors, N.H. Public Television, 1985--, member, State Historical Commission, 1969-76, N.H. American Revolution Bicentennial Commission, 1971-82. Rosamond (Eckfeldt), Jan. 12, 1946. Blair, Oct. 17, 1948, Shepard, May 11, 1951, Alexander, April 25, 1953, Scott, Jan. 2, 1957. Congregational. 14 Middle St., Amherst.

Creeley Shepard Buchanan

Charles Edward Buckley

Charles Edward Buckley

Fine arts consultant, appraiser. South Hadley Center, Mass., April 29, 1919, William Bertram and Alice (Nicholl) Buckley. Elgin (Ill.) High School, 1936, School of the Art Institute of Chicago, B.F.A., 1940, Harvard Univ., M.A., 1948. U.S. Army, 1943-46, sgt. Keeper, W.A. Clark Collection, Corcoran Gallery of Art, Washington, D.C., 1949-51, general curator, Wadsworth Athenaeum, Hartford, 1951-55, director, Currier Gallery of Art, Manchester, 1955-64, director, St. Louis Art Museum, 1964-75, fine arts consultant, appraiser, 1976--. Vice president, trustee, Association of Art Museum Directors, 1960-75, president American Association of Museums, 1972-74, trustee, N.H. Historical Society, 1958-64, Museum of American Textile History, North Andover, Mass., 1981--, Sterling and Francine Clark Art Institute, Williamstown, Mass., 1980--. Congregational. Old Amherst Rd., Mont Vernon.

Jean Kamman Burling

Attorney, judge. Worcester, Mass., July 7, 1946, Zora and Evelyn (Weisler) Kamman. Northfield-Mount Hermon School, Northfield, Mass., 1964, Wellesley College, B.A., 1968, Boston Univ. School of Law, J.D., 1973. Attorney, 1973--, special justice, Claremont District Court, 1979--. Co-owner, manager, Austin Farm, Cornish, 1978--, trustee, Northfield-Mount Hermon School, 1975-79, Franconia College, 1973-76, Green Mountain Horse Association, 1980--, Upper Valley Humane Society, 1985--, trustee, executive committee, Mount Ascutney Hospital and Health Center, 1972-77, director Standardbred Owners and Breeders of N.H., 1985--, director, treasurer, Milo Chocron Inc., Boston, 1971-76, member, Police Standards and Training Council, 1980--, vice chairman, 1982-84. Peter Hoe Burling, June 8, 1969. RR 2, Box 194, Cornish.

Jean Kamman Burling

Robert Phillips Burroughs

Robert Phillips Burroughs

Pension plan designer, retired. Manchester, N.H., Jan. 13, 1900, Sherman and Helen (Phillips) Burroughs. Manchester High School, 1917, Dartmouth College, A.B., 1921, M.B.A., 1922. U.S. Army Air Corps, 1918-19, 1st lt. Salesman, leather buyer, Gale Shoe Manufacturing Co., 1922-26, factory manager, 1924-27; agent, general agent, National Life Insurance Co. of Vt., 1928-66, president, R.P. Burroughs Co., 1948-66. Owner, apple orchard farm, Canterbury, 1941--, director, Loon Mountain Recreation Corp., 1965--, N.H. Insurance Co., 1956-78, honorary, 1978--; Hitchiner Manufacturing Co., 1950-79, American Forestry Association, 1950-75, trustee, Manchester Savings Bank, 1934-70, Society for the Protection of N.H. Forests, 1969-74, member, Dartmouth Alumni Council, 1966-72, board of overseers, Tuck School, 1962-68, Republican National Committeeman, 1932-44. Dorothy (Wellman), April 20, 1927 (dec. 1964). James, Feb. 24, 1929, Helen, July 4, 1930, Harriet, Sept. 12, 1935. Martha (Parsons), June 19, 1965. Episcopal. 1280 Union St., Manchester.

Richard Alden Burt

Art instructor, illustrator, painter. Hanover, N.H., Dec. 11, 1921, Clarence and Mildred (Poland) Burt. Framingham (Mass.) High School, 1951, Plymouth State College, B.A.E., 1965, Dartmouth College, M.A., 1973. U.S. Army Air Force, 1942-46, cpl. Technical illustrator, Workshop Associates, Needham, Mass., freelance commercial artist, 1950-65, freelance artist, Equity Publishing, Orford, 1953-62, art instructor, Chaffee Museum, Rutland, Vt., 1954-65, art coordinator, Lebanon High School, 1965-70, art director, teacher, Cardigan Mountain School, Canaan, 1970-75, art instructor, Lebanon High School, 1975-83. Chairman, N.H. Commission on the Arts, 1974-79, director, N.H. Art Association, 1985--, advisory committee, visual arts, Waterville Valley Arts Festival, 1985--, watercolorist, 1953--. Mary (Emerson), Oct. 19, 1946. Protestant. RR 2, Box 399, Enfield.

Richard Alden Burt

Raymond Stephen Burton

Raymond Stephen Burton

Executive councilor. Burlington, Vt., Aug. 13, 1939, Stephen and Natalie (Hill) Burton. Woodsville High School, 1958, Plymouth State College, B.Ed., 1962. Teaching principal, Warren, Andover, 1962-68, sergeant at arms, N.H. Senate, 1967-68, staff, Rep. James Cleveland, 1969, Gov. Walter Peterson, 1969-72, general partner, Direct Mail Systems, 1973-82, N.H. Executive Council, 1977-79,81--, core faculty member, N.H. College, 1982--. Bath School Board, 1962-78, director, Plymouth State Fair, 1966-76, chairman, Robert Frost Award, Plymouth State College Alumni, 1972, director, No. Community Investment Corp., 1975-80, trustee, N.H. Public Radio, 1978--, Hitchcock Clinic, 1983--, chairman, N.H. Cancer Crusade, 1981-82, member, Governor's Advisory Commission on Highways, 1985--, North Country Council, 1972--, chairman, N.H. Operation Life Saver Rail Safety Committee, 1983--. United Church of Christ. River Rd., Bath.

William Stewart Bushnell

President, chief executive officer, Amoskeag Bank. Oneida, N.Y., May 15, 1930, Stanton and Pauline (Jacobs) Bushnell. Williston Academy, Easthampton, Mass., 1949, Colgate Univ., 1949-52, Utica College, B.A., 1961. Oneida Savings Bank, 1952-68, secretary, treasurer, 1962-68; vice president, Elmira Savings Bank, 1968-70, president, chief executive officer, 1970-80; president, chief executive officer, Amoskeag Bank, 1980--. Chairman, chief executive officer, Amoskeag Bank Shares Inc., 1983--, director, Bank Meridian, 1984--, Amoskeag Investment Co., 1982--, Business and Industry Association of N.H., 1985--, Amoskeag Industries, 1983--, United Way of Greater Manchester, 1983--, Greater Manchester YMCA, 1982-85, Manchester Chamber of Commerce, 1982-85, trustee, N.H. Historical Society, 1984--, Palace Theatre, 1981--, Notre Dame College, 1986--. Dolores (McDuffee), Nov. 1, 1951. Patricia, March 20, 1953, Nancy, Feb. 24, 1955, Diane, March 28, 1957. Presbyterian. 49 Old Sawmill Rd., Bedford.

William Stewart Bushnell

Marilyn Ruth Campbell

State representative. Salem, N.H., July 31, 1932, Howard and Ruth (Kimball) Turner. Woodbury High School, Salem, 1950, Univ. of N.H., B.S., 1954. Occupational therapist, 1958-61, substitute teacher, Salem, 1961-65, co-owner, operator, Kev-Ber-Ken Farm, Salem, 1965--, president, Turner Homestead Inc., 1984--. N.H. House of Rep., 1973--, Current Use Advisory Board, 1981-83, director, Rockingham County Farm Bureau, 1960--, advisory committee, N.H. Vocational Technical College, Manchester, 1979-82, member, Salem Business and Professional Women's Club, 1976--, president, associated women, N.H. Farm Bureau, 1980-84, second vice president, N.H. Farm Bureau, 1984--, member, American Farm Bureau Women's Committee, 1984--, N.H. Advisory Council for Vocational Education, 1984-85, director, Granite State Electric Co., 1986--. Bernard Campbell, April 3, 1955. Bernard, Jan. 9, 1956, Kenneth, April 14, 1957, Kevin, April 14, 1957. Methodist. 79 Brady Ave., Salem.

Gerald Posner Carmen

Former diplomat. Quincy, Mass., July 8, 1930, Edward and Hilda (Holland) Carmen. Manchester Central High School, 1948, Univ. of N.H., B.A., 1952. Owner, various private companies, Manchester, 1959-79, senior consultant, Reagan for President, 1979-80, administrator, General Services Administration, 1981-84, Ambassador and United States Permanent Representative to the United Nations Office and Other International Organizations in Geneva, 1984-86. Chairman, Republican State Committee, 1975-79, commissioner, Manchester Housing Authority, 1969-74, chairman, 1970-71; chairman, N.H. Housing Commision, 1973-74, former chairman, Manchester Heart Fund, former director, N.H. Brotherhood Council. Anita (Saidel), Dec. 17, 1950. Melinda, Nov. 21, 1952, David, April 13, 1957. Jewish. 308 Crestview Circle, Manchester.

Gerald Posner Carmen

John Avery Carter

John Avery Carter

Architect. Nashua, N.H. June 16, 1924, Eliot and Edith (Gardner) Carter. Phillips Academy, Andover, Mass., 1942, Yale School of Engineering, 1942-43, Univ. of Detroit, 1943-44, Yale Univ., B.Arch., 1949. U.S. Army, 1943-46, pfc. Architect, Nashua, 1953--. Director, N.E. region, National-American Institute of Architects, 1980-83, chairman, N.H. Architectural Registration Board, 1970-75, trustee, Nashua Symphony Assn., 1954-60, co-founder, life trustee, Nashua Arts and Science Center, 1957--, trustee, Eaglebrook School, Deerfield, Mass., 1971--, member, Nashua Building Code Board of Appeals, 1955--, chairman, 1979--; trustee, N.H. Historical Society, 1978-86, executive board, 1981; fellow, American Institute of Architects, 1984--. Julie (Macauley), Nov. 4, 1950. Stephen, Nov. 20, 1958, Cocoa Alexandra, Nov. 4, 1960, Julie, March 15, 1962, Robin, March 4, 1963, Christina, Oct. 6, 1965, Perry, Feb. 2, 1970. Episcopal. 14 Bartlett Ave., Nashua.

H. Alfred Casassa

Attorney. Bangor, Maine, Oct. 28, 1930, Herbert and Olga (Tasker) Casassa. Hampton Academy, 1948, Boston College, B.S., 1952, Boston Univ. School of Law, LL.B., 1957. U.S. Naval Reserve, 1953-55. Federal estate tax agent, Internal Revenue Service, Portsmouth, 1958-60, attorney, Hampton, 1960--. Justice, Hampton District Court, 1972-80, president, Rockingham County Bar Association, 1974-75, moderator, Hampton, 1967--, director, legal counsel, Hampton Co-operative Bank, 1968--, vice chairman, 1986--; trustee, Exeter Hospital, 1982--, director, Hampton National Bank, 1962-73, Hampton Planning Board, 1961-72, chairman, 1965-72; vice president, Seacoast Family Service Center, 1963-65, member, N.H. Judicial Council, 1983--, N.H. Constitutional Convention, 1964, board of governors, N.H. Bar Association, 1969. Clarice (Murphy), June 30, 1956. Anne, May 1, 1957, Robert, April 9, 1959, Christine, Nov. 22, 1968. Catholic. 12 Towle Ave., Hampton.

H. Alfred Casassa

Grace Amelia Casey

Grace Amelia Casey

Former executive director, New Hampshire Art Association. Lowell, Mass., March 13, 1917, Charles and Millie (Russon) Barton. Lowell High School, 1934, Cushing Academy, Ashburton, Mass., 1936, Minneapolis School of Art, 1936-38. Art teacher, Belvidere School, Lowell, 1950-52, owner, antiques business, 1952--, Casey Gallery of Antiques, 1957-67, founder, director, N.H. Heritage Forum and Antiques Show, 1961-67, owner, operator, River House Art Gallery, Portsmouth, 1967-68, executive director, N.H. Art Association, 1968-84. President, N.H. chapter, Ceara Partners of the Americas, 1982-86, commissioner, N.H. Commission on the Arts, 1979-83, co-founder, co-producer, Prescott Park Arts Festival, Portsmouth, 1974-85, art consultant, Dunaway Country Store, Strawbery Banke, 1967-68, Manchester Bank, 1967-70, member, National Trust for Historic Preservation, Theatre by the Sea Guild, N.H. Alliance for Art Education. Joseph Casey, March 20, 1942. JoAnn, May 7, 1943, Peter, July 8, 1944. Protestant. Old Towne Rd., Gilmanton Iron Works.

James Coleman Chamberlin

State representative, former selectman, Durham. Marion, Pa., Feb. 16, 1912, James S. and Milicent (Coleman) Chamberlin. Storm High School, Cornwall, N.Y., 1932, Lafayette College, 1932-36. U.S. Army, 1941-46, maj. Investment banker, First Boston Corp., 1936-38, sales representative, Bethlehem Steel Co., 1938-40, N.E. Coca-Cola, 1946-55, co-owner, vice president, Craig Supply Co., Durham, 1955-79. Selectman, Durham, 1951-85, trustee, N.H. Municipal Trusts, 1979-85, former member, budget committee, planning board, safety committee, historic commission, all of Durham, corporator, Wentworth-Douglass Hospital, 1983--, Seacoast Savings Bank, 1982--, N.H. House of Rep., 1980--, president, N.H. Assessor's Association, 1957, N.H. Constitutional Convention, 1974. Nell (Evans), June 12, 1943. James Jr., Sept. 22, 1946, Allan, June 8, 1951, David, Sept. 16, 1954, Catharine, Sept. 16, 1954. Protestant. P.O. Box 516, Durham.

James Coleman Chamberlin

Mary Peyton Chambers

Mary Peyton Chambers

State representative. Poca, W. Va., Aug. 31, 1931, Henry and Hilda (Cary) Peyton. Poca High School, 1948, W. Va. Wesleyan College, A.B., 1952, Vanderbilt Univ., M.A., 1955. Teacher, Putnam County School System, Winfield, W. Va., 1952-54, education supervisor, teacher, consultant, Baird Children's Center, Burlington, Vt., 1956-62, tutor, Bishop DeGoesbriand Hospital, Burlington, 1960-62, counselor, teacher, director, Upper Valley Adult Basic Education, Lebanon, 1974--. N.H. House of Rep., 1973--, director, Baird Children's Center, 1958-67, president, 1961-62,65-66; director, Dartmouth-Hitchcock Mental Health Center, 1976, member, Professional Conduct Committee, N.H. Supreme Court, 1979--, National Council on the Handicapped, 1980-82, Upper Valley Youth Services Board, 1980--, N.H. Developmental Disabilities Council, 1982--. Wilbert Chambers, July 6, 1957. Henry, Dec. 10, 1958, James, July 26, 1960, Jane, June 13, 1966. Congregational. Hanover Center Rd., Etna.

Norman Edmond Champagne

Associate justice, Manchester District Court. Manchester, N.H., Sept. 15, 1941, Laurier and Lillian (Demers) Champagne. Bishop Bradley High School, Manchester, 1959, St. Anselm College, B.A., 1963, Suffolk Univ. Law School, J.D., 1973. Underwriter, Travelers Insurance Companies, 1963-69, division director, N.H. Insurance Department, 1969-75, assistant commissioner, Department of Health and Welfare, 1975-76, attorney, Manchester, 1976-83, associate justice, Manchester District Court, 1983--. N.H. Senate, 1980-83, vice chairman, appellate division, N.H. Department of Employment Security, 1981-83, commissioner, N.H. Data Processing Commission, 1981-82, board of governors, secretary, N.H. Medical Malpractice Joint Underwriting Association, 1978-81, director, N.H. Automobile Reinsurance Facility, 1979-81, board member, Trinity High School, 1981--, chairman, 1982-85. Jocelyne (Desrochers), Nov. 28, 1963. Michelle, May 9, 1965, Susan, June 27, 1967, Joceline, March 20, 1972. Catholic. 8 Kearsarge St., Manchester.

Norman Edmond Champagne

James Edgar Chandler

James Edgar Chandler

Banker. Keene, N.H., July 2, 1924, Harold and Blanche (Chandler) Chandler. Keene High School, 1942, Univ. of Pa., B.S., 1945, Stonier Graduate School of Banking, Rutgers Univ., 1954. First National Bank, Philadelphia, 1945-53, Indian Head National Bank, Nashua, 1953--, president, 1958-73, chairman, 1975--; president, Indian Head Banks Inc., 1960-81, vice chairman, 1981-84, chairman, 1984--. Director, Governor's Management Review, 1981-82, president, N.H. Bankers Association, 1970-72, board of visitors, Whittemore School of Business, 1976--, director, Industrial Development Authority, 1966--, chairman, 1983--; member, Governor's Advisory Committee on N.H.'s Future, 1977-78, director, Crotched Mountain Foundation, 1960--, chairman, 1966--; trustee, Indian Head Banks Inc. Foundation, 1980--, Rivier College, 1984--, director, Pratt Read Corp., 1980--, Edgcomb Steel of N.E., 1958-86. Christine (Wilder), Feb. 25, 1945. Carolyn, Nov. 26, 1947, Harold, Jan. 29, 1950. Episcopal. Town Crier Rd., Amherst.

John Parker Hale Chandler Jr.

State senator. Boston, Mass., Aug. 6, 1911, John P.H. and Madeleine (Vogel) Chandler. Huntington Preparatory School, Boston, 1930, Harvard Univ., B.S., 1934. Editor, publisher, *Kearsarge Independent*, 1943-59, owner, Warner Ski Area, 1946-62. N.H. House of Rep., 1943-47,51-53,73-78, N.H. Executive Council, 1953-59, N.H. Senate, 1947-49,67-71,80--, selectman, Warner, 1961-63, N.H. Constitutional Convention, 1974, executive committee, N.E. Board of Higher Education, 1978, trustee, Sugar River Savings Bank, 1958-72, former president, Warner Historical Society, chairman, N.H. Conservative Union, former trustee, State Industrial School, former president, N.H. Society Sons of the American Revolution, secretary, treasurer, N.E. Council Sons of the American Revolution, member of about 100 civic, fraternal, patriotic, charitable and social organizations. South Main St., Warner.

John Parker Hale Chandler Jr.

Phoebe Ashley Chardon

Phoebe Ashley Chardon

State representative. Washington, D.C., May 5, 1933, Clifford and Sarah (Scudder) Ashley. Miss Hall's School, Pittsfield, Mass., 1950, Vassar College, B.A., 1954. Ski instructor, Henniker, 1962-66, ski instructor, Cannon Mountain Ski School, 1966-76, director, 1976--. Director, executive committee, N.H. Council for Better Schools, 1967-80, director, White Mountain Community Services, 1970-78, president, 1973-75; incorporator, director, No. N.H. Mental Health System, 1971-78, incorporator, N.H. Savings Bank, 1972-83, Jefferson Planning Board, 1975-84, N.H. House of Rep., 1980--, director, Environmental Law Council, 1982--, Weeks State Park Association, 1983--, No. N.H. Foundation, 1985--, incorporator, N.H. Charitable Fund, 1983--, member, Governor's High-Level Waste Task Force, 1985--. Alain Chardon, Sept. 6, 1952. Marc, Nov. 1, 1955, Stephen, April 24, 1957, Jennifer, Nov. 29, 1958. Episcopal. Box 93, RFD 1, Jefferson.

Jere Allen Chase

President, New England College, retired. Seabrook, N.H., March 31, 1915, Jerome and Elizabeth (Dockam) Chase. Amesbury (Mass.) High School, 1932, Univ. of N.H., B.S., 1936, M.Ed.,1946. U.S. Army Air Force, 1941-46,51-52, col. Submaster, teacher, coach, Berwick Academy, 1936-38, Dow Acadamy, Franconia, 1938-41, Univ. of N.H., a number of positions starting in 1946 including executive vice president, assistant to the president, acting president, 1962-63, interim president, 1979-80; president, N.E. College, 1969-73, president, Chase Enterprises, 1973--. N.H. House of Rep., 1959-61, chairman, N.H. Commission on the Arts, 1965-73, chairman, N.H. College and Univ. Council, 1972-73, trustee, Univ. System of N.H., 1976-84, N.E. College, 1963-69,73-83, emeritus, 1983--. Two honorary degrees. Jane (Woodbury), April 17, 1938. Robert, Jan. 2, 1940, Nancy, Nov. 30, 1946. Protestant. Durham Point Rd., Durham.

Malcolm Jerome Chase

Malcolm Jerome Chase

Civil engineer. Seabrook, N.H., July 5, 1911, Jerome and Elizabeth (Dockam) Chase. Amesbury (Mass.) High School, 1928, Univ. of N.H., B.S., 1932. U.S. Army Reserve, 1941-46, lt. col. N.H. Highway Department, survey crew chief, 1932-41, supervisor of construction of tramway at Mt. Sunapee, 1946-48, senior engineer, bridge division, 1948-50, location engineer, 1950-53, state turnpike engineer, 1953--56, chief design engineer, 1954-60, vice president, Davison Construction Co., Manchester, 1960-61, special projects engineer, N.H. Department of Public Works and Highways, 1961-73, special engineering consultant, Wright Pierce, Portsmouth, 1973-78, president, Kimball Chase Co., Portsmouth, 1980--. Trustee, Strawbery Banke, 1973-76, selectman, Durham, 1951-55,69-78, chairman, 1976-77; N.H. Consititutional Convention, 1984, trustee of trust funds, Durham, 1970-75, member, vice chairman, N.H. State Board of Registration for Professional Engineers, 1976--, member, N.H. Oceanographic Foundation, 1976-82, vice president, president, N.H. Society of Professional Engineers, 1974-76. Charlotte (Boothroyd), Dec. 22, 1935. David, Nov. 3, 1936, Malcolm Jr., Oct. 10, 1943. Protestant. Durham Point Rd., Durham.

Russell Cushing Chase

State representative. Dorchester, Mass., Feb. 5, 1907, William and Mabel (Cushing) Chase. Stoneham (Mass.) High School, 1925, Northeastern Univ., B.S., 1929. Shell Oil Co., manager, asphalt department, 1944-52, manager, marketing, 1953-61, manager, personnel, 1961-62, manager, management development and training, 1963-66, family candy business, Wolfeboro, 1967--. N.H. House of Rep., 1969--, N.H. Constitutional Convention, 1984, chairman, N.H. Bicentennial Commission on the U.S. Constitution, 1984--, organizer, Wolfeboro Home for the Aged, 1969, president, 1970-80; trustee, Brewster Academy, 1969--, board member, Huggins Hospital, 1969--, secretary, executive board, 1983--; former president, Wolfeboro Historical Society. Katherine (Owen), Oct. 3, 1931. Barbara, Feb. 23, 1933, Russell Jr., July 14, 1935 (dec.), David, May 6, 1951. Unitarian. Middleton Rd., Wolfeboro.

Russell Cushing Chase

Edwin Irving Chertok

Edwin Irving Chertok

Commissioner, Belknap County. Laconia, N.H., Aug. 26, 1915, Max and Rose (Winner) Chertok. Laconia High School, 1933, Univ. of N.H., B.S., 1937, U.S. Army, 1945, pvt. Retail home furnishing business, Laconia, 1937-80. Laconia City Council, 1971-78, mayor, Laconia, 1974-76, commissioner, Belknap County, 1978--, N.H. Constitutional Convention, 1964,84, director, Retail Merchants Association of N.H., 1966-73, Laconia Industrial Development Corp., 1975--, N.H. Association of Counties, 1980--, trustee, City Savings Bank, 1962-75, Lakes Region General Hospital, 1974-79, Belknap Mill Society, 1976-80, N.H. Savings Bank, 1975-83, director, N.H. Savings Bank Corp., 1983--, member, N.H. Revenue Reform Committee, 1981-83, corporator, Shaker Village, 1980--. Pauline (Shuman), Nov. 19, 1939. Susan, July 15, 1942, Fredda, April 3, 1947, Maxine, June 12, 1952. Judaism. 50 Blueberry Ln., Apt. 2, Laconia.

Charles Halsey Clark

Rector, St. Paul's School. New York, N.Y., Dec. 2, 1926, Alfred and Martha (Keck) Clark. Thacher School, Ojai, Calif., 1944, Yale Univ., B.A., 1948, Yale Divinity School, 1949-51, Va. Theological Seminary, B.D., 1952, Yale Graduate School, M.A., 1956. U.S. Naval Reserve, 1944-46, apprentice seaman. Lecturer, assistant chaplain, Yale Univ., 1953-57, director, International Student Center, Yale, 1953-56, assistant, associate professor, Trinity Theological College, Singapore, 1957-67, dean, St. Andrew's Seminary, Manila, 1967-77, dean, Berkeley Divinity School, Yale, 1977-82, associate dean, Yale Divinity School, 1977-82, director of field education, Yale and Berkeley, 1977-82, rector, St. Paul's School, 1982--. Founder, East Asian Institute of Liturgy and Music, 1975, fellow, Society for Values in Higher Education, director, N.H. Committee on National Security. Two honorary degrees. Priscilla (Hannah), May 15, 1953. Pamela (st. dau.), Nov. 1, 1944, Martha, March 14, 1957, Nathaniel, Nov. 12, 1958, Mary, Oct. 23, 1962, Anne, July 6, 1964. Episcopal. St. Paul's School, Concord.

Charles Halsey Clark

John Alden Clements

John Alden Clements

President, New England Fuel Institute. Hyannis, Mass., Aug. 22, 1930, George and Florence (Pinkerton) Clements. Yarmouth High School, South Yarmouth, Mass., 1948, Yale Univ., B.S.M.E., 1952. U.S. Naval Reserve, 1952-54, lieut. Chief manufacturing engineer, vice president for manufacturing, N.H. Ball Bearings Co., 1954-70, vice president, Sturm, Ruger and Co., Newport, 1971-76, commissioner, N.H. Department of Public Works and Highways, 1976-85, president, National Highway Users Federation, Washington, D.C., 1985-86, president, N.E. Fuel Institute, Boston, 1986--. Director, Indian Head Banks Inc., 1976--, N.H. Business Development Corp., 1973-84, First Citizens National Bank, Newport, 1971-75, Industrial Development Authority, 1969-80, president, National Association of State Highway and Transporation Officials, 1982, president, Business and Industry Association of N.H., 1974-76, selectman, Peterborough, 1965-68, chairman, transportation research board, National Academy of Sciences, 1985. John Jr., April 30, 1958, Katheryn, Jan. 28, 1961. Hannah (Coolidge), Oct. 22, 1969. Episcopal. 110 Patterson Ln., Newington.

Hilary Paterson Cleveland

Lecturer, Colby-Sawyer College. Orange, N.J., Dec. 7, 1927, David and Marjorie (Sclater) Paterson. Abbot Academy, Andover, Mass., 1945, Vassar College, B.A., 1948, Institute of International Relations, Geneva, Switz., M.A., 1950. Associate professor, history, political science, Colby-Sawyer College, New London, 1955-82, lecturer, 1982--, visiting professor, School of International Service, American Univ., Washington, D.C., 1963-64. Trustee, Proctor Academy, 1972-84, director, Abbot Academy Association, 1976-80, Center for N.H.'s Future, 1980--, Public Service Co. of N.H., 1984--, N.H. Commission on the Arts, 1983-85, moderator, New London, 1982--, nominating committee, board of incorporators, Mary Hitchcock Memorial Hospital, 1981-84, corporator, N.H. Savings Bank, 1972-85, incorporator, N.H. Charitable Fund, 1976-85, trustee, Phillips Academy, Andover, Mass., 1976-79. James Cleveland, Dec. 9, 1950. Cotton, April 13, 1952, James, Sept. 8, 1953, David, Oct. 29, 1954, Lincoln, Feb. 12, 1957, Susan, June 24, 1968. Christian. Main St., New London.

James Colgate Cleveland

Former United States congressman, attorney. Montclair, N.J., June 13, 1920, Mather and Susan (Colgate) Cleveland. Deerfield (Mass.) Academy, 1937, Colgate Univ., B.A., 1941, Yale Law School, LL.B., 1948. U.S. Army, 1941-46,51-52, capt. Attorney, Concord, New London, 1949--, U.S. Congress, Second District, 1963-81. N.H. Senate, 1951-63, organizer, incorporator, officer, director, New London Trust Co., 1958--, incorporator, director, King Ridge Ski Area 1960-66, director, N.E. Legal Foundation, 1982--, former trustee, Colgate Univ., former director, New London Hospital, former member, New London Budget Committee. Co-author, *We Propose a Modern Congress*, 1966. Two honorary degrees. Hilary (Paterson), Dec. 9, 1950. (Ch. see Hilary Cleveland.) Christian. Main St., New London.

Charles Elmer Clough

President, Nashua Corporation. Concord, N.H., Aug. 7, 1930, Harold and Raelene (Sawyer) Clough. Concord High School, 1948, Dartmouth College, A.B., 1952, M.B.A., 1953. U.S. Navy, 1953-56, lieut. General Electric Co., 1956-57, Nashua Corp., 1957--, budget director, assistant treasurer, treasurer, assistant general manager; vice president, 1982-83, group vice president, executive vice president, 1983, president, chief executive officer, 1983--. Director, Nashua Corp., 1960--, Pennichuck Water Works, 1960--, trustee, Lawrence Academy, 1980--, former trustee, Matthew Thornton Health Plan, Nashua YMCA, Nashua Arts and Science Center. Martha, Feb. 21, 1961, John, Sept. 21, 1962, David, Jan. 14, 1966, Benjamin, April 29, 1970, Thomas, Dec. 19, 1974. Nancy (Carter), July 18, 1985. Episcopal. RFD 3, Contoocook.

Marshall William Cobleigh

Former speaker, New Hampshire House of Representatives. Nashua, N.H., June 4, 1930, Neal and Dorothy (Esson) Cobleigh. Nashua High School, 1948, Boston Univ., A.A., 1950, B.S., 1957. U.S. Navy, 1951-55, yeoman 3rd cl. Proprietor, Marshall Cobleigh Mutual Insurance Agency, 1957-61, general manager, Independent Mutual Insurance Agents of N.E., 1961-72, N.H. House of Rep., 1963-73, speaker, 1969-73, legislative lobbyist, 1972-74, aide, Gov. Meldrim Thomson Jr., 1974-79, administrative assistant, N.H. Senate president, 1980-81, special assistant, administrator and director of program control office, General Services Administration, 1981-82, executive director, N.H. Job Training Council, 1983-84, N.H. Job Training Coordinating Council, 1985--. Member, National Alumni Council of Boston Univ., 1965--, N.H. Constitutional Convention, 1964,74,84. Carolyn (Foley), Oct. 7, 1961 (div. March 1972). Laura Lee, April 24, 1965, Kimberly, Feb. 10, 1968. Congregational. 36 Edgewood Ave., Nashua.

Marshall William Cobleigh

Stacey Ward Cole

Stacey Ward Cole

Former executive director, New Hampshire Petroleum Council. Keene, N.H., Dec. 4, 1921, Warren and Hazel (Ward) Cole. Vermont Academy, Saxtons River, 1939, Univ. of N.H. 1939-41. Owner, operator, Red Crow Farm, West Swanzey, 1943-66, owner, 1943--; director, radio farm program, 1943-66, executive director, N.H. Petroleum Council, 1966-85, senior agricultural advisor, American Petroleum Institute, Washington, D.C., 1986--. N.H. Air Resources Commission, 1967--, trustee, Univ. System of N.H., 1974--, president, N.H. Farm Bureau, 1954-62, trustee, Keene Savings Bank, 1958--, chairman, 1982--; Governor's Council on Energy, 1973-78, N.H. House of Rep., 1965-67, moderator, Swanzey, 1967--, Governor's Advisory Committee on N.H.'s Future, 1977-78, weekly nature column, *Manchester Union Leader*, 1962--, director, American Farm Bureau, 1956-61. Mildred (Hale), Sept. 18, 1942. Protestant. Red Crow Farm, West Swanzey.

John Joslin Colony III

President, Harrisville Designs. Keene, N.H., March 3, 1945, John Jr. and Marjorie (Page) Colony. Phillips Exeter Academy, 1963, Harvard Univ., B.A., 1967. U.S. Coast Guard, 1968-70, lt. jg. President, Harrisville Designs, 1971--. Trustee, Historic Harrisville, 1971--, Monadnock Music, 1984--, director, Inherit N.H., 1984--, Monadnock Perspectives, 1982--, moderator, Harrisville, 1978--, chairman, Harrisville Route 101 Committee, 1978--, director, Cheshire National Bank, 1986--. Patricia (Smith), Dec. 2, 1978. Timothy, Sept. 19, 1979, Joel, July 3, 1983, Nicholas, July 3, 1983. Congregational. P.O. Box 51, Harrisville.

John Joslin Colony III

Susan Ann Colwell

Former chair, New Hampshire Commission on the Status of Women. Cambridge, Mass., Jan. 19, 1943, Neil and Dorothy (Maguire) Colwell. Hyde Park (Mass.) High School, 1960, Mount St. Mary College, B.A., 1966. Professed as a nun, N.H. Sisters of Mercy, Aug. 15, 1964. Social studies teacher, Diocese of Manchester, 1966-71, housing counselor, community services advisor, U.S. Department of Housing and Urban Development, Manchester, 1971-74, equal opportunity specialist, 1974-84; insurance agent, 1984--. Chair, N.H. Commission on the Status of Women, 1979-85, director, Manchester YWCA, 1978--, president, 1980-82,85--; director, co-founder, N.H. Committee for Fair Housing, 1978, coordinator, Manchester Women Against Rape, 1977-78, member, N.H. Sisters of Mercy, 1961-73, associate member, 1983--; director, co-founder, N.H. Community Loan Fund, 1982-85, director, N.H. Women's Lobby, 1983-85. Catholic. 193 West Mitchell St., Manchester.

Marion Lamson Copenhaver

State representative. Andover, Vt., Sept. 26, 1925, Joseph and Christine (Forbes) Lamson. Chester (Vt.) High School, 1943, Univ. of Vt., 1944-46. Real estate agent, 1972-82. N.H. House of Rep., 1973--, incorporator, Mary Hitchcock Memorial Hospital Corp., 1974--, member, Lebanon Business and Professional Women's Club, 1976--, charter member, Unitarian Fellowship of the Upper Valley, 1956, president of fellowship, 1962-63; member, State Health Co-ordinating Council, 1981-83, United Health Systems Agency, 1976-83, co-chair, Area I Health Council, 1980-81; N.H. Social Welfare Council, 1981--, associate supervisor, Grafton County Soil Conservation District, 1983-86. John Copenhaver Jr., June 30, 1946. John III, May 24, 1947, Margaret, Aug. 25, 1948, Christine, Oct. 25, 1950, Eric, Sept. 10, 1954, Lisa, Nov. 7, 1955. Unitarian. 42 Rayton Rd., Hanover.

Thomas Armstrong Corcoran

President, chief executive officer, Waterville Company Inc. Yokohama, Japan, Nov. 16, 1931, David and Harriet (Armstrong) Corcoran. Phillips Exeter Academy, 1950, Dartmouth College, A.B., 1954, Harvard Business School, M.B.A., 1959. Financial analyst, Capital Enterprise Co., San Francisco, 1960-61, assistant to partner, J. Barth and Co., Los Angeles, 1961-63, assistant to the president, Aspen Ski Corp., 1963-65, president, chief executive officer, Waterville Co. Inc., 1965--. Director, National Ski Areas Association, 1969--, Ski the White Mountains Association, 1979-83, U.S. Ski Team Inc., 1984--, U.S. Ski Association, 1982--, president, Eastern Ski Areas Association, 1973-75, president, Ski 93 Association, 1967-69, chairman, director, Mountain Media Inc., 1970--, director, Carroll Reed Inc., 1974--, selectman, Waterville Valley, 1965--, trustee, U.S. Ski Educational Foundation, 1982--, member, U.S. Olympic Skiing Committee, 1970-80, U.S. Olympic ski team, 1956,60, National Ski Hall of Fame, 1978. St. ch., Linda Fogg, Sept. 26, 1957, Daphne Fogg, March 10, 1959. Ch., Michael, Sept. 4, 1961, Christine, Sept. 2, 1963, Kathleen, Oct. 24, 1964, Kerry, Feb. 28, 1967. Daphne (Andresen), May 28, 1976. Greeley Hill Rd., Waterville Valley.

Robert Walden Corell

Director, Univ. of New Hampshire Marine and Sea Grant Programs. Detroit, Mich., Nov. 4, 1934, George and Grace (Hagland) Corell. North Olmsted (Ohio) High School, 1952, Case Institute of Technology, B.S.M.E., 1956, MIT, M.S.M.E., 1959, Case Institute, Ph.D., 1964. Assistant professor, Univ. of N.H., 1959-60, graduate assistant, research, Case Institute, 1960-64, Univ. of N.H., professor, Mechanical Engineering Department, 1964--, chairman, 1964-72; research professor, Complex Systems Research Center, 1979--, director, Marine Systems Engineering Lab, 1977--, director, Marine and Sea Grant Programs, 1977--. Executive committee, Sea Grant Association, 1976--, president, 1979-80; chairman, advisory committee, Ocean Science Division, National Science Foundation, 1982--, vice chairman, University-National Oceanographic Laboratory Systems, 1984-85. Robert Jr., Nov. 10, 1958, David, May 2, 1960, Beth Anne, April 23, 1964. Andrea Lee (Jarvela), May 11, 1985. P.O. Box 10, Durham.

Bernard Whitehorn Corson

Director, New Hampshire Fish and Game Department, retired. Rochester, N.H., June 16, 1920, Frank and Georgina (Whitehorn) Corson. Rochester High School, 1939, Univ. of N.H., B.S., 1947, M.S., 1948. U.S. Naval Reserve, 1942-45, lieut. N.H. Fish and Game Department, technician, 1947-49, aquatic biologist, 1951-65, chief of fisheries, 1965-67, chief, division of inland and marine fisheries, 1967-68, assistant to the director, 1966-68, director, 1968-78. Consultant, National Audubon Society, 1978-79, consultant, National Rifle Association Task Force, 1980-81, member, N.E. Regional Fishery Management Council, 1983-85, advisor, 1985--, trustee, N.H. Audubon Society, 1980-, member, Citizens Task Force on Acid Rain, 1984, state advisory committee, Water Resources Research Center, Univ. of N.H., 1975-80, member, Water Supply and Pollution Control Commission, 1968-78, Bulk Power Supply Site Evaluation Committee, 1968-78. Martha (Clark), April 22, 1943. Clark, Oct. 20, 1944, Craig, March 21, 1949. Protestant. RFD 1, Box 41, Contoocook.

Bernard Whitehorn Corson

Norris Cotton

United States senator, retired. Warren, N.H., May 11, 1900, Henry and Elizabeth (Moses) Cotton. Phillips Exeter Academy, 1918, Wesleyan Univ., George Washington Univ. Law School, LL.B., 1927. Editor, *Granite Monthly*, 1923-24, secretary, Sen. George Moses, 1924-28, attorney, Concord, 1928-33, Lebanon, 1933-55; clerk, N.H. Senate, 1927-29, county attorney, Grafton County, 1933-39, judge, Lebanon District Court, 1939-44, N.H. House of Rep., 1923-25,43-47, speaker, 1945-47; U.S. Congress, Second District, 1947-54, U.S. Senate, 1954-75. Author, *In the Senate*, 1978. Nine honorary degrees. Ruth (Isaacs), May 11, 1927 (dec. 1978). Eleanor (Brown), May 24, 1980. Methodist. 52 Elm St., Lebanon.

Robert Emmet Craig

Associate professor, Univ. of New Hampshire. New York, N.Y., Sept. 24, 1933, Joseph and Florence (Conroy) Craig. Andrew Jackson High School, Queens County, N.Y., 1951, Adelphi College, B.A., 1960, Univ. of N.C., Ph.D., 1971. U.S. Navy, 1952-56, petty off. 1st cl. Lecturer, Univ. of N.C., 1963-65, Univ. of N.H., 1966-71, assistant professor, 1971-81, associate professor, 1981--. Director, N.H. Council on World Affairs, 1976--, executive committee, 1977-84; public member, N.H. Council for the Humanities, 1979-80, member, Governor's Committee on the UN, 1979-81, Democratic State Committee, 1968-74,77-85, chairman, First Congressional District, 1979-85; administrative assistant, Rep. Norman D'Amours, 1975-76, member, N.H. Public Employee Labor Relations Board, 1980--, chairman, 1981--. Patricia (Lynch), Aug. 20, 1960. Sean, May 28, 1961, Anne Marie, Oct. 6, 1962, Siobhan, April 18, 1964. Mary (Huffer), Sept. 19, 1981. Catholic. P.O. Box 151, Dover.

Robert Emmet Craig

William Henry Craig

Attorney. Manchester, N.H., Aug. 26, 1927, William and Emma (Bousquet) Craig. St. Joseph's High School, Manchester, 1944, St. Anselm College, B.A., 1949, Boston Univ. School of Law, LL.B., 1952. U.S. Navy, 1945-46, seaman. Attorney, Manchester, 1952--, U.S. attorney, District of N.H., 1961-63. Director, Indian Head National Bank, 1964-79, BankEast, 1979--, Business and Industry Association of N.H., 1979--, N.H. House of Rep. 1955-59,61-63,65-67,70, Manchester Planning Board, 1956--, Manchester Historical Association, 1981--, Manchester Historical Commission, 1979-81, trustee, Catholic Medical Center, 1974--, director, Governor's Management Review, 1981-82. James, June 2, 1951, Patricia, Nov. 7, 1953, Joseph, Feb. 13, 1956, Paula, March 21, 1957. Gloria (Carrigan), March 12, 1975. 129 Magnolia Rd., Manchester.

Paul Clarke Cummings Jr.

Publisher, *Peterborough Transcript*. Boston, Mass., Aug. 25, 1913, Paul and Marion (Wells) Cummings. Peterborough High School, 1930, Phillips Exeter Academy, 1931, Dartmouth College, A.B., 1935. U.S. Naval Reserve, 1944-46, lt. jg. *Peterborough Transcript*, 1946--, former managing editor and editor, present publisher and owner. Special justice, Peterborough District Court, 1957-83, former president, N.H. Weekly Press Association, founding director, N.E. Press Association, chairman, Transcript Printing Co., 1973--, vice chairman, Peterborough Planning Board, 1959--. Joanne (Dearborn), June 25, 1938. Betsey, Nov. 10, 1939, Joseph, Feb. 26, 1946. Congregational. 244 Sand Hill Rd., Peterborough.

Linda Stewart Dalianis

Linda Stewart Dalianis

Associate justice, New Hampshire Superior Court. Boston, Mass., Oct. 9, 1948, John Jr. and Irene (Connelly) Stewart. Villa Augustina Academy, Goffstown, 1966, Northeastern Univ., B.A., 1970, Suffolk Univ. Law School, J.D., 1974. Attorney, Nashua, 1974-79, marital master, N.H. Superior Court, 1979-80, associate justice, N.H. Superior Court, 1980--. Director, Nashua YWCA, 1975-78, Nashua YWCA/YMCA Council, 1976-79, Northeastern Univ. National Council, 1983--, director, vice president, Nashua Girls Club, 1975-78, member, Nashua Business and Professional Women's Club, 1974-83. Griffin Dalianis, July 31, 1971. G. Matthew, Jan. 12, 1976, Sarah, April 21, 1979 (dec. Sept. 1, 1979), Benjamin, Dec. 15, 1980. Catholic. Nashua.

Louis Clifford D'Allesandro

Former executive councilor. Boston, Mass., July 30, 1938, Louis and Marion (Viscome) D'Allesandro. Worcester (Mass.) Academy, 1956, Univ. of N.H., B.A., 1961, Rivier College, M.Ed., 1971. Teacher, coach, Conway, Manchester, 1961-66, director of athletics, basketball coach, N.H. College, 1962-74, director of admissions, 1974-76; president, Daniel Webster College, 1976-80, executive assistant to the president, N.E. College, 1981-82, senior vice president, Computer Management Dynamics, Nashua, 1984--. N.H. House of Rep., 1973-75, N.H. Executive Council, 1975-81, trustee, Daniel Webster College, 1975-85, Mount Hope School, Nashua, 1985--, N.H. Constitutional Convention, 1974, director, So. N.H. Association of Commerce and Industry, 1976-80, Granite State Independent Living Foundation, 1974-84, Greater Manchester Child Care, 1976-84, Social Welfare Council of N.H., 1980-85, Partners of the Americas, 1970--, National Council on Alcoholism, 1981--, advisory committee, Campaign for Ratepayers' Rights, 1983--. Patricia (Morganstern), May 27, 1961. Anne-Marie, Sept. 16, 1966, Michael, Nov. 15, 1967, Christina, June 19, 1971. Catholic. 332 St. James Ave., Manchester.

Louis Clifford D'Allesandro

Norman Edward D'Amours

Norman Edward D'Amours

Former United States congressman. Holyoke, Mass., Oct. 14, 1937, Albert and Edna (Laplante) D'Amours. Assumption Preparatory School, Worcester, Mass., 1956, Assumption College, A.B., 1960, Boston Univ. School of Law, LL.B., 1960. Assistant N.H. attorney general, criminal division, 1966-69, attorney, Manchester, 1969-74, city prosecutor, Manchester, 1970-72, instructor, criminal law and evidence, St. Anselm College, 1971-73, U.S. Congress, First District, 1975-85, attorney, Manchester, Washington, D.C., 1985--. Member, Democratic National Charter Commission, 1973-74. Helen (Manning), Sept. 4, 1965. Danielle, Dec. 19, 1967, Susan, Oct. 21, 1969, Norman M., March 1, 1972. Catholic. 617 Coolidge Ave., Manchester.

David Stafford Dana

President, Capital Securities. Dallas, Tex., June 5, 1931, Charles and Eleanor (Naylor) Dana. Staunton (Va.) Military Academy, 1949, Columbia Univ. A.B., 1953. U.S. Army, 1955-57, pfc. Dana Corp., Toledo, engineering, 1953-55, sales engineering, 1957-60, manager, international division, 1960-63; president, founder, Spicer, S.A., Mexico City, 1964-67, vice president, Dana International, Toledo, 1968-70, chairman, Executive Aviation, Toledo, 1970-72, president, Capital Securities, 1972--. Vice chairman, finance committee, Ohio Republican Party, 1970-72, director, Toledo Mental Health Clinic, 1968-72, president, 1972; White Mountains Center for the Arts, 1972-82, president, 1976-82; trustee, Los Angeles Chamber Orchestra, 1979--, president, Dalton Ridge, home development project, 1975--. Randall, Aug. 5, 1947, Charles, Dec. 7, 1951. Patricia (Bodiford), Jan. 11, 1957 (div. 1972). Deborah, Oct. 1, 1957, Stephanie, Sept. 23, 1959, Amy, March 12, 1964. Episcopal. Dalton Ridge, Dalton.

Eugene Sanger Daniell Jr.

Attorney, retired, state representative. Augusta, Maine, Sept. 20, 1904, Eugene and Mary (Haynes) Daniell. Salisbury (Conn.) School, 1922, Harvard Univ., B.S. 1926, Boston Univ. School of Law, LL.B., 1929, Harvard Law School, 1930. U.S. Army, 1942-46, maj. Attorney, 1929-81, practice in Franklin, 1940-81. Mayor, Franklin, 1948-49,57,70-75, N.H. Senate, 1949-51, N.H. House of Rep., 1961-63,71--, Franklin School Board, 1964-65,75--, director, Franklin Developments Inc., 1950--, vice president, 1970-75; former trustee, Franklin Regional Hospital. Eva (Burns), July 4, 1931 (dec. May 11, 1982). Eugene III, May 31, 1946. Unitarian. Daniell Point, Franklin.

Jere Rogers Daniell

Professor, Dartmouth College. Millinocket, Maine, Nov. 28, 1932, Warren and Mary (Holway) Daniell. George Stearns High School, Millinocket, 1950, Phillips Exeter Academy, 1951, Dartmouth College, A.B., 1955, Harvard Univ., M.A., 1960, Ph.D., 1964. U.S. Navy, 1955-58, lt. jg. Head tutor, Heritage Foundation, Old Deerfield, Mass., 1960-64, assistant professor, history, Dartmouth College, 1964-69, associate professor, 1969-74, professor, 1974--. Trustee, N.H. Historical Society, 1977-86, board of editors, Univ. Press of N.E., 1970-72,78--, member, Colonial Society of Mass., 1978--, N.H. Council for the Humanities, 1974-77, N.H. Bicentennial Commission on the U.S. Constitution, 1981--. Author, *Experiment in Republicanism: New Hampshire Politics and the American Revolution*, 1970, *Colonial New Hampshire: A History*, 1981. Sally (Wellborn), Dec. 1955 (div. 1969). Douglas, Sept. 1, 1958, Alexander, Dec. 29, 1960, Matthew, June 16, 1962. Elena (Lillie), July 17, 1969. St. ch., Breena Brodsky, Sept. 17, 1962, Clifford Brodsky, Oct. 19, 1963. 11 Barrymore Rd., Hanover.

Jere Rogers Daniell

James Edward DeCourcy

James Edward DeCourcy

Newspaper editor, publisher, retired. Darien, Conn., April 16, 1912, Frank and Bertha (Schlichting) DeCourcy. Darien High School, 1930, Univ. of Maine, B.A., 1934. Reporter, *Norwalk* (Conn.) *Hour*, 1929-34, staff writer, assistant editor, *Printing Magazine*, 1935-41, public relations director, aide to the president, assistant advertising manager, Bridgeport Brass Co., 1941-46, editor, *Westport* (Conn.) *Town Crier*, 1946-49, editor, *Milford* (Conn.) *Citizen*, 1949-61, editor, publisher, *Argus Champion*, Newport, 1961-81. Director, Keene Publishing Corp., 1961-81, Valley Publishing Corp., 1961-81, member, N.H. Committee on Accreditation of the Courts, 1971-76, executive committee, N.H. Public Broadcasting Council, 1975-80, trustee, Richards Free Library, 1964-78, Newport Hospital, 1966-72, Univ. of Maine Alumni Council, 1970-76, president, International Society of Weekly Newspaper Editors, 1962, president, N.E. Press Association, 1955, president, N.H. Press Association, 1968, columnist, 1981--. Alice (Dyer), Oct. 17, 1936. Jane, March 17, 1940, Thomas, May 20, 1943. Congregational. RD 2, Box 82, Newport.

Charles Allyson DeGrandpre

Attorney. Manchester, N.H., July 8, 1936, Arthur and Andrea (L'Etoile) DeGrandpre. Conant High School, Jaffrey, 1954, Clark Univ., A.B., 1958, Univ. of Mich., LL.B., 1961. Attorney, Manchester, 1961--. Board of governors, treasurer, N.H. Bar Association, 1983--, fellow, American College of Probate Counsel, 1985, trustee, Lou and Lutza Smith Foundation, 1985--, Hitchcock Foundation, 1980--, Manchester Historic District Commission, 1980--, member, N.H. Advisory Commission on Health and Welfare, 1967-70, director, Child and Family Services of N.H., 1966--, president, 1979-85; trustee, 4-H Foundation of N.H., 1977--, Child Welfare League of America, 1984--. Sarah, Nov. 9, 1968, David, Sept. 16, 1970. Patricia (Fielding), Oct. 9, 1983. St. ch., Peter Fielding, Sept. 28, 1964, Lizabeth Fielding, May 12, 1972. Unitarian. 101 Amoskeag Pl., Manchester.

Charles Allyson DeGrandpre

Selma Ruth Deitch

Physician. Manchester, N.H., Nov. 15, 1924, John and Anna (Silver) Deitch. Manchester Central High School, 1941, Tufts Univ., B.S., 1944, Tufts Medical School, M.D., 1949, Harvard School of Public Health, M.P.H., 1965. Residency, Boston Floating Hospital, 1950-53, practice of pediatrics, Needham. Mass., 1953-60, director, prediatric outpatient department, Boston Dispensary, 1958-65, director, Bureau of Maternal and Child Health, N.H. Division of Public Health, 1966-74, director, Institute of Child Health and Development, Manchester, 1974-79, planner, clinical director, Child Health Services, Manchester, 1979--. Adjunct associate clinical professor of maternal and child health, Dartmouth Medical School, 1972--, director, Greater Manchester Mental Health Center, 1963-75, president, 1973-75; Greater Manchester Child Care Association, 1972-79, N.H. Lung Association, 1974-75, chairman, health planning committee, N.H. Pediatric Society, 1978-84. John, Sept. 18, 1953. M. Saul Sigel, Aug. 24, 1960 (dec. April 1982). Richard, April 13, 1963. St. ch., Roberta, Dec. 2, 1939, George, Aug. 31, 1941, Marge, Jan. 9, 1945. 300 North Adams St., Manchester.

Margaret Bowles DeLude

Director of welfare, Claremont, retired. Lynchburg, Va., Nov. 4, 1918, Lester and Elizabeth (Wood) Bowles. Cazenovia (N.Y.) Seminary, 1933, Cazenovia Junior College, 1935. Women's program director, WTSV Radio, Claremont, 1970-75, director of welfare, Claremont, 1978-84. Selectman, Unity, 1983--, chairman, 1985--; director, Sullivan County Rehabilitation Center, 1975-78, N.H. Social Welfare Council, 1976-80, executive committee, N.H. Municipal Association, 1984--, N.H. Commission on the Status of Women, 1971-76, chairman, 1974-76; Unity School Board, 1953-59, chairman, 1956-59; moderator, Unity, 1971-83, N.H. House of Rep., 1953-55,59-61, N.H. Senate, 1957-59,63-65, N.H. Constitutional Convention, 1964. Cortland, Feb. 2, 1946. Floyd DeLude, Nov. 6, 1948 (dec. Jan. 16, 1974). Episcopal. P.O. Box 27, Claremont.

Margaret Bowles DeLude

Vincent Joseph DeNobile

Vincent Joseph DeNobile

President, Frisbie Memorial Hospital. Yonkers, N.Y., May 8, 1928, Donald and Louis (Ippoliti) DeNobile. Yonkers High School, 1946, Westchester Commercial School, 1949-52. U.S. Army, 1946-48, pvt. 1st. cl. Assistant accountant, Yonkers General Hospital, 1951-52, office manager, Lawrence Hospital, Bronxville, N.Y., 1953-54, office manager, St. Luke's Hospital, Newburgh, N.Y., 1954-55, office manager, acting assistant administrator, assistant administrator, Nyack (N.Y.) Hospital, 1956-59, director, Wentworth-Douglass Hospital, Dover, 1959-75, president, Frisbie Memorial Hospital Rochester, 1975--. Chairman, Advisory Commission on Health and Welfare, 1965-70, member, N.H. Hospital Association, 1967--, chairman, 1967-69; member, American College of Hospital Administrators, American Academy of Medical Administrators, charter member, former president, N.H. Health Careers Council. Lavergne (DeWitt), Dec. 18, 1954. Pamela, Oct. 4, 1955, Vincent, Aug. 15, 1957, Ellen, May 30, 1962, Scott, Sept. 6, 1964. Chesley Hill Rd., Rochester.

Walter Newton DeWitt

Chairman, chief executive officer, BankEast. Arlington, Mass., March 12, 1937, Walter and Helena (Chittenden) DeWitt. Brewster Academy, Wolfeboro, 1954, Dartmouth College, A.B., 1958, M.B.A., 1965. U.S. Air Force, 1958-63, 1st lt. Executive training program, The Manchester Bank, 1965-67, vice president, investment manager, 1967-72, chairman, chief executive officer, 1972-- (name changed to BankEast in 1981); chairman, chief executive officer, BankEast Corp. (formerly First Financial Group of N.H.), 1972--. Director, Business and Industry Association of N.H., 1975--, president, 1978-80; Manchester Gas Co., 1977-83, vice chairman, N.E. Council, 1981-83, chairman, 1983-85; government relations council, American Bankers Association, 1984--, board chairman, Brewster Academy, trustee, Franconia College, 1967-71, present director, BankEast Corp. and all subsidiaries, Bald Peak Land Co., Amoskeag Industries, Wildcat Mountain Corp. Dorothy (Collins), Sept. 2, 1961. Walter A., Dec. 1, 1962, William, Sept. 22, 1964, Kathryn, June 9, 1968, Cynthia, May 11, 1970. Protestant. One Wall St., Manchester.

Walter Newton DeWitt

Paul Thomas Doherty

Paul Thomas Doherty

Former director, New Hampshire Division of Parks. Wilton, N.H., June 19, 1919, Edward and Myra (Duval) Doherty. Wilton High School, 1938. U.S. Navy, 1942-45, chief petty officer. Conservation officer, 1947-60, district chief conservation officer, 1960-73, director, N.H. Bureau Off-Highway Vehicles, 1973-78, director, N.H. Division of Parks, 1978-82, consultant, Franconia Notch Parkway Project, 1983--. Member, International Association of Snowmobile Administrators, 1974-79, National Association of State Parks Directors, 1978-82, N.H. Fish and Game Commission, 1975-79, chairman, 1977-79; Mount Washington Commission, 1982--, chairman, Gorham Recreation Commission, 1963-67, chairman, Gorham Conservation Commission, 1971-80, selectman, Gorham, 1985--, N.H. Constitutional Convention, 1984. Barbara (Frye), Feb. 2, 1947 (dec. 1963). Sally (Dyson), Oct. 30, 1965. Protestant. Box 271, Gorham.

James Wells Donchess

Mayor of Nashua. Glen Ridge, N.J., July 25, 1949, Stephen and Mary (Wells) Donchess. Arlington (Ill.) High School, 1967, Yale Univ., B.A., 1971, N.Y.U. School of Law, J.D., 1976. Attorney, Boston, 1976-77, Manchester, 1977-83; mayor, Nashua, 1984--. N.H. Housing Commission, 1981-82, N.H. Housing Finance Authority, 1982--, N.H. Human Rights Commission, 1980-81, advisory board, Nashua Salvation Army, 1979--, director, Nashua Girls Club, 1982-85, advisory board, 1985--; alderman, Nashua, 1978-82, N.H. Constitutional Convention, Concord, 1974, Nashua, 1984. Victoria (Seraichick), May 24, 1978. Caroline, Nov. 13, 1981. Congregational. 14 Ronnie Dr., Nashua.

Charles Gwynne Douglas III

Charles Gwynne Douglas III

Former associate justice, New Hampshire Supreme Court. Abington, Pa., Dec. 2, 1942, Charles Jr. and Elizabeth (Graham) Douglas. William Penn Charter School, Philadelphia, 1960, Wesleyan Univ., 1960-62, Univ. of N.H., B.A., 1965, Boston Univ. School of Law, J.D., 1968. Attorney, Manchester, 1968-70, Concord, 1970-74; legal counsel, Gov. Meldrim Thomson Jr., 1973-74, associate justice, N.H. Superior Court, 1974-76, associate justice, N.H. Supreme Court, 1977-85, attorney, Concord, 1985--. Adjunct faculty, Franklin Pierce Law Center, 1980--, chairman, Supreme Court Rules Committee, 1981-82, judicial representative, Police Standards and Training Council, 1975-78, chairman, N.H. Constitutional Bicentennial Education Commission, 1981-85, president, N.H. Task Force on Child Abuse and Neglect, 1977-78, director, N.H. Mediation Program, 1978--, chairman, 1981-85; president, Merrimack County Bar Association, 1984-86. Author, *New Hampshire Practice, Family Law*, 1982. Martha (Ritzman), Aug. 21, 1965 (div. 1979). Charles IV, March 12, 1969, Thomas, Aug. 5, 1971. Nancy (Carter), April 25, 1981 (div. 1985). Lorenca (Rosal), Feb. 25, 1985. Episcopal. 49 Ridge Rd., Concord.

Delbert Francis Downing

Chairman, Water Resources Board. Malden, Mass., Nov. 18, 1931, Michael and Mary (Dewling) Downing. Christopher Columbus High School, Boston, 1948, Burdett College, Emerson College, Portia Law School. Store general manager, Enterprise/J.M. Fields Department Stores, Boston, 1954-63, marketing, sales representative, H.F. Davis Tractor Co., Southborough, Mass., 1963-73, marketing, Shapiro Equipment Corp., Southborough, 1973-78, co-ordinator, N.H. Trade Adjustment Assistance Program, 1979-81, director, N.H. Business Service Center, 1980-81, chairman, Water Resources Board, 1981--. Salem School Board, 1965-71, chairman, 1967-68,70-71; N.H. Senate, 1971-78, Salem Housing Redevelopment Authority, 1979--, chairman, 1984--; chairman, N.H. Wetlands Board, 1981--, member, Water Supply and Pollution Control Commission, 1981--. Teresa (Crimlisk), Oct. 3, 1953. Michael, Oct. 20, 1954, Karen, Aug. 5, 1956, Patricia, Aug. 18, 1957, Delbert, Sept. 12, 1958, Brian, Dec. 19, 1959, Michele, Dec. 10, 1961, Mark, March 31, 1964, Teresa, Sept. 23, 1968, Suzanne, Nov. 25, 1973. Catholic. 112 North Policy St., Salem.

Delbert Francis Downing

Dudley Webster Dudley

Dudley Webster Dudley

Former executive councilor. Exeter, N.H., Aug. 4, 1936, Robert and Polly (Stevens) Webster. Robinson Female Seminary, Exeter, 1954, Univ. of N.H., B.S., 1959. Instructor, School of Life Studies, Univ. of N.H., 1969, N.H. House of Rep., 1973-76, N.H. Executive Council, 1977-85, coordinator of citizen participation, Strafford Guidance Center, Dover, 1980-82, public relations consultant, 1982-84, director of marketing, Citizens Heat and Power, 1985--. Board of overseers, Dartmouth Medical School, 1979-80, director, Univ. of N.H. Alumni Association, 1977-80, Prescott Park Arts Festival, 1981-83, Seacoast Family Y, 1983, incorporator, N.H. Charitable Fund, 1981--. Thomas Dudley Jr., Oct. 6, 1956. Morgan, July 26, 1960, Rebecca, Feb. 5, 1963. 25 Woodman Ave., Durham.

Barbara Jean Dunfey

Consultant. Miami, Fla., March 6, 1949, Joseph and Dorothy (Saks) Levine. Miami Senior High School, 1967, Ohio Univ., 1967-69. Director of advertising, public relations, Sonesta Hotels, Boston, 1969-72, sports broadcaster, WNAC-TV, Boston, 1972-75, consultant, public relations, marketing, Portsmouth, 1975--. Chairman, N.H. Commission on the Arts, 1978-82, trustee, Theatre by the Sea, 1975-84, Univ. of N.H. Pro-Am Classic, 1980--, executive director, 1982-84; founding director, N.H. Film Bureau, 1979, corporator, Portsmouth Hospital, 1980--, community advisory board, N.H. Public Television, 1981--. Div. Jewish. P.O. Box 152, Portsmouth.

John P. (Jack) Dunfey

John P. (Jack) Dunfey

Vice chairman, Omni/Dunfey Hotels. Lowell, Mass., Jan. 7, 1924, Leroy and Catherine (Manning) Dunfey. Keith Academy, Lowell, 1940, Univ. of N.H., B.S., 1952. U.S. Army Air Force, 1943-46, 1st lt. President, chief executive officer, Dunfey Hotels Corp., 1959-80, vice chairman, chief executive officer, 1980-83, vice chairman, 1983-- (name changed to Omni/Dunfey Hotels, 1984). Founder, Hampton National Bank, 1958, president, 1958-59; founder, former treasurer, WBBX Radio, Portsmouth, 1960, co-developer, Maine Mall Shopping Center, 1971, Bedford Mall Shopping Center, 1969, director, Waterville Valley Co., 1967--, member, National Committee of the American Irish Foundation, 1980--, commissioner, National Academy of Peace and Conflict Resolution, 1979-81, member, finance council, Democratic National Committee, 1977-82, incorporator, Spaulding Youth Center, 1974--, founder, director, Ireland Fund, 1976--. Susan, May 9, 1949, David, April 23, 1952, J. Philip, March 12, 1955, Stephen, April 18, 1957. Catholic. 500 Lafayette Rd., Hampton.

William Leo Dunfey

Vice president, Omni/Dunfey Hotels. Lowell, Mass., Oct. 10, 1925, LeRoy and Catherine (Manning) Dunfey. Keith Academy, Lowell, 1943, Miami (Ohio) Univ., 1947-48, Univ. of N.H., B.A., 1950, M.A., 1954. U.S. Marine Corps, 1943-46, sgt. Vice president, personnel, Dunfey Hotels Corp., 1960-73, vice president, corporate planning, 1973-78, vice president, director, 1978-- (name changed to Omni/Dunfey Hotels, 1984). N.H. Library Commission, 1954-59, trustee, Univ. System of N.H., 1972-76, alternate representative, UN General Assembly, 1979, board of overseers, Dartmouth Medical School, 1980--, chairman, *N.H. Times*, 1981-83, director, vice chairman, *World Paper*, 1979--, member, National Development Committee, Univ. of N.H., 1984--, Democratic National Committeeman, 1960-64, chairman, Democratic State Committee, 1965-67, state coordinator, John F. Kennedy Library, 1964, director, Mediators Productions Inc., 1983--, advisory board, Center for Foreign Journalists, 1984--. Two honorary degrees. Ruth (Thomas), June 14, 1956. Julie, March 9, 1958. Catholic. 500 Lafayette Rd., Hampton.

William Leo Dunfey

Philip Stanley Dunlap

Philip Stanley Dunlap

Trust management. Manchester, N.H., Oct. 10, 1918, Clifton and Hazel (Elliott) Dunlap. Concord High School, 1936, Univ. of N.H., B.S., 1940. President, Dunlap-Johnson Inc., 1946-53, vice president, Morrill and Everett Inc., real estate and insurance agency, 1953-84, director, S.H. Dunlap Realty Trust, 1984--. Director, Northern Railroad, 1952--, vice president, treasurer, 1984--; president, treasurer, Concord Builders, 1957-83, director, manager, N.H. Automatic Equipment, 1955--, director, Aerotronic Associates, 1960-85, Concord National Bank, 1963--, Public Service Co., 1982--, incorporator, N.H. Savings Bank, 1951-73, trustee, Univ. System of N.H., 1969-79, chairman, 1973-78, acting chancellor, 1973-74; N.H. Senate, 1959-65, president, 1963-65; moderator, Hopkinton School District, 1956-58, moderator, Hopkinton, 1959--. Two honorary degrees. Shirley (Holmes), June 11, 1949. William, March 15, 1951, Ann, April 9, 1953, Robert, June 22, 1957, John, March 20, 1959. Congregational. Putney Hill Rd., Hopkinton.

Sylvio Louis Dupuis

President, New England College of Optometry. Manchester, N.H., June 2, 1934, Arthur and Alma (Lizotte) Dupuis. St. Marie High School, Manchester, 1952, St. Anselm College, 1954-55, Ill. College of Optometry, B.S., 1956, O.D., 1957. Optometrist, Manchester, 1957-71, mayor, Manchester, 1971-75, president, Catholic Medical Center, Manchester, 1975-83, commissioner, N.H. Department of Health and Human Services, 1983-85, president, N.E. College of Optometry, Boston, 1985--. Chairman, Federated Arts Campaign, Manchester, 1981, board of visitors, U.S. Military Academy, 1979-83, trustee, St. Anselm College, 1984--, Currier Gallery of Art, 1976--, director, BankEast Corp., 1981--, Energy North, 1982--, N.H. Charitable Fund, 1980--, advisory board, Mount St. Mary College, 1976-78. Two honorary degrees. Cecile (Pellerin), July 14, 1956. Jeanne-Marie, April 24, 1964, Michelle, May 1, 1965, Marc, Feb. 9, 1966, Mary-Carol, Oct. 5, 1969. Catholic. 451 Coolidge Ave., Manchester.

Sylvio Louis Dupuis

John Anthony Durkin

John Anthony Durkin

Former United States senator, attorney. Brookfield, Mass., March 29, 1936, Joseph and Charlotte (Daley) Durkin. St. John's Preparatory, Worcester, 1954, Holy Cross College, B.S., 1959, Georgetown Univ. Law Center, LL.B., 1965. U.S. Navy, 1959-61, lt. jg. Law clerk, Comptroller of the Currency, Washington D.C., 1963-66, assistant attorney general, N.H., 1966-68, commissioner, N.H. Insurance Department, 1968-73, attorney, Manchester, 1973-74, U.S. Senate, 1975-80, attorney, Manchester, 1981--. Moderator, Brookfield, 1959, past president, Merrimack Valley Navy League, member, N.H. Bar Association, 1966--, Mass. Bar Association, 1966--. Patricia (Moses), Aug. 28, 1965 (div. 1983). Andrea, Sept. 20, 1966, John Jr., Dec. 19, 1967, Sheilagh, May 29, 1971. Catholic. 60 Lenz St., Manchester.

Lane Dwinell

Former governor of New Hampshire. Newport, Vt., Nov. 14, 1906, Dean and Ruth (Lane) Dwinell. Lebanon High School, 1924, Dartmouth College, A.B., 1928, M.B.A., 1929. Partner, president, Carter and Churchill Co., sportswear manufacturer, Lebanon, 1936-66, governor, N.H., 1955-59, assistant secretary of state for administration, 1959-60, assistant administrator, Agency for International Development, 1969-71. Special justice, Lebanon Municipal Court, 1944-54, N.H. House of Rep., 1949-53, speaker, 1951-53; N.H. Senate, 1953-55, president, 1953-55; director, National Bank of Lebanon, 1947-80, president, 1960-67, chairman, 1967-79; N.H. Constitutional Convention, 1948,84, president, N.H. Manufacturers Association, 1946-47, trustee, N.H. Savings Bank, 1961-72, Mary Hitchcock Memorial Hospital, 1962-82, Colby-Sawyer College, 1964-77, Dartmouth College, 1955-59, Univ. of N.H., 1955-59. Four honorary degrees. Elizabeth (Cushman), April 1932. Congregational. 94 Bank St., Lebanon.

Lane Dwinell

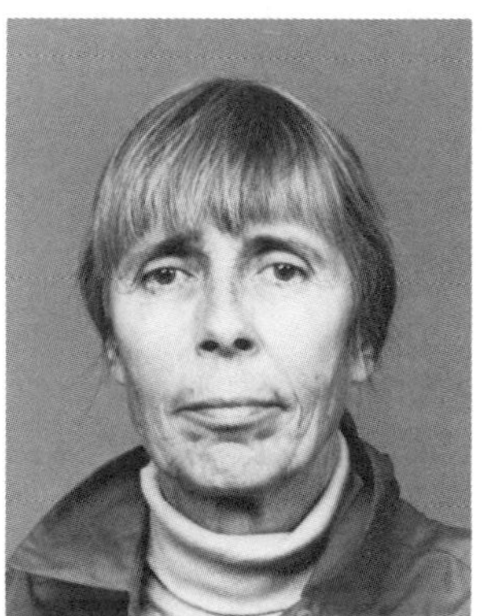
Jayne Elizabeth Dwyer

Jayne Elizabeth Dwyer

Artist. Nashua, N.H., Aug. 1, 1928, Ambrose and Laura (Baker) Dwyer. Nashua High School, 1946, Vesper George School of Art, Boston, 1946-49, Mass. College of Art., B.S., 1954, The Maryland Institute, College of Art, M.F.A., 1970. Supervisor of art, Laconia elementary schools, 1954-57, kindergarten teacher, Laconia, 1957-59, designer of, "Art At Your Fingertips," public television series, 1962-63, art teacher, Memorial Junior High School, Laconia, 1963-64, instructor, assistant professor, department of the arts, Univ. of N.H., 1965-69,71-73, teacher of art classes, Barn Gallery, Ogunquit, Maine, 1979-81,83-84, Durham Art Association, 1975--, co-owner, director, The Gallery, Portsmouth, 1982, teacher of painting, Appalachian Mountain Club, Pinkham Notch, 1985--. Member, N.H. Art Association, 1951--, Ogunquit Art Association, 1968--. Illustrator of book *Nine Children*, 1986. Catholic. 9 Sheafe St., Portsmouth.

Joseph March Eaton

State representative. Salisbury, Mass., Dec. 1, 1901, Stephen and Ellen (Merrill) Eaton. Amesbury (Mass.) High School, 1918, Boston Univ., B.B.A., 1926. Advertising writer, 1926-42, federal investigator, 1942-47, owner, Eaton Furniture, Hillsboro, 1947--. N.H. House of Rep., 1961--, chairman, Republican State Platform Committee, 1972, chairman, Governor's Commission on Welfare, 1973-74, N.H. Constitutional Convention, 1974,84. Mildred (Pehrson), June 28, 1930. Joseph Jr., April 19, 1931, Nancy, Aug. 30, 1933, Pauline, March 22, 1935. 11 Walnut St., Hillsboro.

Joseph March Eaton

Winslow Bryan Eaves

Winslow Bryan Eaves

Sculptor. Detroit, Mich., Sept. 8, 1922, William and Tula (Faulkner) Eaves. Northwestern High School, Detroit, 1940, Cranbrook Art Academy, Bloomfield Hill, Mich., 1941-42, Art Students League, N.Y.C., 1942-43. U.S. Army, 1943-45, cpl. Instructor, Munson-Williams-Proctor Institute School of Art, Utica, N.Y., 1946-49, assistant to the director, League of N.H. Arts and Crafts, 1952-53, instructor, lecturer, Dartmouth College, 1953-55, instructor, Syracuse Univ., 1955-58, assistant professor, Dartmouth College, 1959-68, artist in residence, White Mountains Art and Music Festival, Jefferson, 1973-75, sculptor, 1976--, visiting sculptor, N.H. Hospital, 1982,85, Mascoma Regional High School, 1985. Former president, Andover Creative Arts Association, member, League of N.H. Craftsmen. Faye (Bayer), March 14, 1947. Bryan, June 20, 1950 (dec. 1980), Clifford, July 31, 1951. Route 4A, Potter Place.

Richard Ghormley Eberhart

Poet, professor of English. Austin, Minn., April 5, 1904, Alpha and Lena (Lowenstein) Eberhart. Austin High School, 1921, Univ. of Minn., 1922-23, Dartmouth College, A.B., 1926, Cambridge Univ., B.A., 1929, M.A., 1933. U.S. Naval Reserve, 1942-46, lt. comdr. Tutor, son of King Prajadhipok of Siam, 1930-31, master, English, St. Mark's School, Southborough, Mass., 1933-41, teacher, English, Cambridge School, Kendal Green, Mass., 1941-42, visiting professor of English, poet in residence, Univ. of Wash., 1952-53, professor, English, Univ. of Conn., 1953-54, visiting professor, Wheaton College, Norton, Mass., 1954-55, professor, Princeton Univ., 1955-56, professor, English, Dartmouth College, 1956-70, professor emeritus, 1970--, poet in residence, Dartmouth, 1956--, visiting professor, English, spring term, Univ. of Fla., 1974--. Consultant in poetry, Library of Congress, 1959-61, Pulitzer Prize for poetry, 1966, poet laureate, N.H., 1979-84, honorary president, Poetry Society of America, 1972--. Six honorary degrees. Helen Elizabeth (Butcher), Aug. 29, 1941. Richard B., Oct. 30, 1946, Margaret, May 26, 1951. Episcopal. 5 Webster Terrace, Hanover.

Richard Ghormley Eberhart

Douglas Newton Everett

Douglas Newton Everett

Chairman, Morrill and Everett Inc., retired. Cambridge, Mass., April 3, 1905, Frederic and Gertrude (Lamson) Everett. Concord High School, 1921, Colby Academy, 1922, Dartmouth College, A.B., 1926. Partner, Morrill and Everett, Concord, 1926-52, president, chairman, 1952-85. Corporator, 1928, trustee, 1934, chairman, N.H. Savings Bank, 1962-78; director, Concord National Bank, 1938-72, founder, former president, Concord Regional Development Corp., Concord Planning Board, 1942-70, chairman, 1964-70; trustee, Concord Hospital, 1944-63, president, 1954-58; former vice president, Concord Natural Gas Corp., member, U.S. Olympic hockey team, 1932, U.S. Hockey Hall of Fame, 1974, trustee, Episcopal Diocese of N.H., 1928-78, treasurer, 1951-71. Helen (Foster), Sept. 28, 1928 (div. 1962). Edward, April 13, 1931, Jean, Sept. 28, 1932, Cynthia, Sept. 2, 1944. Vida (Duffett), Oct. 16, 1965 (dec. Nov. 1979). St. ch., Peter Clarke, April 21, 1943, Mary-Ellen Hutchins, April 30, 1949. Episcopal. 297 Pleasant St., Concord.

James Dennis Ewing

Publisher, *Keene Sentinel*. St. Louis, Mo., Jan. 14, 1917, Oscar and Helen (Dennis) Ewing. Hotchkiss School, Lakeville, Conn., 1934, Princeton Univ., A.B., 1938. U.S. Naval Reserve, 1943-46, lieut. Instructor, Taft School, Watertown, Conn., 1939-41, mediation officer, National War Labor Board, Washington, D.C., 1942-43, co-publisher, *Bangor* (Maine) *Evening and Sunday Commercial*, 1946-54, publisher, *Keene Sentinel*, 1954--. President, *Valley News*, 1956-80, vice president, treasurer, *Argus Champion*, 1961-81, vice chairman, *N.H. Times*, 1981-82, director, National Securities and Research Corp., N.Y.C., 1961-70, trustee, Cheshire Hospital, 1970-74, director, Center for N.H.'s Future, 1980--, vice president, treasurer, Center for Foreign Journalists, 1984--, director, MacDowell Colony, 1962-76, vice president, 1967-74; selection committee, Nieman fellows, Harvard Univ., 1980, juror, Pulitzer Prizes in journalism, 1977,80,81. One honorary degree. Ruth (Dewing), Sept. 11, 1943. Carolyn, Jan. 13, 1945, Joan, Oct. 3, 1947, Thomas, Jan. 26, 1950. Unitarian. East Surry Rd., Keene.

James Dennis Ewing

William Joseph Farrell

William Joseph Farrell

President, Plymouth State College. Milwaukee, Wis., Aug. 17, 1936, William and Rita (Taggart) Farrell. Marquette Univ. High School, Milwaukee, 1954, Marquette Univ., B.S., 1958, M.B.A., 1976, Univ. of Wis., M.A., 1959, Ph.D., 1961. Faculty, Univ. of Chicago, 1961-68, visiting professor, Univ. of Calif.-Berkeley, 1967-68, department of English, Marquette Univ., 1968-75, director of foundation support, Marquette, 1970-75, associate vice president for educational development and research, Univ. of Iowa, 1975-84, president, Plymouth State College, 1984--. Trustee, Univ. System of N.H., 1984--, Postsecondary Education Commission, 1984--, N.E. Board of Higher Education, 1984--, N.H. College and Univ. Council, 1984--, American Assocation of State Colleges and Universities, American Council on Education, N.H. Music Festival, 1984--. Carol (Leeming), Aug. 1, 1959. William Jr., May 14, 1960, Charles, June 18, 1961, Elizabeth, Jan. 14, 1964. Catholic. 10 School St., Plymouth.

Oliver Roland Fifield

Insurance company executive, retired. Concord, N.H., Oct. 19, 1926, Roland and Margaret (Smith) Fifield. Penacook High School, 1944, Univ. of N.H., B.S., 1950. U.S. Army Signal Corps, 1944-46, sgt. President, N.H.-Vt. Blue Shield, 1968-77, president, N.H. -Vt. Blue Cross, 1973-77, president, N.H.-Vt. Blue Cross and Blue Shield, 1977-81, president, Northeast Consolidated Services, 1981-85. Trustee, Concord Savings Bank, 1972--, director, Blue Shield Association, Chicago, 1975-77, Blue Cross Association, Chicago, 1977-79, Business and Industry Association of N.H., 1978-85, BCS Financial Corp., Chicago, 1979-82, moderator, Canterbury, 1976--, selectman, Canterbury, 1958-64,67, director, Concord YMCA, 1970-72, member, Snowshoe Club, Concord, 1973--. Mary Ellen (Fife), Oct. 12, 1950. Naomi, Sept. 27, 1951, Ann, Feb. 25, 1953, Janet, Oct. 23, 1954, Stephen, Jan. 24, 1957, Abigail, July 16, 1959. Protestant. Welch Rd., Canterbury.

Oliver Roland Fifield

James Joseph Finnegan

Chief editorial writer, *The Union Leader*. Philadelphia, Pa., Aug. 1, 1930, John and Mary (Nothnagel) Finnegan. Milton Hershey School for Boys, Hershey Pa., 1948, Hershey Junior College, 1950, Boston Univ., B.S., 1952. Staff announcer, news director, news analyst, radio station WKBO, Harrisburg, Pa., 1952-56, staff secretary, Committee on Preventive Medicine and Public Health, Pa. Medical Society, 1956, news commentary, radio station WGIR, Manchester, 1957, editorial writer, chief editorial writer, *Manchester Union Leader*, (name changed to *The Union Leader* in 1980), 1957--. Member, Diocesan Holy Name Society Committee on Human Rights, 1967-68, officer, director, St. Patrick's Holy Name Society, 1964-68, judge, professional and amateur boxing, N.H. Boxing Commission, 1978--. Rita (Cagnoli), Sept. 8, 1951. Kathleen, Sept. 16, 1952, Sharon, March 21, 1956, James Jr., Feb. 5, 1958 (dec.), Joseph, March 31, 1962, John, March 3, 1964. Catholic. 147 Moore St., Manchester.

John Thompson Flanders

Commissioner, Department of Resources and Economic Development. Concord, N.H., May 12, 1926, Ralph and Bessie (Thompson) Flanders. Concord High School, 1944, Univ. of N.H., B.S., 1949. U.S. Army Air Force, 1944-45, aviation cadet. Municipal accounts auditor, State Tax Commission, 1950-52, assistant to State Tax Commission, 1952-57, director, division of accounts, Department of Administration and Control, 1957-61, administrative assistant, Gov. Wesley Powell, 1961, assistant commissioner, N.H. Department of Public Works and Highways, 1961-70, comptroller, Department of Administration and Control, 1970-73, associate commissioner, Department of Public Works and Highways, 1973-85, commissioner, Department of Resources and Economic Development, 1985--. Trustee, Merrimack County Savings Bank, 1967--, Concord Hospital, 1975--, director, Bancroft Products, 1981--, president, Concord Board of Education, 1975-78,79-82. Jeannine (Smalldon), Feb. 9, 1951 (div. 1973). Susan, June 14, 1953, John II, Dec. 31, 1955, Richard, July 9, 1957, James, Aug. 23, 1962. Diane (Moulton), Feb. 20, 1975 (div. 1986). Congregational. 203 Loudon Rd., Building 2A, Apt. 7, Concord.

John Thompson Flanders

Robert Winthrop Flanders

Robert Winthrop Flanders

Former state treasurer. Concord, N.H., Nov. 3, 1930, Ralph and Bessie (Thompson) Flanders. Concord High School, 1948, Univ. of N.H., 1949-50. Municipal accounts auditor, State Tax Commission, 1950-55, accountant, state treasurer, 1955-59, supervisor of business management, Department of Education, 1959-61, director, division of accounts, Department of Administration and Control, 1961-62, deputy state treasurer, 1962-64, state treasurer, 1964-84, vice president, treasurer, Robert C. Carr & Co., 1984--. Chairman, N.H. Retirement System, 1967-77, member, N.H. School Building Authority, 1964-84, N.H. Municipal Bond Bank, 1977-84, chairman, 1980-82. Rosamond (Leathers), Nov. 11, 1950. Jef, Oct. 5, 1953, Robert II, May 13, 1955, Bruce, July 17, 1957, Jay, March 13, 1959. Methodist. 80 Portsmouth St., Concord.

Hilda Wallerstein Fleisher

Attorney. Richmond, Va., Dec. 24, 1929, Robert and Hilda (Weil) Wallerstein. Thomas Jefferson High School, Richmond, 1947, Univ., of N.C.-Greensboro, B.A., 1951, Franklin Pierce Law Center, J.D., 1981. Attorney, Manchester, 1982--. Director, N.H. Child and Family Services, 1963--, president, 1974-79; national board, Child Welfare League of America, 1976-83, incorporator, N.H. Charitable Fund, 1973-83, director, N.H. Social Welfare Council, 1970-74, United Way of N.H., 1976-80, president, 1978-79; N.H. Constitutional Convention, 1974, N.H. House of Rep. 1975-76, N.H. Commission on the Status of Women, 1979-83, Manchester Model City Agency, 1967-72, Charter Revision Committee, Manchester, 1964, Manchester Airport Authority, 1983--, trustee, Norwin and Elizabeth Bean Foundation, 1980-83. Edward Fleisher, Dec. 19, 1954. Leslie, Oct. 18, 1955, Mark, April 14, 1957, Adam, April 9, 1959, Cary, May 12, 1961. Jewish. 251 North Bay St., Manchester.

Hilda Wallerstein Fleisher

Margaret Quill Flynn

Margaret Quill Flynn

Associate justice, New Hampshire Superior Court. Stoughton, Mass., July 9, 1922, John and Bridget (Crimmins) Quill. Stoughton High School, 1939, Boston Univ., A.B., 1943, LL.B., 1944. Attorney, Boston, 1946-58, Nashua, 1958-86; associate justice, N.H. Superior Court, 1986--. Lecturer, Rivier College, 1978-82, N.E. Aeronautical Institute, 1965-68, member, N.H. Board of Bar Examiners, 1978-86, Nashua Police Commission, 1974-86, chairman, 1984-86; N.H. Higher Education and Health Facilities Authority, 1979-86, chairman, 1984-86; advisory board, Rivier College, 1973--, Daniel Webster College, 1977-82, chairman, 1980-82; Citizens Task Force, 1969-70, N.H. Constitutional Convention, 1974,84, Nashua Board of Education, 1960-74, president, 1972-74; director, St. Joseph Hospital, 1974--, secretary of board, 1980-83, vice chairman, 1984--. One honorary degree. Charles Flynn, May 27, 1950. Katherine, Jan. 8, 1959, Margaret, Nov. 5, 1963. Catholic. 9 Anders Ln., Nashua.

Eileen Foley

Former mayor of Portsmouth. Portsmouth, N.H., Feb. 27, 1918, Charles and Mary Ellen (Carey) Dondero. Portsmouth High School, 1936, Syracuse Univ., B.A., 1940. Women's Army Corps, 1944-45, cpl. City clerk, Portsmouth, 1946-51, assistant to the special service officer, Portsmouth Naval Shipyard, 1961-66, manager, area office, Sen. Thomas McIntyre, 1968-78, state disaster director, director, Civil Defense Agency, 1979-83. N.H. Senate, 1965-78, Portsmouth City Council, 1968-72,83--, mayor, Portsmouth, 1968-72,84-86, Portsmouth Board of Education, 1958-61,64-67,80-83, Commission on the Status of Women, 1972-73, incorporator, N.H. Charitable Fund, 1973-78, president, Council of Senior Citizens, 1985--, director, N.H. Social Welfare Council, 1977-78, Great Bay School and Training Center, 1960--, Greater Portsmouth Community Foundation, 1981--, Prescott Park Arts Festival, 1981--. John Foley, June 12, 1948. Mary, Nov. 24, 1950, John Jr., Jan. 29, 1952, Barry, June 18, 1956. Catholic. 39 Sunset Rd., Portsmouth.

John Franklin Fort III

John Franklin Fort III

President, chief executive officer, Tyco Laboratories. New York, N.Y., Oct. 12, 1941, John II and Florence (Baumrucker) Fort. Landon School, Bethesda, Md., 1959, Princeton Univ., B.S., 1963, MIT, M.S., 1966. Vice president, general manager, Simplex Wire and Cable Co., Newington, 1970-74, president, 1974-79; vice president-operations, Tyco Laboratories, Exeter, 1979-82, senior vice president-operations, 1982, president, chief executive officer, 1983--. Director, Greater Portsmouth Chamber of Commerce, 1970-72, Theatre by the Sea. 1974-80, Greater Portsmouth Community Foundation, 1983--. Nancy (Barnett), Feb. 18, 1967. John, April 13, 1969, Alexandra, Aug. 12, 1971, Tucker, Dec. 11, 1974, Elizabeth, April 24, 1983. Salt Marsh Farm, Rye.

Robert Harding Foster

Publisher, *Foster's Daily Democrat*. Portland, Maine, May 17, 1921, Frederick and Mabel (McCuddy) Foster. Dover High School, 1939, Univ. of N.H., B.S., 1943. U.S. Army, 1943-45,51-52, 1st lt. *Foster's Daily Democrat*, 1946--, production manager, advertising manager, business manager, publisher, 1957--. Director, N.E. Daily Newspapers, 1975-79, Merchants National Bank, Dover, 1970--, trustee, Univ. System of N.H., 1975-79, member, Northam Colonists, 1953--, president, 1966-68; Elks, 1946--, exalted ruler, 1952-53; Dover-Durham Rotary International, 1948--. Therese (Durnin) Foster, Sept. 8, 1951. Catherine, Sept. 28, 1953, Robert F., June 15, 1955, Patrice, June 2, 1959. Catholic. P.O. Box 727, Dover.

Robert Harding Foster

Priscilla Kingsbury Frechette

Priscilla Kingsbury Frechette

Corporate director. Keene, N.H., June 29, 1920, Edward and Lillian (Williamson) Kingsbury. Keene High School, 1937, Smith College, A.B., 1942, Univ. of Mass., M.S.B.A., 1979. Director, Kingsbury Machine Tool Corp., 1964--, Public Service Co., 1977-85, Ashuelot National Bank (merged with Indian Head Bank, Keene), 1976--, Indian Head Banks Inc., 1985-86, trustee, Elliot Community Hospital, Keene, 1959-70, Keene Board of Education, 1966-76, executive council, N.H. School Boards Association, 1970-77, president, 1975-76; trustee, N.E. College, 1977--, chairman, 1985--; Dartmouth College, 1979--, incorporator, N.H. Charitable Fund, 1981--, director, Center for N.H.'s Future, 1981--, Keene Clinic, 1984--. Henry Frechette, May 1, 1943 (dec. Jan. 25, 1976). David, May 7, 1945, James, March 18, 1947, Jocelyn, June 14, 1950, Henry Jr., April 18, 1952, Edward, Jan. 22, 1959, Peter, June 8, 1960. M. Douglas Maynard, Jan. 4, 1986. United Church of Christ. 76 Bradford Rd., Keene.

Elenore Shirley Freedman

Executive director, New Hampshire Association of School Principals. Brockton, Mass., Jan. 15, 1926, Benjamin and Dora (Markovitz) Finklestein. Brockton High School, 1943, Radcliffe College, B.A., 1947. Executive director, N.H. Council for Better Schools, 1957-69, program coodinator, publications director, administrative assistant, Center for Educational Field Services and N.H. School Boards Association, 1970-74, executive director, N.H. Association of School Principals, 1974--. Director, N.H. Charitable Fund, 1972-82, chair, 1981-82, incorporator, 1983--; trustee, Currier Gallery of Art, 1975--, executive committee, N.H. Council for Better Schools, 1970-78, director, Corporate Council for Critical Skills, 1982-85, N.H. Council on Economic Education, 1985--, board of governors, N.H. Public Television, 1986--. Peter Freedman, June 8, 1947. Dorrie, April 29, 1950, Hal, July 15, 1953. Jewish. 20 Kalmia Way, Bedford.

George Edward Freese Jr.

George Edward Freese Jr.

State senator, president, Globe Manufacturing Company. Pittsfield, N.H., Nov. 9, 1920, George and Elizabeth (Sweet) Freese. Pittsfield High School, 1938, New Hampton School, 1939, Univ. of N.H., class of 1943. U.S. Army Air Force, 1942-45, cpl. Globe Manufacturing Co., Pittsfield, 1945--, president, 1953--, general manager, Ski Wear Division, 1945-75, director, chairman, 1953--. Member, National Advisory Board of Ski Industries of American, 1973-74, trustee, director, N.H. Savings Bank, 1979--, advisory board, N.H. Small Business Development Center, 1985--, Pittsfield School Board, 1947-49, N.H. House of Rep., 1947-49, N.H. Senate, 1981--, N.H. Air Pollution Control Commission (now N.H. Air Resources Commission), 1973-79, chairman, N.H. Coalition for Liability Law Reform, 1985--. Florence (Greene), Aug. 28, 1948. Barbara, Aug. 21, 1949, Patricia, Nov. 11, 1950, George III, July 13, 1954, John, Nov. 3, 1956, Robert, March 20, 1965. Protestant. Indian Meadow Farm, Tilton Hill Rd., Pittsfield.

J. Fred French

Banker, retired. Chichester, N.H., June 23, 1902, Frank and Agnes (Greeley) French. Concord High School, 1920, Bentley School of Accounting, Boston, 1920. Proprietor, Manchester Credit Bureau, 1926-37, asssistant treasurer, Amoskeag Savings Bank, 1937-43, vice president, 1943-51, president, 1951-68, chairman, 1968-74, honorary chairman, 1974-75, chairman emeritus, 1975--. Chairman, N.H. Association of Savings Banks, 1965-67, trustee, Univ. System of N.H., 1961-72, board of visitors, Whittemore School of Business, Univ. of N.H., 1965-77, director, N.H. Insurance Co., 1952-78, honorary, 1978--; advisory board, *Manchester Union Leader*, 1961-75, director, Amoskeag Industries, 1954--. Two honorary degrees. Florence (Heath), June 1, 1926. Shirley, Dec. 6, 1942. Congregational. 150 North St., Manchester.

Martha McDanolds Frizzell

Former state representative. Branchville, N.J., Nov. 18, 1902, George and Kate (Roe) McDanolds. Littleton High School, 1920, Univ. of N.H., B.S., 1924. Chemist, Royal Baking Powder Co., 1924-27. N.H. House of Rep., 1951-78, N.H. Constitutional Convention, 1956,64,74, president, N.H. Library Trustees Association, 1962, former secretary, Fort Four Associates, president, N.H. Order of Women Legislators, 1963-64, former moderator, town and school districts, Charlestown, executive committee, N.E. Board of Higher Education, 1960-64,69-70. Author, *Second History of Charlestown, New Hampshire*, 1955, *A History of Walpole, New Hampshire* , 1963. Theodore Frizzell, June 9, 1927. Katherine, April 4, 1928, Theodora, June 5, 1929, Elizabeth, Oct. 8, 1933, Robert, March 19, 1939, James, Oct. 26, 1943. Congregational. Charlestown.

Joachim William Froehlich

President, Saint Anselm College. Waterbury, Conn., June 27, 1944, George and Anna (Praines) Froehlich. Sacred Heart High School, Waterbury, 1962, Saint Anselm College, B.A., 1967, So. Univ. of N.Y., M.A., 1970, Catholic Univ. of America, Ph.D., 1977. Professed as a monk, Saint Anselm Abbey, Order of St. Benedict, July 2, 1965. Faculty, Saint Anselm College, 1973--, chairman of the economics department, 1975-79, president, 1979--. Director, N.E. Education Loan Marketing Corp., 1983--, N.H. Higher Education Assistance Foundation, 1982--, board of governors, St. Joseph College, 1982-85, member Postsecondary Education Commission, 1981--, chairman, 1984--; director, United Way of Greater Manchester, 1985--, Manchester Rotary Club, 1984-85, National Association of Independent Colleges and Universities, 1986--. Catholic. Saint Anselm Abbey, Goffstown.

Joachim William Froehlich

Irene Carbonneau Gallen

Irene Carbonneau Gallen

Littleton, N.H., Dec. 25, 1926, William and Alice (Rousseau) Carbonneau. Littleton High School, 1944. Secretary, N.E. Power Co., 1945-53. Former member, North Country Home Health Agency, N.H. Art Association, Littleton League of Women Voters, 1971-72, director, N.H. Charitable Fund, 1983--, member, N.H. chapter, Partners of the Americas, 1979--. Hugh Gallen, Oct. 16, 1948 (dec. Dec. 29, 1982). Kathleen, Oct. 16, 1952, Michael, Aug. 2, 1954, Sheila, Nov. 25, 1956. Catholic. 16 West Elm, Littleton.

Edith Bumpus Gardner

State senator, retired. Wareham, Mass., Jan. 1, 1899, Bradford and Alice (Holt) Bumpus. Wareham High School, 1917, Nashua Memorial Hospital, 1921, registered nurse, 1922. Supervisor of obstetrics, Polyclinic Hospital, Harrisburg, Pa., 1924-25, public health nurse, Lake Sunapee Nursing Association, 1930-32, postmaster, Springfield, 1932-33. N.H. House of Rep. (Springfield), 1943-47, (Gilford), 1953-57, N.H. Senate, 1961-80, N.H. Constitutional Convention, 1956, Laconia Hospital Nurses Association, 1953-55, Gilford Historical Society, 1952-82, president, 1953; director, Belknap County Committee on Alcohol and Drug Abuse, 1964-69, president, 1969; life member, Laconia Business and Professional Women's Club, 1944--, president, 1957-58; N.H. Order of Women Legislators, 1943--, president, 1969; National Order of Women Legislators, 1943--, president, 1969-70; president, N.H. Federation of Republican Women's Clubs, 1962. One honorary degree. Gilbert Brown, Sept. 11, 1922 (div. 1929). Margaret, Aug. 5, 1923. M. Walter Gardner, Sept. 11, 1933. Walter III, Aug. 26, 1935 (dec. 1953). Protestant. RFD 2, Box 473, Newport.

Edith Bumpus Gardner

William Michael Gardner

New Hampshire secretary of state. Manchester, N.H., Oct. 26, 1948, William G. and Mildred (Claus) Gardner. Bishop Bradley High School, Manchester, 1966, Univ. of N.H., B.A., 1970, London School of Economics, 1972, Univ. of N.C.-Greensboro, M.Ed., 1973, Harvard Univ., M.P.A., 1985. N.H. secretary of state, 1976--. N.H. House of Rep., 1973-76, adjunct lecturer, N.E. College, 1979-80,82, Keene State College, 1982, chairman, N.H. Municipal Records Board, 1978--, incorporator, N.H. Charitable Fund, 1978--, N.H. Savings Bank, 1979-83, trustee, Japanese Charitable Fund, 1976--, Belanger-Gardner Fund, Bishop's Univ., Canada, 1985--, secretary, N.H. Bicentennial Commission on the U.S. Constitution, 1982--, director, Cystic Fibrosis Foundation, No. N.E. chapter, 1979--. Edited, *Towns Against Tyranny*: *Hillsborough County New Hampshire During the American Revolution 1775-1783*, 1976. Kathleen (Gordon), May 21, 1978. William G., Sept. 11, 1980, Kathleen, April 7, 1984. Catholic. 181 Highview Terrace, Manchester.

Odore Joseph Gendron

Bishop, Diocese of Manchester. Manchester, N.H., Sept. 13, 1921, Francois and Valida (Rouleau) Gendron. St. Charles Borromeo Seminary, Sherbrooke, Canada, 1942, St. Paul's Seminary, Univ. of Ottawa, 1942-47. Ordained, Roman Catholic priest, May 31, 1947. Associate pastor, Guardian Angel Parish, Berlin, 1947-52, Sacred Heart Parish, Lebanon, 1952-60, St. Aloysius Parish, Nashua, 1960-65, pastor, Our Lady of Lourdes Parish, Pittsfield, 1965-67, St. Augustine Parish, Manchester, 1967-71, monsignor, 1970, vicar for religious, 1966-75, episcopal vicar for clergy, 1972-75, Roman Catholic bishop, Diocese of Manchester, 1975--. Chairman, Diocesan Personnel Board, 1974-75, member, N.H. Catholic Charities, incorporator, trustee, Catholic Medical Center, 1975--, citizens advisory council, N.H. Department of Corrections, 1984--, member, N.H. Council of Churches, N.H. Council on World Affairs. Catholic. 657 North River Rd., Manchester.

Odore Joseph Gendron

Thomas William Gerber

Newspaper editor, retired. Portland, Oreg., May 2, 1921, Thomas and Mary Anne (Smith) Gerber. New Milford (Conn.) High School, 1939, Dartmouth College, A.B., 1948. U.S. Air Force, 1942-45,51-52, 1st lt. Reporter, United Press, Boston, 1948-51,52-53, manager, Rhode Island bureau, 1953; reporter, *Boston Traveler*, 1953-55, assistant sports editor, 1955-56; Washington correspondent, *Boston Herald and Traveler*, 1956-61, general manager, *Concord Monitor*, 1961-68, editor, assistant publisher, 1968-83. Director, Monitor Publishing Co., 1962-78, Telecable Inc., 1968-73, Concord branch, Bank of N.H., 1962--, trustee, Concord Hospital, 1962-73, alumni advisory board, Dartmouth Public Affairs Center, 1974--, president, N.E. Society of Newspaper Editors, 1967, member, N.H. Judicial Council, 1972-74, Citizens Task Force, 1969-70, vice chairman, N.H. Council for the Humanities, 1972-74, member, American Society of Newspaper Editors, 1978--. Gail (Graham), Jan. 20, 1951 (div. 1969). Cheryl, March 12, 1952, Linda, July 12, 1954. Electra (Bilmazes), Dec. 26, 1971. Protestant. Carter Hill Rd., Concord.

Harlan Leighton Goodwin

Banker. Dover, N.H., Oct. 31, 1909, Frank and Mabel (Tuttle) Goodwin. Concord High School, 1926, Rutgers Univ. Graduate School of Banking, 1940-42. U.S. Army, 1944-46, pfc. First National Bank of Concord, 1927-44,46-55, First National Bank of Portsmouth, executive vice president, 1955-56, president, 1956-76, chief executive officer, 1956-84, chairman of the board, 1976--; chairman, chief executive officer, First Coastal Banks Inc., 1984--. Director, First National Bank of Portsmouth, 1955--, First Coastal Banks Inc., 1984--, Morley Co., 1960--, Public Service Co. of N.H., 1962-83, trustee, Rannie Webster Foundation, 1976--, trustee, treasurer, Chase Home for Children, 1958--. Doris (Fuller), Aug. 15, 1931. Episcopal. 189 Washington Rd., Rye.

Harlan Leighton Goodwin

J. Joseph Grandmaison

J. Joseph Grandmaison

Political consultant. Nashua, N.H., May 19, 1943, Oscar and Irene (Bouchard) Grandmaison. Nashua High School, 1960, Burdett College, 1960-63. Salesman, Sears, Roebuck and Co., Nashua, 1961-66, assistant to the president, Consolidated Foods, Nashua, 1966-71, national staff, McGovern for President, 1971-72, campaign manager, Dukakis for Governor, Massachusetts, 1973-74, director, federal/state relations, Massachusetts, 1975, federal co-chairman, N.E. Regional Commission, Boston, 1977-81, political consultant, 1981--. Chairman, Federal Regional Council of N.E., 1979-81, alderman, Nashua, 1970-71, American Council of Young Political Leaders, Washington, D.C., 1970--, director, Robert F. Kennedy Action Corps, Boston, 1974--, board of visitors, Boston Univ. School of Economics, 1978-81, director, Center for Social Responsibility, Rivier College, 1980. Catholic. 1627 Ocean Blvd., Rye.

Herbert Arthur Grant Jr.

President, chief executive officer, Kingston-Warren Corporation. Amesbury, Mass., Jan. 28, 1937, Herbert and Iva (Colby) Grant. Phillips Exeter Academy, 1955, Dartmouth College, B.A., 1959, M.S., 1960. U.S. Marine Corps, 1960-64, capt. Production engineer, Electropak, Peterborough, 1964-66, Kingston-Warren Corp., 1966--, executive vice president, 1970-75, president, chief executive officer, 1975--. Director, Indian Head Bank and Trust, Portsmouth, 1972--, Edgcomb Steel of N.E., 1981-86, Kingston-Warren Corp., 1972--, Hampton Machine Co., 1984--, Business and Industry Association of N.H., 1985--, trustee, Custom Roll Forming Institute, 1978-85, chairman, 1982-83; Kensington Planning Board, 1970-75, trustee, Exeter Hospital, 1974-75,85--, Strawbery Banke, 1985--. Jennifer, May 12, 1962, Susan, Feb. 26, 1964. Protestant. Bayridge Rd., Greenland.

Herbert Arthur Grant Jr.

Jane Burgess Grant

Jane Burgess Grant

Conservationist. Portland, Maine, March 24, 1914, George and Dorothy (Bates) Burgess. Beaver Country Day School, Chestnut Hill, Mass., 1932, Wellesley College, B.A., 1936, M.A., 1939. Trustee, Audubon Society of N.H., 1960--, president, 1976-80; director, Environmental Law Council, 1979-83, trustee, N.H. Energy Coalition, 1979-83, executive committee, N.H. Environmental Coalition, 1974-82, president, Concord Maternal Health Association, 1943-44, co-chair, Concord chapter, Zero Population Growth, 1969-71, chairman, Dunbarton Conservation Commission, 1968-77, overseer of welfare, Dunbarton, 1955-63, member, Governor's Advisory Council on Growth, 1979-81, incorporator, N.H. Charitable Fund, 1980--, trustee, N.E. Coalition on Nuclear Pollution, 1982--, vice president, 1983--; director, Inherit N.H., 1984--. George Grant Jr., July 20, 1940 (dec. May 26, 1973). Anne, June 20, 1941, Sarah, Sept. 24, 1943. Episcopal. Pages Corner, Dunbarton.

William Segal Green

Attorney. Presque Isle, Maine, Dec. 21, 1917, Saul and Julia (Segal) Green. Manchester Central High School, 1935, Dartmouth College, A.B., 1939, Harvard Univ., LL.B., 1947. U.S. Marine Corps, 1942-46, maj. Attorney, Concord, 1947-49, assistant attorney general, N.H., 1949-50, deputy attorney general, 1950-51, attorney, Manchester, 1951--. Director, Merchants Savings Bank (now Numerica Savings Bank), 1956--, Waterville Co., 1965--, Edgcomb Steel of N.E., 1964--, Northern Data Systems, 1984-85, member, N.H. Legislative Council, 1951-57, chairman, State Board of Education, 1969-73, Ballot Law Commission, 1966-68, trustee, N.H. College, 1968--, Elliot Hospital, 1954--, president, 1969-70. Joan (Jacobson), June 27, 1942. William, May 20, 1946, Nancy, July 30, 1948, Richard, Dec. 4, 1953. Jewish. 291 Ray St., Manchester.

William Segal Green

Elizabeth Alice Greene

State representative. North Hampton, N.H., May 21, 1906, Herbert and Mildred (Prescott) White. Portsmouth High School, 1923, Univ. of N.H., B.A., 1927. High school teacher, Farmington, Bartlett, Warner, 1927-34. N.H. House of Rep., 1961--, chairman, N.H. Air Pollution Control Commission, 1972-73, trustee, N.H. Oceangraphic Foundation, 1972-75, member, N.H. Acid Rain Coordinating Committee, 1980--. Edward Greene, Jan. 16, 1934. Prescott, July 16, 1935, Elizabeth, Oct. 16, 1943, William, Jan. 2, 1945. Protestant. 399 South Rd., Rye.

Hugh Gregg

Former governor of New Hampshire. Nashua, N.H., Nov. 22, 1917, Harry and Margaret (Richardson) Gregg. Phillips Exeter Academy, 1935, Yale Univ., A.B., 1939, Harvard Law School, LL.B., 1942. Special agent, U.S. Army Counter Intelligence Corps., 1942-46,50-52. Attorney, Nashua, 1946--, governor, N.H., 1953-55, president, Gregg and Son Inc., 1947-70. Alderman, Nashua, 1948-50, mayor, Nashua, 1950, director, Indian Head Banks Inc., 1964--, chairman, 1964-84; Indian Head National Bank, 1947--, chairman, 1955-64; Wildcat Corp., 1958-67, secretary, Computer Mart of N.H., 1980-84, manager, Waumbek Village Properties, 1970--, co-publisher, *N.H. Profiles*, 1959-65, member, National and Canadian Kitchen Cabinet Associations, 1946-81, trustee, Crotched Mountain Rehabilitation Center, 1954-85, owner, manager, Greenhouse Restaurant, Sarasota, Fla., 1977-81, president, Resources of N.H. Inc., 1982--, president, N.E. Council, 1956-58. Three honorary degrees. Catherine (Warner), July 24, 1940. Cyrus, June 26, 1943, Judd, Feb. 14, 1947. Congregational. Gregg Rd., Nashua.

Judd Alan Gregg

Judd Alan Gregg

United States congressman. Nashua, N.H., Feb. 14, 1947, Hugh and Catherine (Warner) Gregg. Phillips Exeter Academy, 1965, Columbia Univ., A.B., 1969, Boston Univ. School of Law, J.D., 1972, LL.M., 1975. Attorney, Nashua, 1972-80, U.S. Congress, Second District, 1981--. N.H. Constitutional Convention, 1974, N.H. Executive Council, 1979-81, director, Indian Head National Bank, 1974-79, board member, Greater Nashua United Way, 1977--, Nashua Community Council, 1977-83, president, 1978; Nashua Fresh Air Camp, 1977--, advisory board, N.H. Salvation Army, 1976-80, Crotched Mountain Foundation, 1974-76, trustee, 1976--; N.H. commissioner, National Conference of Commissioners on Uniform State Laws, 1975-78. Kathleen (MacLellan), Sept. 22, 1973. Molly, July 29, 1978, Sarah, Jan. 24, 1980, Joshua, Aug. 5, 1983. Congregational. Pine Ridge Rd., Greenfield.

Frederick Welby Griffin

Insurance executive, retired. Manchester, N.H., May 28, 1917, Vaughn and Grace (Coan) Griffin. Phillips Academy, Andover, Mass., 1935, Harvard Univ., B.A., 1940. U.S. Naval Reserve, 1942-46, lt. sg. Trainee, N.H. Insurance Co., 1941-42, special agent, 1946; agent, William Berry Insurance Agency, 1946-49, partner, 1949-56; partner, Berry and Edgerly Insurance, 1956-68, partner, Burpee, Griffin and Perkins, 1968-82, executive vice president, Kendall Insurance, Manchester, 1982-83. Trustee, Manchester Savings Bank, 1952-68, director, BankEast, 1968-82, president, N.H. Association of Independent Insurance Agents, 1968-69, member, Currier Gallery Advisory Council, 1984--, trustee, Norwin and Elizabeth Bean Foundation, 1967-85, chairman, 1980-81; trustee, Audubon Society of N.H., 1984--, director, chairman, Northern N.H. Foundation, 1985--, director, N.E. Ski Museum, 1982--. Ruth (Dickson), Sept. 20, 1941. Barbara, Sept. 20, 1943, Frederick Jr., Aug. 24, 1947, Robin, March 11, 1950, Bonnie, Nov. 20, 1952. Protestant. Wallace Hill Rd., Franconia.

Robert Frederick Griffith

Robert Frederick Griffith

Associate justice, New Hampshire Supreme Court, retired. Claremont, N.H., June 12, 1911, Murrie and Grace (Bickford) Griffith. Nashua High School, 1929, Univ. of N.H., B.A., 1933, Boston Univ. School of Law, J.D., 1936. U.S. Army, 1944-46, 1st lt. Attorney, Nashua, 1936-52, associate justice, N.H. Superior Court, 1952-67, associate justice, N.H. Supreme Court, 1967-77. Director, Second National Bank, Nashua, 1954-60, president, Nashua YMCA, 1948-52, chairman, Nashua chapter, American Red Cross, 1956-58. Mabel (Brown), June 18, 1938. John, May 6, 1939, Nancy, Feb. 3, 1941. Unitarian-Universalist. 12 Berkeley St., Nashua.

William Alvan Grimes

Chief justice, New Hampshire Supreme Court, retired. Dover, N.H., July 4, 1911, Frank and Annie (Ash) Grimes. Dover High School, 1930, Univ. of N.H., B.S., 1934, Boston Univ. School of Law, LL.B., 1937. U.S. Naval Reserve, 1942-45, lt. sg. Attorney, Rochester, 1937-47, city solicitor, Dover, 1946-47, associate justice, N.H. Superior Court, 1947-66, associate justice, N.H. Supreme Court, 1966-79, chief justice, 1979-81. Distinguished visiting professor, Calif. Western School of Law, 1981-85, Univ. of San Diego School of Law, 1986--, faculty, National Judicial College, Reno, 1964--, chairman, judicial administration division, American Bar Association, 1978, N.H. House of Rep., 1933-35,37-39, N.H. Constitutional Convention, 1939. Three honorary degrees. Barbara (Parsons), June 22, 1940. Gail, Sept. 12, 1947, Gordon, Feb. 24, 1949. Christian. 60 Portland Ave., Dover.

Martin Louis Gross

Attorney. New York City, N.Y., Oct. 22, 1938, Walter and Harriet (Shoben) Gross. Trinity School, New York City, 1956, Harvard Univ., A.B., 1960, Victoria Univ., New Zealand, 1960-61, Harvard Law School, J.D., 1964. Law clerk, U.S. District Court, Concord, 1964-65, attorney, Concord, 1965--. Legal counsel, Gov. Walter Peterson, 1970-72, special counsel, Gov. Hugh Gallen, 1982, Concord City Council, 1970-82, mayor pro tem, Concord, 1974-75, mayor, 1976-82; N.H. Constitutional Convention, 1974,84, State Prison Board of Trustees, 1972-78, N.H. Board of Bar Examiners, 1969--, chairman, 1974--; director, BankEast, 1981--, legislative affairs chairman, Business and Industry Association of N.H., 1980-81, executive committee, N.H. Municipal Association, 1970-77, Arts Council of Greater Concord, 1971-74, incorporator, N.H. Charitable Fund, 1985--, trustee, Concord Hospital, 1983--, Capital Area Health Care, 1985--, Granite State Public Radio, 1982--, chairman, 1984-85; advisory committee, U.S. Court of Appeals for First Circuit, 1983--. Caroline (Lord), Nov. 5, 1960. 15 Rumford St., Concord.

Robert David Gross

Executive director, New Hampshire Legal Assistance. Cleveland, Ohio, Oct. 29, 1945, Merrill and Martha (Perlick) Gross. Shaker Heights (Ohio) High School, 1963, Williams College, A.B., 1967, Case Western Reserve Univ., J.D., 1972. N.H. Legal Assistance, 1972--, fellow, 1972-74, director of legislation, legislative counsel, 1974-75, director of litigation, 1975-76, executive director, 1976--. N.H. Bar Association, 1972--, vice chairman, N.H. Pro Bono Referral System, 1985--. Snook Rd., Goffstown.

May Gruber

Textile company executive. New York, N.Y., March 6, 1912, Morris and Bertha (Greenberg) Blum. Evander Childs High School, Bronx, N.Y., 1927, N.Y.U., B.A., 1931, Columbia Univ., 1933-34. Partner, Nile Knitting Mills, N.Y.C., 1931-32, partner, Brookshire Knitting Mills, 1934, (firm eventually became Pandora Industries), president, 1964-77, chairman, 1977-83; president, One Dow Court Inc., Manchester, 1983--. Director, Gruber Foundation, 1968--, Brookshire Foundation, 1964--, Anna Philbrook Foundation for Children, 1968--, Child Health Services, 1980-85, charter member, Manchester League of Women Voters, 1944--, publisher, *Manchester Free Press*, 1960-64. Author, *Pandora's Pride*, 1985. Saul Sidore, Oct. 11, 1931. Sara, May 14, 1936, Gene, June 24, 1938, Ralph, Sept. 14, 1944, Rebecca, June 13, 1947, Micala, Aug. 18, 1949. Samuel Gruber, Oct. 27, 1967. Jewish. Addison Rd., Goffstown.

May Gruber

Gordon Arthur Haaland

Gordon Arthur Haaland

President, University of New Hampshire. Brooklyn, N.Y., April 19, 1940, Ole and Ellen (Hansen) Haaland. Butler (N.J.) High School, 1958, Wheaton College, A.B., 1962, State Univ. of N.Y., Buffalo, Ph.D., 1966. Univ. of N.H., assistant professor, 1965-69, associate professor, 1969-74, professor, 1974, chairman, department of psychology, 1970-74; dean, College of Arts and Sciences, professor, Univ. of Maine-Orono, 1975-79; vice president for academic affairs, professor, Univ. of N.H., 1979-83, interim president, 1983-84, president, 1984--. Director, Council of Colleges of Arts and Sciences, 1977-79, Center for N.H.'s Future, 1980--, N.H. Psychological Association, 1967-70,73-74, trustee, Theatre by the Sea, 1980-83, corporator, Bangor Savings Bank, 1976-79, incorporator, N.H. Charitable Fund, 1985--. Carol (Anderson), Jan. 19, 1963. Lynn, Aug. 6, 1967, Paul, Dec. 7, 1970. Protestant. Thompson Hall, Durham.

Elizabeth Sears Hager

State representative. Washington, D.C., Oct. 31, 1944, Hess and Betty (Harper) Sears. St. Mary's Hall, Faribault, Minn., 1962, Wellesley College, B.A., 1966, Tufts Univ., 1966-67, Univ. of N.H., M.P.A., 1979. Principal, Philbrook Center, Concord, 1969-71, coordinator, community resources, Concord School District, 1976-78, fundraising consultant, 1982--. N.H. House of Rep., 1973-76,84--, N.H. Constitutional Convention, 1974,84, Concord City Council, 1982--, trustee, Concord YMCA, 1982--, N.H. Civil Liberties Foundation, 1979--, chair, 1980-82; chair, director, N.H. Women's Lobby, 1980-82, member, Commission on the Status of Women, 1972-75,79-83, chair, N.H. International Women's Year Coordinating Committee, 1976-77, director, United Way of Greater Concord, 1976-81, president, 1979-80. Dennis Hager, Sept. 3, 1966. Annie, July 9, 1969, Lucie, Aug. 4, 1971. Episcopal. 5 Auburn St., Concord.

Elizabeth Sears Hager

Judson Drake Hale Sr.

Judson Drake Hale Sr.

Editor, *Yankee Magazine*. Boston, Mass., March 16, 1933, Roger and Marian (Sagendorph) Hale. Choate School, Wallingford, Conn., 1951, Dartmouth College, B.A., 1955. U.S. Army, 1955-57, spec. 4. *Yankee Magazine*, *The Old Farmer's Almanac*, assistant editor, 1958-60, associate editor, 1960-62, managing editor, 1962-70, editor, 1970--. Trustee, Monadnock Community Hospital, 1975-84, president of the board, 1983-84; director, MacDowell Colony, 1973--, president, Task Force for Historic Preservation in N.H., 1983-84, director, Inherit N.H., 1984--, Yankee Publishing, 1965--, Society for a New England Biography, 1972-79, member, Committee for Dublin By-Pass, 1976--, civil defense director, Dublin, 1960-67. Author, *Inside New England*, 1982. One honorary degree. Sally (Huberlie), Sept. 6, 1958. Judson Jr., July 30, 1959, Daniel, Nov. 29, 1960, Christopher, Jan. 4, 1965. Episcopal. P.O. Box 251, Dublin.

Donald Hall

Writer. New Haven, Conn., Sept. 20, 1928, Donald and Lucy (Wells) Hall. Phillips Exeter Academy, 1947, Harvard Univ., B.A., 1951, Oxford Univ., B. Litt., 1953. Writer, first book of poetry, *Exiles and Marriages*, 1955, first book of prose, *String Too Short to be Saved*, 1961, junior fellow, Harvard, 1954-57, assistant professor, Univ. of Mich., Ann Arbor, 1957-61, associate professor, 1961-66, professor, 1966-77. Poetry editor, *Paris Review*, 1953-62, Guggenheim fellow, 1963,72, poetry board, Wesleyan Univ. Press, 1958-64, consultant, Harper and Row, 1964-81, poet laureate, N.H., 1984--. Three honorary degrees. Kirby (Thompson), Sept. 13, 1952 (div. 1969). Andrew, April 15, 1954, Philippa, June 26, 1959. Jane (Kenyon), April 17, 1972. Congregational. Eagle Pond Farm, Danbury.

Donald Hall

Fred William Hall Jr.

Fred William Hall Jr.

Attorney. Franklin, N.H., Sept. 22, 1920, Fred and Grace (Canney) Hall. Nashua High School, 1937, Univ. of N.H., B.S., 1941, Univ. of Mich. Law School, LL.B., 1948. U.S. Army, 1941-46,51-52, maj. Attorney, Rochester, 1948--. County attorney, Strafford County, 1951, city solicitor, Rochester, 1960-61, N.H. Executive Council, 1963-65, N.H. Constitutional Convention, 1956,74,84, Citizens Task Force, 1969-70, State Prison Board of Trustees and Board of Parole, 1957-61, director, First National Bank of Rochester, 1969-82, chairman, 1975-82; BankEast Corp., 1982--, member, N.H. Bar Association, 1948--, president, 1965-66; American College of Probate Counsel, 1978--, trustee, Univ. System of N.H., 1966-73, chairman, 1968-72; Austin Cate Academy, 1950-76, civilian aide, secretary of the Army, state of N.H., 1970-78. Jane (Coe), Sept. 23, 1950. Marcella, Oct. 17, 1952, Susan, Oct. 17, 1954, John, March 31, 1961. Episcopal. 18 Eastern Ave., Rochester.

George Twombly Hamilton

Banker. Philadelphia, Pa., June 13, 1924, Frank and Katherine (Twombly) Hamilton. Tilton School, 1942, Springfield College, B.S., 1949, M.Ed., 1963. U.S. Army Air Force, 1943-46, sgt. Conservation officer, N.H. Fish and Game Department, 1952-55, assistant manager, huts system, Appalachian Mountain Club, 1955-58, manager, 1959-66; assistant planning director, resources and outdoor recreation, Office of State Planning, 1968-70, special assistant for planning, Office of the Governor, 1970-71, director, Parks and Recreation, state of N.H., 1971-77, vice president, municipal services, Manchester Bank, 1978-80 (name changed to BankEast in 1981), regional president, BankEast, Concord, 1980--. President, White Mountains Region Association, 1964, chairman, advisory committee, N.H. Statewide Trail System, 1971-77, member, Water Supply and Pollution Control Commission, 1971-77, N.H. Council of Resources and Development, 1971-77, secretary, treasurer, National Association of State Park Directors, 1974-77, director, National Society for Park Resources, 1976-77, trustee, N.H. Historical Society, 1980-83. Robert, Aug. 20, 1958. Helen (Strong), June 26, 1966. Christopher, Sept. 3, 1972. Protestant. Pond View Dr., Bow.

George Twombly Hamilton

Richard Freeman Hamilton

Richard Freeman Hamilton

President, White Mountains Attractions Association. North Conway, N.H., Feb. 13, 1936, Carroll and Esther (Brackett) Hamilton. Kennett High School, Conway, 1954. U.S. Air Force, 1954-56, airman 2nd cl. Sales manager, Eastern Slope Inn, North Conway, 1959-63, assistant manager, Indianhead Mountain Ski Area, Bessemer, Mich., 1963-66, founder, executive director, Ski 93 Association, 1966-70, president, White Mountains Attractions, 1970--, executive vice president, Ski the White Mountains Association, 1976--, photographer. Founder, president, N.H. Travel Council, 1973-78, director, 1978--; director, Littleton Area Historical Society, 1979-83, N.H. Hospitality Association, 1978--, Lincoln-Woodstock Chamber of Commerce, 1972-84, Better Business Bureau of N.H., 1983--, board of governors, Postsecondary Vocational-Technical Education, 1984--, member, Governor's High-Level Waste Task Force, 1985--, Society of American Travel Writers, 1976--, National Press Photographers Association, 1966--. Sandra (Hakanson), Aug. 25, 1962. Lisa Ann, Feb. 8, 1963, Trevor, Jan. 29, 1968, Scott, March 28, 1970. Episcopal. 61 Cottage St., Littleton.

Mary Louise Hancock

Planning consultant. Franklin, N.H., July 5, 1920, Herbert and Amanda (Lambert) Hancock. Concord High School, 1937, Univ. of N.H., B.A., 1942. Stenographer, N.H. Department of Education, 1942-43, secretary, N.H. Travel Division, 1943-44, N.H. Planning and Development Commission, Department of Resources and Economic Development, Office of State Planning, 1944-76, research librarian, planning associate, assistant planning director; director, 1960-76; planning consultant, 1976-79,81--, executive assistant to the regional administrator, U.S. Department of Housing and Urban Development, 1979-81. Concord School Board, 1955-64, Concord Planning Board, 1967-72, N.H. Senate, 1976-79, trustee, Audubon Society of N.H., 1978-84, Univ. System of N.H., 1979--, Concord Hospital, 1979--, director, N.H. Art Association, 1974--, corporator, Shaker Village, 1978-84, advisory committee, Campaign for Ratepayers' Rights, 1983--, board of governors, N.H. Public Television, 1979--, N.H. Water Supply and Pollution Control Commission, 1960-73. Unitarian. 33 Washington St., Concord.

Mary Louise Hancock

Parker Lambert Hancock

Parker Lambert Hancock

Warden, New Hampshire State Prison, retired. Newport, N.H., July 31, 1912, Herbert and Amanda (Lambert) Hancock. Concord High School, 1929, Univ. of N.H., B.S., 1934, Boston Univ., M.S., 1949. U.S. Army, 1943-45, pvt. Overseer of public welfare, city of Concord and Merrimack County, 1941-43,46-50, warden, N.H. State Prison, 1950-72. Correctional consultant, 1972-74, faculty, Dartmouth Medical School, 1972-75, faculty, St. Anselm College, 1973-79, director, American Correctional Association, 1951-72, president, 1967-68; president, Wardens Association of America, 1969-70, member, Governor's Commission on Crime and Delinquency, 1969-72, chairman, 1979; president, N.H. Social Welfare Council, 1958-60, N.H. House of Rep., 1939-41, executive secretary, N.E. Correctional Coordinating Council, 1974-77. Eleanor (Blackwood), June 4, 1938. Parker B., Oct. 11, 1940, David, Dec. 23, 1942, Jonathan, Dec. 24, 1953. Unitarian. 58 Ridge Rd., Concord.

Robert James Hankins

Director, State Council on the Arts. Elkhorn, Wis., July 25, 1946, Earl and Gudrun (Hammerstrom) Hankins. Delavan (Wis.) High School, 1968, Univ. of Wis., B.A., 1972, M.A., 1974. Director, Wausau (Wis.) Area Performing Arts Foundation, 1974-79, director, El Paso (Tex.) Arts Resources Department, 1979-82, director, State Council on the Arts, 1982--. N.E. Foundation for the Arts, 1982--, Association of College, University and Community Arts Administrators, 1979-82. Methodist. 40 North Main St., Concord.

George Russell Hanna

Attorney. West Swanzey, N.H., Jan. 19, 1918. Edward and Grace (Russell) Hanna. Keene High School, 1935, Dartmouth College, B.A., 1939, Boston Univ. School of Law, LL.B., 1949. U.S. Army, 1941-46, maj. Attorney, Keene, 1948--. Trustee, Keene Savings Bank, 1966--, Keene Public Library, 1957-85, Univ. System of N.H., 1963-71, Franklin Pierce College, 1975-80, member, Keene Rotary Club, 1948--, president, 1958. Shirley (Garfield), Feb. 2, 1946. Thomas, July 31, 1949, Susan, July 2, 1951, Katherine, Sept. 5, 1953, Lucy, June 4, 1959. United Church of Christ. 693 West St., Keene.

Selden James Hannah

Skier, farmer, innkeeper, pioneer in ski area development. Berlin, N.H., Nov. 9, 1913, Frank and Mary (McKenna) Hannah. Berlin High School, 1931, Dartmouth College, A.B., 1935. Civilian advisor on mountain warfare, 503rd paratroops, 1941-42. Owner, operator, Ski Hearth Farm, Franconia, 1938--, designer of ski areas, 1934--, advisor, winter sports planner, U.S. Forest Service, 1936-70, founder, president, Sno-Engineering, 1954-69. Member, Franconia Ski Club, 1938--, president, 1938-39; U.S. Olympic ski team, 1940, U.S. Eastern downhill champion, 1941, National Ski Hall of Fame, 1968, co-founder, director, N.E. Ski Museum, director, N.H. Potato Growers Association, 1950-60, president, 1955-56; president, Franconia Chamber of Commerce, 1946. Pauline (Lee), June 27, 1938. Joan, April 27, 1939, Lucy, Oct. 28, 1940, Frank, April 18, 1942, Selden L., Aug. 27, 1943. Ski Hearth Farm, Franconia.

Selden James Hannah

John Parker Hansel

John Parker Hansel

President, Filtrine Manufacturing Company. Cranford, N.J., Sept. 11, 1924, Charles and Kathryn (Denman) Hansel. Lawrenceville (N.J.) School, 1942, Princeton Univ., B.A., 1946. U.S. Marine Corps Reserve, 1942-45, 1st lt. Salesman, Filtrine Manufacturing Co., 1947--, president, 1954--. Founder, publisher, *National Building News*, 1964--, founder, executive director, Elm Research Institute, 1967--, director, Business and Industry Association of N.H., 1980--, Suffield (Conn.) School, 1966-68, Monadnock Family and Health Service, 1982--, chairman, No East West Highway Committee, 1972--, director, Governor's Management Review, 1981-82. Frances (Soule), July 20, 1945. Carla, Jan. 7, 1947, Parker, April 15, 1948, Peter, April 2, 1950, Turner, Sept. 19, 1954, David, Nov. 18, 1955. Episcopal. Cobb Hill Farm, Harrisville.

Arnold Philip Hanson

Attorney. Berlin, N.H., July 11, 1924, Arnold and Evelyn (Renaud) Hanson. Berlin High School, 1942, Univ. of N.H., A.B., 1948, Boston Univ. School of Law, LL.B., 1951. U.S. Navy, 1943-46, 1st cl. petty officer. Attorney, Berlin, 1951--. County attorney, Coos County, 1952-56, partner, North Country TV Cable Co., 1962--, director, Berlin Co-operative Bank, 1961-75, chairman, Berlin City Bank, 1975--, president, N.H. Bar Association, 1974-75, director, Univ. of N.H. Alumni Association, 1974-77, trustee, Androscoggin Valley Hospital, 1976-85, vice chairman, 1982-85; member, N.H. Court Accreditation Committee, 1970-77. Della (Lavernoich), June 26, 1948. Arnold Jr., Nov. 24, 1949, Caryl, Jan. 19, 1951, Julie, July 15, 1954. Lutheran. 119 Prospect St., Berlin.

Arnold Philip Hanson

John Robertson Hardie

John Robertson Hardie

Chairman, New Hampshire Savings Bank. Brooklyn, N.Y., Aug. 22, 1926, Allan and Isabel (Burchell) Hardie. Choate School, Wallingford, Conn., 1944, Yale Univ., B.A., 1947. Franklin Savings Bank, 1949-52, N.H. Savings Bank, 1952--, assistant treasurer, 1958, treasurer, 1963, treasurer, secretary, 1965, first vice president, 1968, president, 1972-85, chairman, 1982--, chairman, N.H. Savings Bank Corp., 1983--. Director, N.H. Savings Bank, 1972--, N.H. Business Development Corp., 1965-71, president, 1970-71; chairman, N.H. Association of Savings Banks, 1980-81, trustee, Society for the Protection of N.H. Forests, 1972-78,85--, treasurer, 1972-76; director, N.H. Housing Finance Agency, 1979-80, former director, Concord Regional Development Corp., former president, Family Financial Counseling Service, member, N.E. advisory committee, Federal Reserve, Boston. Drusilla (Penn), June 4, 1949. John, Oct. 11, 1951. Episcopal. Hopkinton Rd., Hopkinton.

Frederick John Harrigan

Attorney, judge, newspaper publisher. Bethlehem, N.H., Feb. 21, 1920, Carl and Fanny (Seymour) Harrigan. Lisbon High School, 1938, Harvard Univ., A.B., 1942, Georgetown Univ. Law School, LL.B., 1947. U.S. Naval Reserve, 1942-46, lt. comdr. Attorney, Colebrook, 1947--, justice, Colebrook District Court, 1949-84, judge of probate, Coos County, 1951--, owner, publisher, *News and Sentinel*, Colebrook, 1960--. Director, Andover Wood Products, 1954-70, treasurer, News and Sentinel Inc., 1960--, director, Coos Junction Press, 1981--, Blue Cross and Blue Shield, 1972-73, trustee, Society for the Protection of N.H. Forests, 1966-70, Daniel Webster Home, North Country YMCA, charter member, Colebrook Ambulance Corps, 1970-80. Esther (White), Aug. 15, 1942. Susan, April 5, 1945, John, April 22, 1947, Peter, July 28, 1948, Mary, Nov. 19, 1959. Catholic. South Hill, Box 62, Colebrook.

Frederick John Harrigan

John Dennis Harrigan

Editor, publisher, *Coos County Democrat*. Littleton, N.H., April 22, 1947, Frederick and Esther (White) Harrigan. Colebrook Academy, 1964, Maine Central Institute, 1965, N. Mex. State Univ., 1965-66. Reporter, *Nashua Telegraph*, 1968-71, *N.H. Sunday News*, 1971-76, editor, *News and Sentinel*, Colebrook, 1976-78, editor, publisher, *Coos County Democrat*, Lancaster, 1978--. Outdoor columnist, *N.H. Sunday News*, 1972--, president, Coos Junction Press, 1981--, president, trustee, Fenton Hardwick Foundation, 1980--, member, Pontook Reservior State Regulating Committee, 1985--, president, N.H. Press Association, 1979-80. Belinda (Ramirez), March 19, 1967 (div. 1982). Karen, April 15, 1970, John, April 10, 1973, Kathryn, July 23, 1978. P.O. Box 28, Lancaster.

Robert Joseph Harrison

President, chief executive officer, Public Service Company of New Hampshire. St. Charles, Mo., June 21, 1931, Daniel and Marie (Riney) Harrison. St. Joseph's Preparatory School, Muskogee, Okla., 1948, Muskogee Junior College, A.A., 1950, Univ. of Okla., B.B.A., 1957. U.S. Air Force, 1951-55, staff sgt. Public Service Co. of N.H., 1957--, assistant to the president, 1971, vice president, 1973, vice president, treasurer, 1977, financial vice president, 1978-80, president, 1980--, chief financial officer, 1980-81, chief operating officer, 1981-83, chief executive officer, 1983--. Director, Public Service Co. of N.H., 1979--, Maine Yankee Atomic Power Co., 1983--, Vt. Yankee Nuclear Power Corp., 1983--, Yankee Atomic Electric Co., 1984--, United Way of Greater Manchester, 1970-78, Governor's Management Review, 1981-82, corporator, director, Merchants Savings Bank (now Numerica Savings Bank), 1973--, former director, Business and Industry Association of N.H. Monique (Gilbert), June 18, 1955. David, March 11, 1957, Gregory, July 17, 1959, Elizabeth, June 10, 1965, Thomas, Feb. 20, 1969. Catholic. 234 Mayflower Dr., Manchester.

Robert Joseph Harrison

William Baird Hart Jr.

William Baird Hart Jr.

President, Dunfey Brothers Capital Group. Brooklyn, N.Y., Sept. 17, 1943, William and Christine (Ballantyne) Hart. Hopkins Grammar School, New Haven, 1961, Yale Univ., B.A., 1965. Dean of students, teacher, Hopkins Grammar School, 1967-70, executive director, Historic Windsor (Vt.) Inc., 1973-74, executive director, trustee, Historic Harrisville Inc., 1971-74, regional director, N.E. Field Services Office, Boston, 1974-75, director, advisory services, National Trust for Historic Preservation, Washington, D.C., 1975-79, president, N.H. Charitable Fund and Affiliated Trusts, 1979-86, president, Dunfey Brothers Capital Group, 1986--. Trustee, Society for the Preservation of N.E. Antiquities, 1984--, director, Harris Center, Hancock, 1982--, Center for N.H.'s Future, 1984--. Constance (Eaton), Aug. 5, 1980. Halliday, Aug. 20, 1981. Bonney Rd., Marlborough.

Edward John Haseltine

Business executive, retired. Merrimack, N.H., Jan. 23, 1909, John and Mabel (Lowell) Haseltine. Merrimack High School, 1927, Univ. of N.H., B.S., 1931. U.S. Army Air Force, 1942-46, lt. col., Army and Air Force Reserves, 1931-66, brigadier gen. N.H. Bureau of Labor Unemployment Compensation, 1936-42, president, Haseltine Brothers, lumber manufacturing, Merrimack, 1946-54, president, treasurer, N.E. Pole and Wood Treating Corp., Merrimack, 1955-68, executive director, Associated General Contractors of N.H., Concord, 1968-72, president, Bank of N.H., National Association, 1972-74, vice chairman, 1974-80. Judge, Merrimack Municipal Court, 1952-68, selectman, Merrimack, 1947-70, State Personnel Commission, 1973-75,83--, director, Bank of N.H., N.A., 1968-79, St. Joseph Hospital, Nashua, 1970--, International Paper Box Machine Co., Nashua, 1980--, chairman, Public Employee Labor Relations Board, 1975-81, N.H. House of Rep., 1963-65. Eleanor (Metcalfe), July 16, 1938. John, Oct. 3, 1939, Mark, Jan. 19, 1945, Paul, Sept. 28, 1960. Congregational. P.O. Box 820, Merrimack.

Edward John Haseltine

John Woodsum Hatch

John Woodsum Hatch

Artist, art educator, retired. Saugus, Mass., Nov. 1, 1919, Herbert and Florence (Woodsum) Hatch. Saugus High School, 1937, Mass. School of Art., 1937-41, Yale Univ. School of Fine Arts, B.F.A., 1948, M.F.A., 1949. U.S. Army, 1941-45, staff sgt., T-4. Landscape and portrait artist, 1940--, Univ. of N.H., instructor in the arts, 1949-55, assistant professor, 1955-57, associate professor, 1957-63, professor, 1963-85. President, N.H. Art Association, 1958-60, advisory board, Thorne Art Gallery, Keene State College, 1971-75, executive board, Yale Arts Association, 1972-75, co-chairman, traveling exhibitions, N.H. Art Association, 1951-58, visual arts committee, N.H. Commission on the Arts, 1968-70, juror, Boston Arts Festival, 1961, Durham Conservation Commission, 1974--, chairman, 1976-78; vice chairman, Lamprey River Watershed Association, 1982--. Maryanna (Eckman), Aug. 25, 1946. Johanna, Dec. 11, 1947, Rebecca, April 23, 1950. 28 Mill Rd., Durham.

James Henry Hayes

Former executive councilor. Hyde Park, Mass., Aug. 19, 1908, John and Carrie (Shuman) Hayes. Quincy (Mass.) High School, 1926, Thayer Academy, South Braintree, Mass., 1928, Univ. of N.H., B.A., 1932, Harvard Univ., 1932-33,36-37. Trooper, Mass. State Police, 1933-37, captain and executive officer, N.H. State Police, 1937-39, director of safety, National Fireworks, West Hanover, Mass., 1940-45, president, N.H. Distributors Inc., 1946-73, chairman and chief executive officer, 1973--. N.H. House of Rep., 1953-55, N.H. Executive Council, 1959-77, president, N.H. Wholesale Beverage Association, 1950-51, trustee, N.H. Savings Bank, 1960-71, N.H. Historical Society, 1972-73, director, Concord National Bank, 1960-85, Concord General Life Insurance Co., 1975--, Concord General Mutual Insurance Co., 1975--. One honorary degree. Claire (Short), Dec. 11, 1935. Robert, Sept. 10, 1936, Patricia, Oct. 25, 1939, Gail, Feb. 25, 1944, Margaret, Aug. 22, 1946, Elizabeth, Jan. 16, 1948, James Jr., Feb. 26, 1953. Catholic. 32 Westbourne Rd., Concord.

James Henry Hayes

William Andrew Healy

Executive director, New Hampshire Water Supply and Pollution Control Commission. Brookline, Mass., Nov. 30, 1912, John and Bridget (Halloran) Healy. Chauncy Hall School, Boston, 1932, MIT, B.S., 1936. N.H. Health Department, district sanitary engineer, 1937-42, senior sanitary engineer, 1942-45, associate sanitary engineer, 1949-50, director, division of sanitary engineering, 1950-65, executive director, N.H. Water Supply and Pollution Control Commission, 1965--. Chairman, N.H. Bulk Power Supply Site Evaluation Committee, 1971--, chairman, N.H. Energy Facility Evaluation Committee, 1974--, member, N.H., N.E. American Water Works Associations, 1940--, member, N.E. Water Pollution Control Association, 1950--, N.H. commissioner, N.E. Interstate Water Pollution Control Commission, 1951--, chairman, N.E. Interstate Water Pollution Control Commission, 1972, diplomate, American Academy of Environmental Engineers, 1958--, life member, Water Pollution Control Federation, 1980--. Mary (McKinney), Jan. 3, 1942. Elizabeth, Dec. 4, 1946, John, Feb. 11, 1949. Catholic. 30 Union St., Concord.

Edgar James Helms Jr.

Consultant. Cambridge, Mass., March 27, 1945, Edgar and Shirley (Colby) Helms. Milford (Mass.) High School, 1962, Drew Univ., B.A., 1967, Univ. of N.H., M.A., 1971. U.S. Army, 1967-70, 1st lt. Associate planner, N.H. Office of Comprehensive Health Planning, 1971-72, research planning technician, 1972-74; legislative assistant, Sen. Thomas McIntyre, 1974-75, field representative, 1975-78; executive assistant, Gov. Hugh Gallen, 1979, commissioner, N.H. Department of Health and Welfare, 1979-83, consultant, Concord, 1983--. Chairman, human services planners, N.H. Planners Association, 1973, trustee, Merrimack Valley Day Care Center, 1978-79, member, Downtown Revitalization Committee, Concord, 1975-76, member, Gov. Walter Peterson's Select Task Force on Drug Abuse, 1971-72, trustee, Spaulding Youth Center, 1985--. Sally (Hess), June 27, 1970. Margaret, Aug. 16, 1982. Protestant. 9 Tahanto St., Concord.

Jean Lande Hennessey

Jean Lande Hennessey

Director, Dartmouth Institute on Canada. Seattle, Wash., Feb. 1, 1927, Clarence and Adelia (Babcock) Lande. Highline High School, Seattle, 1945, Vassar College, A.B., 1948. Executive director, N.H. Charitable Fund, 1968-77, president, Women and Foundations/Corporate Philanthropy, 1977-78, budget director, Gov. Hugh Gallen, 1979, commissioner, International Joint Commission, Washington, D.C., 1979-81, consultant on foundation, corporate and individual philanthropy, Hanover, 1981--, research fellow, Dartmouth College, 1981--, director, Dartmouth Institute on Canada, 1986--. Trustee, Environmental Law Institute, 1978-84, Population Resource Center, 1979--, N.E. Natural Resources Center, 1973--, director, Council on Foundations, 1974-80, incorporator, N.H. Charitable Fund, 1978--, member, Governor's Task Force on Discrimination in State Employment, 1982, N.H. Commission on the Status of Women, 1971-73, Democratic National Committee, 1979-81, board of visitors, Whittemore School of Business, 1976--. Two honorary degrees. John Hennessey Jr., June 26, 1948. John III, Sept. 5, 1952, Martha, Feb. 2, 1954. 4 Webster Terrace, Hanover.

John William Hennessey Jr.

Professor. Danville, Pa., March 25, 1925, John and Martha (Braun) Hennessey. William Penn High School, York, Pa., 1941, Princeton Univ., A.B., 1948, Harvard Univ., M.B.A., 1950, Univ. of Wash., Ph.D., 1956. U.S. Army, 1943-46, 1st lt. Instructor, associate professor, Univ. of Wash., 1950-57, professor, Amos Tuck School of Business Administration, Dartmouth College, 1957--, associate dean, 1962-68, dean, 1968-76. Trustee, Educational Testing Service, 1975-85, chairman, 1978-80,84-85; Univ. of Vt., 1986--, Dartmouth Savings Bank, 1970-76, Mary Hitchcock Memorial Hospital, 1962--, chairman, 1977-83; director, American Assembly of Collegiate Schools of Business, 1970-77, president, 1975-76; Controlled Environment Corp., 1972-75, Conn. Mutual Life Insurance Co., 1971--, Zayre Corp., 1980--, Encyclopedia Britannica Educational Corp., 1985--, Milbank Memorial Fund, 1983--. Three honorary degrees. Jean (Lande), June 26, 1948. John III, Sept. 5, 1952, Martha, Feb. 2, 1954. Presbyterian. 4 Webster Terrace, Hanover.

John William Hennessey Jr.

Lyle Edward Hersom

Lyle Edward Hersom

New Hampshire Liquor Commission. Groveton, N.H., Aug. 9, 1928, Edward and Ethel (Thompkins) Hersom. Groveton High School, 1948. U.S. Army, 1952-54, sgt. Owner, operator, service station and garage, 1948-50, foreman and envelope manufacturing adjuster, 1950-52, educational sales representative, 1955-77, commissioner, N.H. Liquor Commission, 1977--. N.H. House of Rep., 1957-59, N.H. Executive Council, 1971-77, N.H. Constitutional Convention, 1960, N.H. State Racing Commission, 1960-64, N.H. Prison Board of Trustees, 1974-76, moderator, Groveton, 1958-80, moderator, Northumberland School District, 1958-80, director, Lancaster Fair, 1964--, president, 1975-77; director, Groveton National Bank, 1975-83, chairman, Northumberland Historical Society, 1960--. Ruth (McFarland), Feb. 2, 1949. Methodist. 1 Preble St., Groveton.

Robert Joseph Hill

President, New Hampshire Savings Bank, retired. Quincy, Mass., Sept. 1, 1907, Joseph and Mary (Noyes) Hill. Roxbury (Mass.) Latin School, 1925, Amherst College, A.B., 1930. Securities analyst, 1930-53, N.H. Savings Bank, treasurer, 1953-59, executive vice president, 1959-61, president, 1961-72. Trustee, N.H. Savings Bank, 1961-81, director, National Association of Mutual Savings Banks, 1962-71, president, 1968-69; Mechanicks National Bank, Concord, 1959-70, member, Mount Washington Commission, 1970--, vice chairman, Mount Washington Planning Committee, 1966-70, chairman, N.H. Water Supply and Pollution Control Commission, 1972-80, president, trustee, Land Use Foundation of N.H., 1966-72, Canterbury Planning Board, 1968-77, chairman, 1969-76; trustee, Shaker Village, 1976--, president, 1980-82; member, Appalachian Mountain Club, 1948--. Virginia (Walters), June 1, 1935. Robert Jr., Nov. 28, 1937, Virginia, Feb. 3, 1941, Gregory, Feb. 7, 1944. Miriam (Thomas), June 30, 1961. Christian Scientist. 4 Amoskeag Rd., Concord.

John Henry Hoben

City coordinator, Manchester. Manchester, N.H., Nov. 12, 1946, John and Margaret (Enright) Hoben. Bishop Bradley High School, Manchester, 1964, Middlebury College, B.A., 1969, Case Western Reserve Univ., M.P.M.S., 1971. Administrative trainee, Manchester Housing Authority, 1967-68, administrative assistant, Model Cities Agency, Manchester, 1968-69, independent consultant, municipal planning and finance, 1969-70, director of research, state of W. Va., 1970-71, director of business taxes, W. Va. State Tax Department, 1971-72, city coordinator, Manchester, 1972--, president, Greater Manchester Development Corp., 1985--. Incorporator, Merchants Savings Bank, 1978-82, Catholic Medical Center, 1976--, member, Charter Revision Commission, 1982, N.H. Air Resources Commission, 1978-80, director, Federated Arts of Manchester, 1978-81, Manchester Institute of Arts and Sciences, 1978-80. Mary (Vial), Oct. 27, 1972. David, Dec. 4, 1963, Elizabeth, Feb. 9, 1970. Catholic. 535 East High St., Manchester.

Russell Adams Holden

President, Granite State Electric Company. Somerville, Mass., Jan. 3, 1925, Charles and Augusta (Lerner) Holden. Belmont (Mass.) High School, 1941, Chauncey Hall Preparatory School, Boston, 1942, Tufts Univ., B.S., 1945. U.S. Navy, 1945-46, lieut. Vt. Hardware Co., 1947-62, commissioner of highways, Vt. 1962-67, assistant vice president, New England Power Co., 1967-69, vice president, 1969--; president, Granite State Electric Co., 1973--. Chairman, N.E. Electric Transmission Corp., 1981--, Northeast Consolidated Services, 1981--, director, Concord General Mutual Insurance Co., 1971--, Concord Group Insurance Co., 1971--, member, Association of N.H. Utilities, 1979--, director, 1982--, president, 1979-80; member, Vt. Electrical Association, 1950--, Vt. Society of Engineers, 1964--, Business and Industry Association of N.H., 1971--, Associated Industries of Vt., 1967--. Gwen, April 5, 1948, Russell Jr., Aug. 4, 1949, Robin, Nov. 6, 1951, Bruce, Oct. 27, 1953, Mark, May 12, 1955, Sandra, Aug. 2, 1963, Jo-Ann, July 17, 1966. Episcopal. 111 Mountain Rd., Concord.

Russell Adams Holden

Edith Elizabeth Holland

Register of deeds, Rockingham County, retired. Boston, Mass., June 25, 1914, George and Elise (Schwartz) Young. Quincy (Mass.) High School, 1931, Burdett College, Northeastern Univ. School of Law, LL.B., 1940. Independent title abstracter, 1951-63, register of deeds, Rockingham County, 1963-85. Exeter Planning Board, 1973-76, former vice president, Exeter League of Women Voters, former committee chairman, Girl Scouts of America, Exeter, former director, Land Information Systems International, honorary member, N.H. Land Surveyors Association. Everett Holland, Aug. 3, 1940. Nancy, Sept. 6, 1941, George, Nov. 15, 1942, Janette, Oct. 30, 1944, Everett P., Nov. 2, 1946 (dec. 1969), John, Aug. 19, 1951 (dec. 1975), Martha, Sept. 7, 1954. Congregational. 20 Hampton Falls Rd., Exeter.

John Sullivan Holland

Attorney. Boston, Mass., April 24, 1928, Daniel and Katherine (Kelly) Holland. Boston Latin School, 1945, Maryknoll Seminary, A.B., 1949, Boston College Law School, LL.B., 1960. U.S. Navy, 1952-55, lt. jg. Attorney, Manchester, 1960--. Bedford School Board, 1967-70, chairman, N.H. Board of Education, 1979-83, Democratic National Committeeman, 1968-72, legislative counsel, Gov. John King, 1965, director, Manchester Association of Retarded Citizens, 1974-76, chairman, Governor's Task Force on Education of the Handicapped, 1981-82, member, American College of Probate Counsel, 1978--. Patricia (O'Brien), Jan. 14, 1956. Maria, March 24, 1957, Christian, May 28, 1958, Martha, April 7, 1960, Anne, Dec. 5, 1962, Anthony, April 24, 1972, Catholic. 5 Glen Rd., Bedford.

Paul Jackson Holloway Jr.

Paul Jackson Holloway Jr.

President, Dreher-Holloway Buick-Pontiac. Philadelphia, Pa., Sept. 11, 1938, Paul and Elizabeth (Fricke) Holloway. Germantown High School, Philadelphia, 1956, Temple Univ., B.S., 1961. Salesman, Atlantic Refining, Philadelphia, 1960-61, district manager, Buick Motor Division, Flint, Mich., 1961-67, president, Dreher-Holloway Buick-Pontiac, Exeter, 1967--. President, N.E. Buick Dealers Association, 1976-78, member, Exeter Budget Committee, 1973-79, president, Seacoast Regional Development Commission, 1975-76, member, Portsmouth Maritime Association, 1982--, chairman, Exeter Area School District Building Committee, 1973-75, trustee, Berwick (Maine) Academy, 1977-80, Univ. System of N.H., 1972--, chairman, 1985--; Public TV Board of Governors, 1978-80, director, Indian Head Banks Inc., 1985--. Anna (Baer), April 1, 1961. Paul S., Sept. 26, 1963, Debra, Jan. 2, 1966. Congregational. 80 Front St., Exeter.

Nelle Louise Weathers Holmes

Educator, retired, former state senator. Elkton, Ky., June 22, 1903, George and Elizabeth (McKinney) Weathers. Peabody Demonstration School, Nashville, Tenn., 1920, Barnard College, A.B., 1924, Columbia Univ., M.A., 1937. Teacher, history, government, Oxford School, West Hartford, Conn., Packer Collegiate Institute, Brooklyn, Sarah Dix Hamlin School, San Francisco. N.H. House of Rep., 1951-57, N.H. Senate, 1957-65, former trustee, Amherst Town Library, charter member, former president, Amherst Historical Society, director, Council for Better Schools, 1960, trustee, N.H. Historical Society, 1955-79, honorary, 1979--; N.H. Higher Education Loan Plan, 1962-79, member, Rivier College Advisory Board, 1962-79, honorary, 1979--; member, N.H. Historical Commission, 1978-82, member, N.H. planning committee, White House Education Conference, 1955, member, State Historical Marker Advisory Committee. Two honorary degrees. Philip Holmes, Sept. 6, 1925 (dec. 1985). Episcopal. Hunt Community, Nashua.

Mildred McAfee Horton

Mildred McAfee Horton

President, Wellesley College, retired. Parkville, Mo., May 12, 1900, Cleland and Harriet (Brown) McAfee. Francis W. Parker School, Chicago, 1916, Vassar College, B.A., 1920, Univ. of Chicago, M.A., 1928. Director, Women's Reserve, U.S. Naval Reserve, 1942-46, capt. Acting professor, economics, sociology, Tusculum College, Greenville, Tenn., 1923-25, dean of women, professor of sociology, Centre College, Danville, Ky., 1927-32, dean of college women, Oberlin College, 1934-36, president, Wellesley College, 1936-49. Director, National Broadcasting Co., 1950-61, Radio Corp. of America, 1951-61, co-chairman, National Women's Committee for Civil Rights, 1963, president, Association of American Colleges, 1947, member, Fund for Advancement of Education, Ford Foundation, 1950-67, vice president, National Council of Churches, 1954-57, director, Havenwood Retirement Community, 1975-84, trustee, Univ. System of N.H., 1963-74, chairman, 1972-73. Thirty-one honorary degrees. Douglas Horton, Aug. 10, 1946. United Church of Christ. Randolph.

Ralph Degnan Hough

State senator. Hanover, N.H., May 21, 1943, Frank and Renna (Degnan) Hough. Kimball Union Academy, Meriden, 1962, St. Michael's College, B.A., 1967. U.S. Army, 1967-69, sgt. Insurance broker, Lebanon, 1969--. N.H. House of Rep., 1973-78, N.H. Senate, 1978--, N.H. Association of Independent Insurance Agents, 1969--, Veterans of Foreign Wars, American Legion, Elks. Susan (Rector), Nov. 8, 1971. Anna, Oct. 4, 1972, David, May 14, 1975. Catholic. RFD 1, Poverty Ln., West Lebanon.

Ralph Degnan Hough

John Jeremiah Houlihan

John Jeremiah Houlihan

Dentist. Bellows Falls, Vt., May 27, 1930, Maurice and Dorothy (Wolfe) Houlihan. Bellows Falls High School, 1948, St. Michael's College, B.S., 1952, Loyola Univ., D.D.S., 1956. U.S. Army Dental Corps, 1956-58, capt. General practitioner of dentistry, Claremont, 1958--, staff, Claremont Hospital, 1959--. Member, National Board of Dental Examiners, 1971-73, Citizens Task Force, 1969-70, incorporator, Connecticut Valley Health Compact, 1969-71, president, N.H. Dental Society, 1969-70, charter member, director, president, N.H. Dental Service Corp., 1967-68, member, N.H. Division of Public Health Oral Cancer Screening Team, 1973-76, trustee, American Dental Association, 1973-79, treasurer, 1978-79, president-elect, 1979-80, president, 1980-81; dental health coordinator, Claremont School District, 1960-75, director, Indian Head National Bank, Claremont, 1981-84. Mary (Abbott), June 18, 1955. John A., June 28, 1956, Kevin, May 17, 1958, Mary, Jan. 19, 1963, Ann, Sept. 27, 1966. Catholic. Highland Ave. Ext., Claremont.

Leslie Stoddard Hubbard

Chairman, Hubbard Farms, retired. Walpole, N.H., April 25, 1904, Ira and Gertrude (Lamb) Hubbard. Walpole High School, 1922, Univ. of N.H., B.S., 1927. Engineer, N.Y. Telephone Co., 1927-28, manager, Niagara Poultry Farm, Ransonville, N.Y., 1928-32, branch manager, Hubbard Farms, Lancaster, Pa., 1932-55, vice president of sales, Hubbard Farms, Walpole, 1955-69, chairman, 1969-74. Director, Hubbard Farms, 1939-69, Hubbard Euro-Poultry S.A., Oudenaarde, Belguim, 1960-69, chairman, 1962-64; trustee, Lancaster General Hospital, 1938-62, director, Farmers Bank and Trust Co., Lancaster, 1949-62, chairman, Walpole Conservation Commission, 1973--, director, Connecticut River Watershed Council, 1971-80, executive committee, Citizens Scholarship Foundation of America, 1972-81, national chairman, Campaign for Distinction, Univ. of N.H., 1980-84, president, National Poultry Producers Federation, 1948-52, president, Poultry and Egg National Board, 1955-56. One honorary degree. Iola (McCracken), Sept. 23, 1932. Marcia, March 12, 1936, John, Sept. 3, 1940. Protestant. Sparhawk Hill, Walpole.

Leslie Stoddard Hubbard

Oliver Wentworth Hubbard

Oliver Wentworth Hubbard

President, general manager, Hubbard Farms. Walpole, N.H., Dec. 19, 1928, Oliver J. and Dorothy (Penniman) Hubbard. Loomis School, Windsor, Conn., 1946, Univ. of N.H., B.S., 1950. U.S. Army, 1951-53, sgt. Hubbard Farms, research specialist, 1950-51,53-56, director of research and development, 1956-62, president, general manager, 1962--. Director, former president, N.H. Poultry Growers Association, 1959-64, director, former chairman, American Egg Board, 1971-76, director, American Broiler Council, 1979--, member, N.H. Agricultural Advisory Board, 1981--, director, Southeastern Poultry and Egg Association, 1985--, First Vt. Financial Corp., 1972--, board of visitors, Whittemore School of Business, Univ. of N.H., 1972--, trustee, Vt. Academy, 1979--, member, former chairman, school board, Walpole, 1954-63, president, N.E. Kurn Hattin Homes, 1978--, trustee, former chairman, 4-H Foundation of N.H., 1974-80. Janet, Aug. 17, 1954, Dale, Aug. 7, 1956, Heidi, Dec. 29, 1957, Jeffrey, June 2, 1962. Protestant. RFD, Walpole.

Gordon John Humphrey

United States senator. Bristol, Conn., Oct. 9, 1940, Gordon C. and Regina (Berio) Humphrey. Bristol High School, 1958, George Washington Univ., 1962-63, Burnside-Ott Aviation Institute, Dallas. U.S. Army Air Force, 1958-62, airman 1st cl. Ferry pilot, 1965-66, Universal Air Transport, Detroit, 1966-67, co-pilot, Allegheny Airlines, 1967-78, U.S. Senate, 1979--. Co-founder, coordinator, N.H. Conservative Caucus, 1977-78, member, Airline Pilots Association. Patricia (Green), July 2, 1978. Daniel, adopted, Aug. 1985. Baptist. Chichester.

Gordon John Humphrey

David Oliva Huot

Attorney, judge. Laconia, N.H., April 4, 1942, J. Oliva and Irene (Fournier) Huot. Sacred Heart High School, Laconia, 1960, St. Anselm College, A.B., 1964, Georgetown Univ. Law School, J.D., 1967. Attorney, Laconia, 1967--. Justice, Laconia District Court, 1979--, N.H. House of Rep., 1971-75, incorporator, Lakes Region Hospital, 1976--, director, Lakes Region Mutual Fire Aid Association, 1968-82, board of governors, N.H. Bar Association, 1978-80, member, Knights of Columbus, 1960--, state advocate, 1969-75. Patricia Ann (Hawkins), Aug. 8, 1981. Matthew, Jan. 18, 1983. Catholic. 62 Walker St., Laconia.

Harold Eldred Hyde

President, Plymouth State College, retired. Hartwick, N.Y., July 22, 1911, Howard and Bertha (Eldred) Hyde. Hartwick High School, 1926, Hartwick College, B.S., 1933, Albany (N.Y.) State College for Teachers, M.S., 1939, N.Y.U., Ed.D., 1950. Business teacher, vice principal, Spencer (N.Y.) High School, 1934-37, business teacher, Nyack (N.Y.) Junior and Senior High School, 1937-39, assistant principal, director of guidance, Vestal (N.Y.) Central School, 1939-44, director of guidance, Endicott (N.Y.) Public Schools, 1944-48, chief, division of educational research, N.H. Department of Education, 1948-51, president, Plymouth State College, 1951-77. President, N.H. College and Univ. Council, 1974, president, American Association of State Colleges and Universities, 1972-73, trustee, Univ. System of N.H., 1963-77, N.H. College, 1977-82, member, Postsecondary Education Commission, 1973-78. Four honorary degrees. Mary Rita (Oliver), April 10, 1941. Mary Anne, Oct. 10, 1947. Protestant. Coxboro Rd., Holderness.

Harold Eldred Hyde

William Aron Ingram

Attorney, judge. New York, N.Y., Sept. 12, 1939, Edward and Jeanette Ingram. Tabor Academy, Marion, Mass., 1958, Yale Univ., 1958-60, Univ. of N.H., A.B., 1968, Boston College Law School, J.D., 1971. Attorney, Lancaster, 1971--. Associate justice, Lancaster District Court, 1983--, chairman, Weathervane Theatre Players, 1975-85, incorporator, N.H. Charitable Fund, 1985--, No. N.H. Foundation, 1985--, N.H. Commission on the Arts, 1983--, member, Weeks State Park Association, president, Coos County Bar Association, 1976, board of governors, Coos County, N.H. Bar Association, 1977-79, at-large, 1979-80; co-owner, Spalding Inn & Club, Whitefield, 1985--. Flora (Bullock), Aug. 28, 1965. Edward, Sept. 10, 1968, William Alexander, May 24, 1970. 67 Elm St., Lancaster.

Alice Peters Irwin

Executive, Hartford Element Co., retired. New York, N.Y., Sept. 6, 1920, John and Charlotte (Hodge) Peters. Prospect Hill School, New Haven, 1937, Radcliffe College, 1937-39. Hartford Element Co., Newport, clerk, 1953-54, bookkeeper, office manager, 1954, treasurer, office manager, 1955-57, treasurer, production manager, personnel manager, 1957-81. Overseer of welfare, Sunapee, 1981--, director, Sullivan County Mental Health Association, 1973-77,83--, president, 1984--; director, Sullivan County Rehabilitation Center, 1973-79,80--, president, 1983-85; director, N.H. Association for Mental Health, 1975-80, member, Governor's Commission for the Handicapped, 1972-74,81--, director, N.H. Social Welfare Council, 1976-78,83--, board member, United Way of N.H., 1978--, president, 1980--; Planned Parenthood League of the Upper Valley, 1978-80, trustee, Claremont General Hospital, 1979. David Irwin, Dec. 16, 1939. Nancy, Dec. 13, 1940, David, March 26, 1942, Charles, Aug. 26, 1946, Dorothy, April 24, 1948. Lake Ave., P.O. Box 707, Sunapee.

Alice Peters Irwin

Lotte Jacobi

Photographer. Thorn, West Prussia, Germany, Aug. 17, 1896, Sigismund and Maria (Lublinski) Jacobi. Wagner School, Posen, Germany, 1912, Academy of Posen, 1912-16, Bavarian State Academy of Photography and Univ. of Munich, 1925-27, Univ. of N.H., 1961-62. Photographer, specializing in portraits, Jacobi Studio, Berlin, 1927-35, N.Y.C., 1935-55, Deering, 1955-85. Honorary curator of photography, Currier Gallery, 1972--, former member, Deering Conservation Commission. Six honorary degrees, N.H. Governor's Award for the Arts, 1980. Fritz Honig, 1916 (div. 1926). John, March 17, 1917 (dec. June 30, 1985). Erich Reiss, Oct. 7, 1940 (dec. May, 1951). Havenwood Retirement Community, Concord.

Alf Edgar Jacobson

Professor, state representative. Spokane, Wash., April 4, 1924, Carl and Emmy (Burgess) Jacobson. Lewis and Clark High School, Spokane, 1942, North Park College, A.A., 1948, Northwestern Univ., B.S., 1952, Tufts Univ., M.A., 1954, Harvard Univ., S.T.B., 1954, S.T.M., 1955, Ph.D., 1963. U.S. Marine Corps, 1943-46, sgt. Professor of social science, Colby-Sawyer College, 1958--. N.H. Senate, 1969-78, president, 1975-78; N.H. House of Rep., 1983--, New London Planning Board, 1965-71, moderator, New London, 1970-73, selectman, New London, 1973-85, moderator, Kearsarge Regional School District, 1968-84, trustee, Lake Sunapee Savings Bank, 1976--, N.H. Municipal Workers Fund, 1984--, member, National Archive Advisory Council, 1981-84, library trustee, New London, 1960-63, member, Peace Corps Advisory Council, 1982-84. Sonja (Torstenson), Dec. 8, 1951. Kurt, July 9, 1959, Brent, March 1, 1963. American Baptist. Burpee Hill Rd., New London.

Alf Edgar Jacobson

Frank Austin Jillson

Frank Austin Jillson

President, New Hampshire Blue Cross and Blue Shield. Concord, N.H., July 15, 1930, Austin and Claudia (Twiss) Jillson. Concord High School, 1948, N. E. College, 1948-49, Fisher Business School, Boston, 1949-50, Univ. of N.H., B.S., 1959. U.S. Air Force, 1951-55, staff sgt. N.H. Blue Cross and Blue Shield, 1959--, vice president, provider and professional affairs, 1980-82, president, 1982--. Director, National Blue Cross and Blue Shield, 1985--, N.H. Health Systems Agency, 1977-81, State Health Coordinating Council, 1981-83, Health Planning Advisory Council, 1983-85, N.H. Association for Mental Health, 1977--, Concord Red Cross, 1984--. Beverly (Bartkus), Nov. 19, 1954. David, Nov. 27, 1955, Karen, Oct. 18, 1959, Kathie, Oct. 18, 1959, Jenifer, March 24, 1967. Methodist. 7 Cote St., Concord.

Owen Johnson

Lumber company owner, retired. Wayne, Maine, April 25, 1887. Oliver and Minnie (Foss) Johnson. Thayer Academy, So. Braintree, Mass. Co-owner, B.H. Piper Co., 1910-14, president, treasurer, Johnson Lumber Co. and Johnson Building Materials, Manchester, 1916-75. Trustee, Cogswell Benevolent Trust, 1955--, executive committee, Society for the Protection of N.H. Forests, 1951-64, treasurer, 1965-71; director, N.H. Business Development Corp., 1956-59, member, N.H. Forestry and Recreation Commission, 1940-60, Manchester Police Commission, 1927-34, corporator, Amoskeag Savings Bank, 1957-63, chairman, Governor's Timber Salvage Committee, 1939-40, member, Manchester Historical Association, 1966--, N.H. Historical Society, 1945--, former director, president, Northeastern Lumber Manufacturers Association. Ruth (Cheney), Dec. 7, 1910 (dec. 1935). Barbara, March 16, 1912. Elizabeth (Coleman), Jan. 2, 1937. Protestant. 73 Liberty St., Manchester. Owen Johnson died on June 29, 1986.

Owen Johnson

William Reynold Johnson

Associate justice, New Hampshire Supreme Court. Excelsior, Minn., Oct. 21, 1930, Reynold and Nettie (Cunningham) Johnson. Excelsior High School, 1949, Dartmouth College, A.B., 1953, Harvard Law School, J.D., 1958. U.S. Army, 1956-58, 1st lt. Attorney, Lebanon, Hanover, 1958-69, adjunct professor of business law, Amos Tuck School, Dartmouth College, 1959--, associate justice, N.H. Superior Court, 1969-85, associate justice, N.H. Supreme Court, 1985--. President, Lebanon College, 1962-65, president, Grafton County Bar Association, 1965-66, N.H. House of Rep., 1963-65,69, N.H. Senate, 1965-67, chairman, Republican State Committee, 1965-66. Nancy (Preston), Aug. 14, 1954. Catherine, Aug. 30, 1959, Susan, July 21, 1962. Congregational. 14 Rayton Rd., Hanover.

E. Leo Kanteres

President, Kanteres Real Estate. Manchester, N.H., Jan. 22, 1926, Vaios and Merope (Kakou) Kanteres. Manchester Central High School, 1943, Univ. of N.H., 1945-46, Hesser Business College, 1946-47. U.S. Army Air Force, 1944-45, sgt. Owner, Kanteres Insurance Agency, 1952-59, owner, Kanteres Real Estate, 1952--, president, 1985--. Partner, Riley-Kanteres Construction Co., Laurel Acres, Bell Building, corporator, Manchester Savings Bank, advisory committee, BankEast, director, N.H. Business Development Corp., 1980-83, director, Industrial Development Authority, 1981-83, former president, vice president, director, N.H. Association of Realtors, former director, Small Business Advisory Council, former chairman, So. N.H. Planning Commission, advisory committee, Campaign for Ratepayers' Rights, 1983--. Zoe (Economou), Feb. 6, 1949. Lynda Ann, Feb. 7, 1950, William, April 21, 1952. Greek Orthodox. 629 Kearney Circle, Manchester.

E. Leo Kanteres

John Jacob Karol Jr.

John Jacob Karol Jr.

Producer-filmmaker. Mount Kisco, N.Y., April 1, 1935, John and Ann (Hale) Karol. Deerfield (Mass.) Academy, 1953, Williams College, B.A., 1958, Yale Law School, LL.B., 1962. Attorney, N.Y.C., 1962-64, parliamentary draftsman, Zomba, Malawi, Africa, 1964-67, deputy commissioner, general counsel, Vt. Department of Taxes, 1967-69, producer-filmmaker, Orford, 1969--. Member, Citizens Advisory Council, Dartmouth-Hitchcock Mental Health Center, 1973-77, Task Force on Historic Preservation in N.H., 1983-85, director, Inherit N.H., 1985--. Angelisse, Feb. 5, 1962, Christopher, May 29, 1964. Portia (Fitzhugh), June 21, 1980. Fitzhugh, May 31, 1982. Episcopal. Main St., Orford.

Howard Wadleigh Keegan

President, Amoskeag Bank Shares. Greenfield, Mass., Nov. 17, 1923, Frank and Helen (Wadleigh) Keegan. Deerfield (Mass.) Academy, 1943, Amherst College, A.B., 1948, Harvard Univ., M.B.A., 1950. U.S. Army Air Force, 1943-45, 2nd lt. Vice president, National Shawmut Bank, Boston, 1950-62, Amoskeag National Bank and Trust Co., Manchester, 1962-86, chief executive officer, 1973-86, chairman, 1982-86; president, Amoskeag Bank Shares, 1986--. Incorporator, Catholic Medical Center, 1982--, director, Federated Arts of Manchester, 1975--, president, 1975-76; N.H. Sweepstakes Commission, 1983--, chairman, 1985--; N.H. Commission on the Arts, 1981--, trustee, N.H. Symphony Orchestra, 1983-85, advisory council, 1985--; Derryfield School, 1969-74, director, N.H. Bankers Association, 1965-66,74-81, president, 1976-77; co-chairman, Liberty Centennial Campaign, N.H. chapter, 1985--. Janet (Davis), June 21, 1945. Lynda, Feb. 4, 1949, Gary, Oct. 31, 1950, Geoffrey, Oct. 17, 1958. Protestant. 1029 Ray St., Manchester.

Howard Wadleigh Keegan

Jean Alexander Kemeny

Jean Alexander Kemeny

Writer. Burlington, Vt., Oct. 26, 1930, Robert and Laura (Bliss) Alexander. Cape Elizabeth (Maine) High School, 1949, Smith College, 1949-50. First lady, Dartmouth College, 1970-81. Member, Handel Society, Authors Guild, Dartmouth Players, Madrigal Singers, Hanover Democratic Committee, chairman of fund drives for Friends of Hanover Schools, Hopkins Center for the Arts, Montshire Museum. Author, *It's Different at Dartmouth*, 1979, *Strands of War*, 1984. Two honorary degrees. John Kemeny, Nov. 5, 1950. Jennifer, Sept. 27, 1954, Robert, Sept. 20, 1955. Congregational. Woods End Rd., Etna.

John George Kemeny

Professor, former president, Dartmouth College. Budapest, Hungary, May 31, 1926. Tibor and Lucy (Fried) Kemeny. George Washington High School, N.Y.C., 1943, Princeton Univ., B.A., 1947, Ph.D., 1949. U.S. Army, Los Alamos project, 1945-46. Research assistant, Dr. Albert Einstein, Institute for Advanced Study, 1948-49, instructor, research fellow, mathematics, Princeton Univ., 1949-51, assistant professor of philosophy, 1951-53; Dartmouth College, 1953--, professor of mathematics, 1953-70, Albert Bradley Third Century Professor, 1969-72, president, 1970-81, professor of mathematics and computer science, 1981--. Consultant, Rand Corp., 1953-70, chairman, U.S. Commission on Mathematics Instruction, 1958-60, Hanover School Board, 1961-64, chairman, President's Commission on the Accident at Three Mile Island, 1979, chairman, Consortium on Financing Higher Education, 1979-80, trustee, Carnegie Foundation for the Advancement of Teaching, 1972-78, director, Honeywell Inc., 1978-79. Author, co-author of 15 books, co-inventor, computer language, BASIC. Eighteen honorary degrees. Jean (Alexander), Nov. 5, 1950. Jennifer, Sept. 27, 1954, Robert, Sept. 20, 1955. Jewish. Woods End Rd., Etna.

John George Kemeny

Kennett Russell Kendall Jr.

Kennett Russell Kendall Jr.

President, Kendall Insurance. Rochester, N.H., March 31, 1938, Kennett and Mary (Neal) Kendall. Phillips Exeter Academy, 1957, Dartmouth College, B.A., 1961. Kendall Insurance, Rochester, 1963--, president, 1973--. Director, Kendall Real Estate, 1965--, BankEast Corp., 1982--, WNDS-TV, 1984--, Governor's Management Review, 1981-82, Loon Mountain Recreation Corp., 1975--, Assurex International, 1980-83, president, 1982-83; trustee, Frisbie Memorial Hospital, 1975--, treasurer, 1982--; vice chairman, Business and Industry Association of N.H., 1980--, board president, Berwick Academy, 1979-81, incorporator, N.H. Charitable Fund, 1983--. Patricia (Cox), Sept. 8, 1961. Sheldon, March 9, 1966, Kennett III, May 18, 1968, Stephanie, April 28, 1971. Protestant. 3 Dartmouth Ln., Rochester.

Donald Edward Kent

Meteorologist. Boston, Mass., Sept. 29, 1917, Horace and Maizie (Wilson) Kent. North Quincy (Mass.) High School, 1935, evening division, Boston Univ., 1935-38, special weather course, MIT, 1937-38. U.S. Coast Guard, 1942-45, ensign. Weather broadcasting, WJDA Radio, Quincy, 1947-51, WBZ Radio, 1951-85, WBZ-TV, 1955-83, freelance weather reporting, Sanbornton, 1983--, rug salesman, 1936-42, operator, carpet store, 1947-60, manufacturing, marketing, weather instruments, 1962-76, alternative energy retailer, 1974-80, wholesaler, solar heating products, 1979--. Chairman, board of directors, Northeast Surf Patrol, 1960, trustee, Weymouth Savings Bank, 1980-83, official forecaster, America's Cup, 1968-80. Miriam (Hanson), Dec. 27, 1942. Douglas, June 27, 1950, David, Feb. 6, 1952, Nancy, Jan. 15, 1954, Jeffrey, July 12, 1956. Protestant. Gulf Rd., Sanbornton.

Donald Edward Kent

William Foster Kidder

William Foster Kidder

State representative. New London, N.H., Sept. 16, 1912, William M. and Edna (Foster) Kidder. Proctor Academy, Andover, 1932, Univ. of N.H., B.S., 1936. U.S. Army, 1942-45, maj. Partner, president, Kidder Garage, New London, 1937-70. President, New London Trust Co., 1958-84, chairman, 1985--, town clerk, New London, 1941-42,46-83, president, N.H. Association of Town Clerks, 1979-80, N.H. House of Rep., 1971--, director, King Ridge Ski Area, New London Trust Co., 1958--, Univ. of N.H. Alumni Board, 1978-84, trustee, Univ. System of N.H., 1984--. Harriett (Gott), April 17, 1937. William Jr., Dec. 11, 1944, David, March 5, 1948. Protestant. Barrett Rd., New London.

Jon Edward Kimbell

Theatre producer. Detroit, Mich., Jan. 30, 1943, Roy and Lydia (Redmann) Kimbell. Central High School, Phoenix, Ariz., 1960, Univ. of S. Dak., B.F.A., 1965, Sacramento State College, 1965-67, London Academy of Music and Dramatic Arts, 1967-68. Actor, director, various stage, national tours, regional and stock theatre, TV, 1968--, associate producer, WENH-TV, Durham, 1977-78, producer, Prescott Park Arts Festival, Portsmouth, 1975-82, producing director, Theatre by the Sea, Portsmouth, 1974-83, producer, North Shore Music Theatre, Beverly, Mass., 1983--. Consultant, National Endowment for the Arts, 1978-80, evaluator, N.H. Touring Program, 1980-83, executive board, League of Resident Theatres, 1979, advisory board, Playwrights Platform, Boston, 1983--, Pontine, Portsmouth, 1983--, member, Actors Equity Association, 1970--, Council of Stock Theatres, 1983--. Protestant. Rye.

Jon Edward Kimbell

Francis Walter King

Francis Walter King

Psychologist. Washington, D.C., Dec. 13, 1918, Francis and Ellen (Lockwood) King. Haverhill (Mass.) High School, 1936, Bowdoin College, B.S., 1940, Boston Univ., A.M., 1941, Harvard Univ., Ph.D., 1952. U.S. Army, 1942-45, capt. Psychologist, head of social service department, State Farm, Mass., 1941-42, instructor in social science, Boston Univ., 1946-48, Dartmouth College, associate in counseling, instructor in psychology, 1949-52, clinical psychologist, 1952-67, assistant professor of psychology, 1952-57, associate professor of psychology, 1957-60, adjunct professor of psychology, 1960-67, professor of psychiatry, 1960-84, assistant director, College Health Service, 1967-84, professor emeritus of psychiatry, 1984--, private practice, 1984--. Chairman, N.H. Board of Examiners of Psychologists, 1963-70, associate clinical staff, Mary Hitchcock Memorial Hospital, 1952-79, associate consulting staff, 1979-84; member, Advisory Commission on Health and Welfare, 1975-81, chairman, 1979-81; president, N.H. Psychological Association, 1959-60. Dorothy (Cushman), July 3, 1943 (div. Nov. 3, 1976). Marilyn, May 6, 1950, Michael, Sept. 25, 1952. Ruth (Moser), Dec. 12, 1976. 21 Low Rd., Hanover.

John William King

Chief justice, New Hampshire Supreme Court, former governor. Manchester, N.H., Oct. 8, 1916, Michael and Anna (Lydon) King. St. Joseph's High School, Manchester, 1934, Harvard Univ., A.B., 1938, Columbia Univ., M.A., 1941, Columbia Univ. Law School, LL.B., 1944. Attorney, N.Y.C., 1943-48, Manchester, 1948-69, governor, N.H., 1963-69, associate justice, N.H. Superior Court, 1969-79, associate justice, N.H. Supreme Court, 1979-81, chief justice, 1981-86. Instructor, business law, St. Anselm College, 1948-50, N.H. House of Rep., 1957-63, N.H. Ballot Law Commission, 1952-54, N.H. Constitutional Convention, 1956, chairman, N.H. Court Accreditation Committee, 1971--, editor, founder, *N.H. Bar Journal*, 1958-63, board of editors, 1963--; trustee, St. Anselm College, 1970--, chairman, Professional Conduct Committee, N.H. Supreme Court, 1985--. Seven honorary degrees. Anna (McLaughlin), Oct. 13, 1945. Catholic. Connemara Farm, Kennedy Hill Rd., Goffstown.

John William King

Thomas Joseph King

Chief of police, Manchester. Manchester, N.H., June 15, 1922, Thomas and Bridget (O'Malley) King. Manchester Central High School, 1941. U.S. Navy, 1943-46, boatswain's mate, 2nd cl. Manchester Police Department, patrolman, 1950, sergeant, 1958, lieutenant, 1964, captain, 1967, deputy chief, 1969, chief, 1975--. Executive board, N.H. Association of Chiefs of Police, member, former president, N.H. Police Association, member, International Association of Chiefs of Police, Manchester Rotary Club, American Legion, Knights of Columbus, executive board, N.E. Association of Chiefs of Police. Barbara (Lee), April 1945. Linda, 1946, Colleen, 1956, Barbara, 1958, Colin, 1960, John, 1962, Christopher, 1966. Catholic. 2101 Goffs Falls Rd., Manchester.

Alice Tirrell Knight

State representative. Manchester, N.H., July 14, 1903, Nathan and Clara (Stiles) Tirrell. Manchester High School, 1921, Univ. of N.H., B.A., 1925. Principal, Bartlett School, Goffstown, 1932-35, home lighting specialist, Public Service Co. of N.H., 1935-39, teacher, merchandising, Mount Ida Junior College, Newton Centre, Mass., 1939-45, home service director, Boyd Corp., Portland, 1945-47, district home economist, Frigidaire Sales Corp., Boston, 1948-64. N.H. House of Rep., 1967-75,76-78,80--, member, Governor's Committee on Alcoholism, 1972-74, Statewide Health Coordinating Council, 1977-78, director, Greater Manchester Visiting Nurse Association, 1983--, Greater Manchester Community Concerts, 1981--, president, 1985; Goffstown Budget Committee, 1965-71, president, Greater Manchester Business and Professional Women, 1972-74, member, National Order of Women Legislators, 1967--, treasurer, 1968-71. Norman Knight, Nov. 15, 1952 (dec. Jan. 1974). Protestant. 4 West Union St., Goffstown.

Alice Tirrell Knight

Vasilike Kounas

Vasilike Kounas

Executive director, New Hampshire Industrial Development Authority. Manchester, N.H., June 18, 1926, Nicholas and Fannie (Boukas) Kounas. Manchester Central High School, 1943, Boston Univ., A.A., 1954, B.S., 1956, Radcliffe College, 1956-57. Report writer, Dun and Bradstreet, clerk, U.S. government, secretary, loan interviewer, Amoskeag Savings Bank, 1943-53, industrial assistant, industrial agent, research and promotion, assistant to the director, N.H. Office of Industrial Development, 1957-68, executive secretary, N.H. Industrial Development Authority, 1968-84, executive director, 1984--. Charter member, Northeastern Industrial Developers Association, president, 1982; director, Merchants National Bank, 1975--, Federated Arts of Manchester, 1981--, Manchester Institute of Arts and Sciences, 1969-72, corporator, Merchants Savings Bank, 1973-75, director, treasurer, N.H. Business Development Corp., 1976-81, member, N.H. Small Business Administration Advisory Council, 1975--, trustee, Notre Dame College, 1982--, N.E. College, 1975-78, co-founder, charter member, N.H. Industrial Agents Association, 1976--, secretary, 1984--. Greek Orthodox. 117 Oak St., Manchester.

Elaine Shirley Krasker

State representative. Portsmouth, N.H., April 18, 1927, Albert and Sophie (Shapiro) Sados. Portsmouth High School, 1945, Univ. of N.H., B.A., 1949. Instructor, Univ. of N.H., 1964, N.H. House of Rep., 1975--, incorporator, N.H. Charitable Fund, 1978--, director, Retired Senior Volunteer Program, 1975-78, Portsmouth Community Health Services, 1975-77, trustee, Strawbery Banke, 1958-60,85--, Portsmouth Board of Education, 1969-73, N.H. Constitutional Convention, 1974, executive committee, Greater Portsmouth Community Foundation, 1984, member, chairman, Wentworth-Coolidge Commission, 1979--, National Task Force on the Arts, 1979-81, trustee, Portsmouth Public Library, 1969-73, Portsmouth Zoning Board, 1964-67, director, Rockingham County Day Care Consortium, 1981-83, Seacoast Task Force on Elderly Abuse, 1980--. Sheldon Krasker, Oct. 31, 1948. Kathy, Nov. 12, 1949, William, July 15, 1952, Thomas, April 5, 1959. Jewish. Little Harbor Rd., Portsmouth.

Elaine Shirley Krasker

Maxine Winokur Kumin

Maxine Winokur Kumin

Poet and author. Philadelphia, Pa., June 6, 1925, Peter and Doll (Simon) Winokur. Cheltenham High School, Elkins Park, Pa., 1942, Radcliffe College, A.B., 1946, A.M., 1948. Freelance writer, 1953--. Staff member, Bread Loaf Writers Conference, 1969,70,71,73,75,77, adjunct professor of writing, Columbia Univ., 1975, Hurst professor of literature, Brandeis Univ., 1975, visiting senior fellow and lecturer, Princeton Univ., 1977, Hurst professor of literature, Washington Univ., St. Louis, 1977, Bell visiting scholar, Randolph-Macon Woman's College, 1978, visiting lecturer, Princeton Univ., spring 1979, fall 1981, spring 1982; Woodrow Wilson visiting fellow, 1979-82, consultant in poetry, Library of Congress, 1981-82, visiting professor, MIT, spring 1984, Pulitizer Prize for poetry, 1973. Author of eight books of poetry, four novels, one collection of short stories, one collection of essays, 20 children's books. Six honorary degrees. Victor Kumin, June 29, 1946. Jane, Oct. 20, 1948, Judith, May 5, 1950, Daniel, June 13, 1953. Warner.

Stephen Guild Kurtz

Principal, Phillips Exeter Academy. Buffalo, N.Y., Sept. 9, 1926, George and Nellie (Crowther) Kurtz. Stony Brook School, Long Island, 1944, Princeton Univ., A.B., 1947, Univ. of Pa., M.A., 1948, Ph.D., 1952. U.S. Naval Reserve, 1944-45, midshipman. History teacher, Kent (Conn.) School, 1951-55, dean of students, assistant to the president, dean of faculty, Wabash College, 1956-66, editor of the papers of John Marshall, director of the Institute of Early American History, Williamsburg, Va., 1966-72, professor of history, dean of the college, Hamilton College, 1972-74, principal, Phillips Exeter Academy, 1974--. Trustee, Athens College, Greece, 1979--, Phillips Exeter Academy, 1974--, director, Exeter Banking Co., 1974--, National Association of Independent Schools, 1977-82, Exeter Historic District Commission, 1976-79. Author, *The Presidency of John Adams*, 1957. Jeanne (Godolphin), Sept. 7, 1947. Sharon, Aug. 6, 1949, Thomas, Feb. 16, 1951, Stephen Jr., April 10, 1959. Protestant. 31 Elliot St., Exeter.

Philip deGaspe Labombarde

Philip deGaspe Labombarde

Manufacturing company executive, retired, state representative. Boston, Mass., Jan. 29, 1921, Harold and Beatrice (Legendre) Labombarde. Nashua High School, 1939, Univ. of Okla., 1943-44, MIT, B.S., 1947. U.S. Army, 1942-45, pfc. International Paper Box Machine Co., Nashua, draftsman, engineer, chief engineer, 1947-56, president, 1956-74, senior vice president, 1974-84. Director, Bank of N.H., 1964--, former director, So. N.H. Association of Commerce and Industry, president, 1978-79; Nashua Airport Authority, 1961-86, chairman, 1963-86; director, St. Joseph Hospital, 1974--, president, 1980-83; trustee, Rivier College, 1969-81, chairman, 1980-81; member, N.H. Advisory Committee to the U.S. Civil Rights Commission, 1956-60, N.H. House of Rep., 1978--, N.H. Constitutional Convention, 1974,84. Frances (Merritt), Jan. 15, 1946. Peter, Aug. 25, 1954, Ann, Nov. 23, 1956, Joan, Sept. 24, 1959. Catholic. 60 Indian Rock Rd., Nashua.

Paul Irving LaMott
State representative. Orford, N.H., June 30, 1917, Elwyn and Lela (Willis) LaMott. Woodsville Union High School, 1934. U.S. Army, 1941-45, sgt. Service manager, T. Borden Walker Enterprises, Woodsville, 1946-58, mechanical contractor, 1958-80. Director, N.H. Plumbing and Heating Contractors, 1963-69, president, 1967-69; president, N.E. Plumbing and Heating Contractors, 1969-72, National Association of Plumbing and Heating Contractors, 1970-72, former president, N.H. Council for Better Schools, N.H. House of Rep., 1961-63, 71--, supervisor of the checklist, Haverhill, 1952--, department commander, Veterans of Foreign Wars, 1960-61. Muriel (Spooner), Nov. 23, 1938. Marcia, Oct. 9, 1946. Court St. Ext., Box 56, Haverhill.

Stewart Lamprey

Stewart Lamprey
Realtor, former legislative leader. Dorchester, Mass., April 8, 1921, Robert and Mary (Campbell) Lamprey. Meredith High School, 1939, Concord Business College, 1940. U.S. Army, 1942-45, tech. 5th cl. Partner, Lamprey and Lamprey Realtors, 1945-79, president, Lamprey Insurance, 1952-82, treasurer, Lamprey Enterprises, 1957-83, partner, Direct Mail Services, 1975-82, owner, N.H. Business Sales, 1979--. N.H. House of Rep., 1951-53,55-65, speaker, 1959-65; N.H. Senate, 1965-69, president, 1965-69; federal co-chairman, N.E. Regional Commission, 1969-71, senior executive officer, Gov. Walter Peterson, 1971-73, president, National Association of National Legislative Leaders, 1969-71, vice chairman, Belknap College, 1975-78, trustee, Mary Hitchcock Hospital, 1972-79, chairman, Centralized Data Processing Commission, 1967-72,81-84, trustee, City Savings Bank, Laconia, 1966-69. Two honorary degrees. Margaret (Watson), July 10, 1941. Diane, July 19, 1947, George, June 25, 1951. Methodist. Fox Hollow Rd., Moultonborough.

Roy Younker Lang

Director, Personnel Commission, retired. Concord, N.H., June 10, 1920, Fred and Viney (Younker) Lang. Concord High School, 1937, Vermont Academy, Saxtons River, 1938, Springfield College, B.S., 1942. U.S. Army, 1942-46, 1st lt. Teacher, track coach, Gorham, 1946-47, assistant personnel manager, Tileston and Hollingsworth Paper Co., Hyde Park, Mass., 1947-48, personnel director, Office of the Comptroller, N.H., 1948-50, director, Personnel Commission, N.H., 1950-83. Executive director, N.H. Reclassification Study Commission, 1948-50, member, N.H. Social Security Study Commission, 1951-52, Concord Zoning Board, 1955-65, N.H. Technical Institute Advisory Committee, 1975-78, N.H. Horse and Trail Association, 1962--, N.H. Farm Bureau, 1973--, Hopkinton Planning Board, 1985--, chairman, Hopkinton Capital Budget Committee, 1985--. Elizabeth (Corser), Sept. 13, 1943. Karen, Nov. 27, 1949, Marcia, June 2, 1953. Methodist. Crowell Rd., Hopkinton.

Roy Younker Lang

Albert Dennis Leahy Jr.

Albert Dennis Leahy Jr.

Attorney, judge. Claremont, N.H., June 22, 1933. Albert and Helen (Farrington) Leahy. Stevens High School, Claremont, 1951, Yale Univ., B.A., 1955, Harvard Law School, J.D., 1961. U.S. Marine Corps, 1955-58, 1st lt. Attorney, Claremont, 1961--. Justice, Claremont District Court, 1972--, director, Claremont National Bank, 1967-81, trustee, Claremont Savings Bank, 1981--, board of governors, N.H. Judges Association, 1980-85, president, 1983-84; board of governors, N.H. Bar Association, 1969-72, member, N.H. Board of Bar Examiners, 1971-75, president, Stevens High School Alumni Association, member, Claremont Industrial Development Authority, 1978--, incorporator, Valley Regional Hospital, 1975-85. Patricia (Henry), Sept. 10, 1960. Alison, July 12, 1962, William, May 1, 1967. Episcopal. Highland Ave. Ext., Claremont.

Charles Farrington Leahy

Attorney. Claremont, N.H., Feb. 27, 1935, Albert and Helen (Farrington) Leahy. Stevens High School, Claremont, 1953, Yale Univ., B.A., 1957, Harvard Univ., J.D., 1963. U.S. Army, 1957-60, cpl. Attorney, Concord, 1963--. Director, executive committee, Bank of N.H., N.A., 1971-81, director, United Life and Accident Insurance Co., 1978-81, Chubb Securities Corp., 1981--, Fidelity Bank and Trust Co., 1983--, Blue Cross and Blue Shield, 1984--, legislative counsel, Gov. Walter Peterson, 1971-72, Citizens Task Force, 1969-70, trustee, White Mountain School, 1966-71, chairman, 1968-71; Concord Board of Education, 1977-82, board of visitors, Antioch/N.E. Graduate Center, 1981--, board of governors, N.H. Public Television, 1986--. Siobhan, Aug. 13, 1961, Charles Jr., Dec. 1, 1963, Matthew, Aug. 14, 1965, Susan, March 10, 1967, Jonathan, Dec. 19, 1969. Mary Susan (Stein), Oct. 22, 1977. Episcopal. 10 Bishopsgate, Concord.

Mary Susan Leahy

Attorney. New River, N.C., March 27, 1944, Edwin and Catherine (Wagner) Stein. Needham (Mass.) High School, 1962, Mount Holyoke College, A.B., 1966, Boston Univ. School of Law, J.D., 1970. Economist, U.S. Bureau of Labor Statistics, 1966-67, law clerk, N.H. Supreme Court, 1970-71, attorney, Concord, 1971--. Trustee, Downtown Concord Revitalization Corp., 1984-85, chair, Merrimack County Task Force Against Domestic Violence, 1984--, trustee, Capital Region Health Care Corp., 1985--, Concord Hospital, 1984-85, N.H. Savings Bank, 1980-83, director, 1983--; director, Greater Concord Chamber of Commerce, 1975-80, president, 1978-79; Concord Regional Development Corp., 1976-81, chair, N.H. Guardian Advisory Council, 1979-81, director, N.H. Feminist Health Center, 1976-77, incorporator, N.H. Charitable Fund, 1982--, director, Central N.H. Community Mental Health Center, 1986--. Charles Leahy, Oct. 22, 1977. Catholic. 10 Bishopsgate, Concord.

Emile Joseph Legere

President, owner, Emile J. Legere Management Co. Troy, N.H., Feb. 24, 1934, Emile and Cecile (Fortier) Legere. Keene High School, 1953. U.S. Army, 1954-55, sgt. President, owner, Emile J. Legere Management Co., Keene, 1962--, developer, owner, Colony Mill Marketplace, Keene, 1981--. Papal volunteer, housing program, Chile, 1964-66, member, Home Builders Association of Southwestern N.H., 1970--, president, 1971; National Association of Home Builders, 1970--, Multi-Family Council, 1970--, International Council of Shopping Centers, 1983--, N.H. Association of Industrial Agents, 1985--, Greater Keene Chamber of Commerce, 1983--, Keene Downtown Renovation Committee, 1985--, director, First Northern Bank (formerly Keene Co-op), 1971-82. One honorary degree. Nancy Ann (Roberts), July 7, 1956. Lisa, July 29, 1961, Stephen, Oct. 31, 1965. Catholic. Spofford Lake, Spofford.

Richard Wilson Leonard

Attorney. Nashua, N.H., Aug. 6, 1919, Thomas and Cecelia (Cone) Leonard. Nashua High School, 1937, Univ. of Va., B.A., 1941, LL.B., 1947. U.S. Air Force, 1941-45, capt., 1950-53, maj., 1961-62, lt. col. Attorney, Nashua, 1948--. N.H. House of Rep., 1965-67, N.H. Senate, 1967-73, State Aeronautics Commission, 1953-58, Nashua Planning Board, 1954-58, Nashua Airport Authority, 1959-63, Nashua School Board, 1964-70, chairman, N.H. Parole Board, 1978-84, president, Nashua Bar Association, 1972-73, director, president, Colonial Bank/BankEast, 1969-79, member, N.H. Air National Guard, 1947-58, Mass. Air National Guard, 1958-65. Janet, Nov. 22, 1945. Andrea (Desmond), 1950 (dec. Feb. 22, 1984). Catholic. 7 Farmington Rd., Nashua.

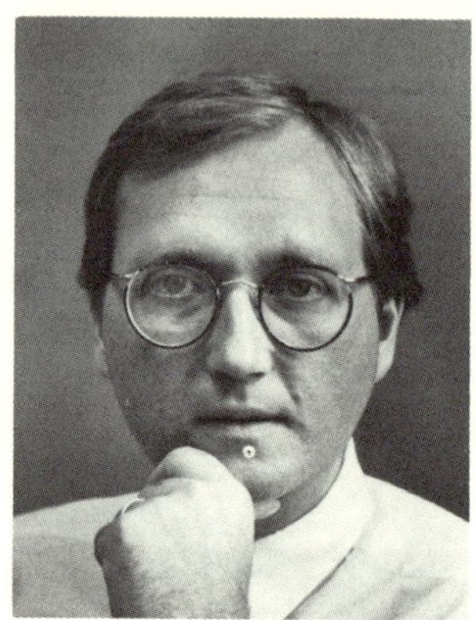

Leo Everett Lessard

Leo Everett Lessard

State senator. Rochester, N.H., May 1, 1950. Norman and Beatrice (Wyman) Lessard. Nute High School, Milton, 1969, Univ. of N.H., A.A., 1976, School for Lifelong Learning, B.G.S., 1983. Employee, Univ. of N.H., 1970-77, real estate investor, 1976--, owner, Lessard Properties, Dover, 1976--. N.H. House of Rep., 1974-80, N.H. Senate, 1980--, director, Univ. of N.H. Alumni Association, 1983--, Southeastern N.H. Alcohol and Drug Abuse Service, 1982--, American Cancer Society, Strafford County unit, 1984--. Pamela (Frazer), Oct. 11, 1975. Michael, Oct. 9, 1979, Jonathan, Nov. 27, 1982. Catholic. 7 West Concord St., Dover.

Calvin Jacob Libby

Artist. Barton, Vt., June 22, 1931, Calvin and Evelyn (Gay) Libby. Stowe (Vt.) High School, 1949, Univ. of Vt., 1949-51, N.E. School of Art, 1956-59. U.S. Air Force, 1952-56, staff sgt. Freelance painter, 1956--, silkscreening, 1971--, art director, Young Rubicam, N.Y.C., 1959-64, Harold Cabot Advertising, Boston, 1965-75. Former instructor, League of N.H. Craftsmen, instructor, advertising design, silkscreen printing, Rivier College, 1976--, instructor, design, Manchester Institute of Arts and Sciences, 1980--, president, N.H. Art Association, 1969-71,81-83, council member, League of N.H. Craftsmen, 1975-76, N.H. Commission on the Arts, 1979--, former board member, Nashua Arts and Science Center. Ann Carol (Espejo), Sept. 1, 1956. Dorcas, July 25, 1961, Melissa, May 7, 1963. Unitarian-Universalist. 346 Broad St., Nashua.

Calvin Jacob Libby

Elizabeth Kitchel Lincoln

Elizabeth Kitchel Lincoln

Lecturer, Plymouth State College. Englewood, N.J., Jan. 3, 1912, Cornelius and Edith (Ray) Kitchel. Masters School, Dobbs Ferry, N.Y., 1929, Vassar College, B.A., 1933, Radcliffe College, M.A., 1938, Univ. of Pittsburgh, M.S.W., 1964, Univ. of No. Colo., Ed.D., 1979. Community field consultant, Department of Mental Health, Montpelier, Vt., 1965-68, research associate, Univ. of Vt. Medical School, 1967-70, director, N.H. State Council on Aging, 1968-73, adjunct faculty, White Pines College, Chester, 1973-83, chairman, department of social work, White Pines College, 1980-83, lecturer, Plymouth State College, 1983--, lecturer, N.H. School for Lifelong Learning, 1986--. Trustee, Meredith Public Library, 1946-62, incorporator, Laconia Hospital, 1950--, N.H. Charitable Fund, 1971-81, N.H. Commission on the Status of Women, 1971-74, trustee, Spaulding Youth Center, 1975-82, director, Lakes Region Mental Health Center, 1977--, N.H. Social Welfare Council, 1967-77, president, 1977-79; trustee, White Pines College, 1985--, incorporator, Shriver Center for Mental Retardation, 1986--. Alexander Lincoln Jr., May 25, 1937. Eleanor, April 2, 1941, Alexander III, Dec. 1, 1943, Robert, Feb. 27, 1946, Margaret, July 19, 1949. Protestant. P.O. Box 979, Meredith.

Nackey Scripps Loeb

President, publisher, Union Leader Corp. Los Angeles, Calif., Feb. 24, 1924, Robert and Margaret (Culbertson) Scripps. Bishop's School, La Jolla, Calif., 1942, Scripps College, 1942-44. Vice president, treasurer, Union Leader Corp., Manchester, 1957-81, president, publisher, 1981--. George Gallowhur, 1944 (div). Nackey, Oct. 13, 1945. William Loeb, July 15, 1952 (dec. Sept. 3, 1981). Edith, Nov. 7, 1956. Baptist. P.O. Box 366, Goffstown.

Nackey Scripps Loeb

Harlan deBaun Logan

Harlan deBaun Logan

Publisher, corporate executive, retired. Starkville, Miss., April 30, 1904, William and Janette (deBaun) Logan. Bloomington (Ind.) High School, 1921, Ind. Univ., A.B., 1925, A.M., 1926, Columbia Univ., 1926-27, Rhodes scholar, Oxford Univ., 1928-30. Associate professor, English, N.Y.U., 1927-35, editor in chief, *Scribners Magazine*, 1936-39, *Look Magazine*, 1939-40, vice president, Cowles Magazines, 1940-46, president, Visual Enterprises, 1947-51, chief of press services, U.S. Information Agency, 1951-52, director, public relations, Steuben and Corning Glass, 1952-55, vice president, General Foods, 1956-61. Trustee, Mary Hitchcock Memorial Hospital, 1969-74, Society for the Protection of N.H. Forests, 1969-75, chairman, 1973-75, emeritus, 1975--; chairman, State Advisory Committee on Aging, 1971-72, trustee, White Mountain School, 1973-76, emeritus, 1976--; N.H. House of Rep., 1967-71. One honorary degree. Barbara (Rollins), June 14, 1929 (dec. 1956). Deborah, June 30, 1930, Lois, Dec. 1, 1934, Penelope, Sept. 30, 1937 (dec. Feb. 1983), Haven, Feb. 24, 1944. Audrey (Olena), July 11, 1958. Methodist. P.O. Box 128, Meriden.

Martin Francis Loughlin

United States District Court judge. Manchester, N.H., March 11, 1923, Martin and Mary (Kendrigan) Loughlin. St. Joseph's High School, Manchester, 1940, St. Anselm College, B.A., 1947, Suffolk Univ. Law School, LL.B., 1951. U.S. Army, 1943-46, cpl., 1951-52, 1st lt. Attorney, Manchester, 1953-63, associate justice, N.H. Superior Court, 1963-78, chief justice, 1978-79; judge, U.S. District Court, 1979--. Former instructor, criminal justice, St. Anselm College, Franklin Pierce Law Center, cemetery trustee, Manchester, 1958-60, water commissioner, Manchester, 1960-64. One honorary degree. Margaret (Gallagher), Sept. 9, 1950. Helen, July 18, 1951, Margaret, Feb. 7, 1953, Shane, Dec. 11, 1956, Mary, March 18, 1959, Sheila, Oct. 1, 1961, Martina, April 22, 1965, Caitlin, April 9, 1971. Catholic. 135 Pepperidge Dr., Manchester.

Cabot Lyford

Sculptor, art instructor. Sayre, Pa., May 22, 1925, Frederic Jr. and Eleanor (Cabot) Lyford. Scarsdale (N.Y.) High School, 1942, Skowhegan School, 1947, Cornell Univ., B.F.A., 1950, Sculpture Center, New York City, 1951-52. U.S. Army, 1943-46, tech. 5th cl. Producer, director, motion pictures and television, New York and Boston, 1950-59, program manager, WENH-TV, Durham, 1959-63, art instructor, Phillips Exeter Academy, 1963-86, chairman, art department, 1964-74, director, Lamont Gallery, 1964-74. Joan (Richmond), June 22, 1953. Matthew, Dec. 10, 1955, Julia, Oct. 19, 1957, Thaddeus, Nov. 9, 1967. 9 Centre St., Exeter.

Kasper Carroll Marking

Vice president, Daniel Webster College. Edgemont, S. Dak., May 21, 1924, William and Theresa (Carroll) Marking. Brigham Young Univ. High School, Provo, Utah, 1942, Univ. of Portland, B.A., 1952, St. Bonaventure Univ., M.A., 1954, Wash. State Univ., Ed.D., 1967. U.S. Army, 1943-46, sgt. Teacher, junior, senior high school, Idaho, 1954-57, instructor, Skagit Valley College, 1957-61, academic dean, 1961-65; assistant professor, Northern Mich. Univ., 1965-67, academic dean, Columbia Basin College, 1967-69, academic vice president, dean of faculty, Minot State College, 1969-72, president, Briar Cliff College, 1972-77, president, Plymouth State College, 1977-83, chancellor, Univ. System of N.H., 1983-86, vice president for academic affairs, dean of faculty, Daniel Webster College, 1986--. Member, Postsecondary Education Commission, 1978-86, chairman, 1978-80,83-84; trustee, Univ. System of N.H., 1977-86. Jamie (Divan), Jan. 22, 1952. Christopher, Oct. 21, 1952, Nicholas, March 15, 1954, Gregory, May 24, 1955, Timothy, March 6, 1958, Randall, Jan. 14, 1960, Raissa, Jan. 13, 1964. Catholic. 47 Bow St., Portsmouth.

Kasper Carroll Marking

James Alfred Masiello

James Alfred Masiello

President, chief operating officer, Masiello Agency. Keene, N.H., June 5, 1940, Alfred and Bertha (Payne) Masiello. Keene High School, 1958, Burdett College, 1958-61. Life insurance agent, Keene, 1961--, Masiello Agency, insurance, real estate, 1965--, president, chief operating officer. President, Monadnock Regional Life Underwriters Association, 1966, president, N.H. Life Underwriters Association, 1969-70, Keene Planning Board, 1969-75, Keene City Council, 1967-71, mayor, Keene, 1972-76, executive committee, N.H. Municipal Association, 1973-75, Governor's Emergency Energy Committee, 1973, Keene Industrial Development and Park Authority, 1976-80, chairman, 1979-80; chairman, State Board of Education, 1983-85, corporator, Keene Savings Bank, 1976--, incorporator, Cheshire County Savings Bank, 1979--, president, Greater Keene Chamber of Commerce, 1975-76. Wendy (Campbell), Oct. 7, 1961. Christopher, Aug. 3, 1962, Lisa, Nov. 24, 1964, Matthew, July 25, 1971. Catholic. 111 Jordan Rd., Keene.

George Thomas Matarazzo

Chairman, Matarazzo Design Inc. North Caldwell, N.J., June 9, 1941, Carmine and Antoinette (Polvarsic) Matarazzo. Grover Cleveland High School, Caldwell, N.J., 1958, State Univ. of N.Y., A.A.S., 1960, Univ. of Ga., B.L.A., 1963, Harvard Univ., M.L.A., 1965. President, Manchester office, Hanslin Planning Association, New London, 1968-76, president, Garden One Inc., Concord, 1974-78, chairman, Matarazzo Design Inc., Concord, 1976--. President, Land Use Group Inc., 1983--, vice president, Brownfields Partnership, 1984--, director, BankEast, 1984--, member, design review committee, Concord Planning Board, 1980--, design critic, Harvard Graduate School of Design, 1970--, member, American Society of Landscape Architects, Home Builders of N.H., N.H. Landscape Association, Urban Land Institute, associate member, National Association of Home Builders, professional affiliate, American Institute of Architects. Patricia (Johnson), Nov. 24, 1967. Macy, Nov. 30, 1968, Tina, April 20, 1970. Catholic. 5 Hillside Rd., Concord.

George Thomas Matarazzo

Sharon Christa McAuliffe

High school teacher. Boston, Mass., Sept., 2, 1948, Edward and Grace (George) Corrigan. Marian High School, Framingham, Mass., 1966, Framingham State College, B.A., 1970, Bowie State College, M.Ed., 1978. Teacher, Benjamin Foulois Junior High School, Morningside, Md., 1970-71, Thomas Johnson Junior High School, Lanham, Md., 1971-78, Rundlett Junior High School, Concord, 1980-81, Bow Memorial School, 1981-82, Concord High School, 1982--. Member, N.H. Council of Social Studies, Concord Teachers Association, N.H. Education Association, National Education Association. Selected, primary candidate, NASA Teacher in Space Project, July 19, 1985. Steven McAuliffe, Aug. 23, 1970. Scott, Sept. 11, 1976, Caroline, Aug. 24, 1979. Catholic. 8 Park Ridge, Concord. Sharon Christa McAuliffe died on Jan. 28, 1986. Biography has not been verified by the biographee.

Rita Cloutier McAvoy

State representative. Lewiston, Maine, June 9, 1917, Gideon and Eva (Lambert) Cloutier. Lewiston High School, 1934. Hotel operations, Lewiston, 1936-48, owner, operator, Thayers Hotel, Littleton, 1946-69, Crawford House Resort, Crawford Notch, 1967-73. N.H. House of Rep., 1976--, executive director, N.H. Commission on the Status of Women, 1976-77, member, Republican State Committee, 1950--, trustee, Littleton Hospital, 1973--, N.H. Board of Probation, 1974-79, director, North Country United Way, 1982--, president, 1984-85; director, legislative consultant, N.H. Association of Hospital Auxiliaries, 1974-79, director, Peoples National Bank, 1978--, United Health Systems Agency, 1979-83, White Mountain Seniors Association, 1982--, president, 1983-85; member, State Health Coordinating Council, 1976-80. George McAvoy, 1948. Richard, Suzanne. Episcopal. Bethlehem Rd., Littleton.

Hannah Mary McCarthy

Hannah Mary McCarthy

President, Daniel Webster College. Boston, Mass., July 17, 1946, Leo and Kay (Pucci) McLaughlin. Villa Augustina Academy, Goffstown, 1964, Simmons College, B.S., 1968, Rivier College, 1973-75. Director of admissions, Rivier College, 1972-76, dean of admissions, Daniel Webster College, 1976-80, acting president, 1980, president, 1980--. Chair, Continuing Education Network of the N.H. College and Univ. Council, 1981-85, trustee, Chamberlayne Junior College, 1981-85, president, chairman of the board, Airport Properties, 1980-84, director, N.E. Association of College Admissions Counselors, 1980-81, executive board, N.E. Association of Collegiate Registrars and Admissions Officers, 1974-77, director, So. N.H. Association of Commerce and Industry, 1984--, Boys Club of Nashua, 1982--, N.H. Higher Education Assistance Foundation, 1980--, incorporator, N.H. Charitable Fund, 1982--. Phillip Rutledge, May 19, 1979. Catholic. 54 Old Manchester Rd., Amherst.

Paul Michael McEachern

Attorney. Portsmouth, N.H., Dec. 30, 1937, Archibald and Ann (Regan) McEachern. Portsmouth High School, 1955, Univ. of N.H., B.A., 1963, Boston Univ. School of Law, LL.B., 1966. U.S. Navy, 1956-60, guided missileman, 2nd cl. Attorney, Portsmouth, 1966--. N.H. House of Rep., 1963-65,73-75, Portsmouth City Council, 1968-72, assistant mayor, 1968-70; counsel, Gov. Hugh Gallen, 1979-80, N.H. Bar Association, board of governors, 1978-79, vice president, 1979-80, president-elect, 1980-81, president, 1981-82; director, Theatre by the Sea, 1972-81, trustee of trust funds, Portsmouth (Prescott Park), 1972-78, executive committee, Greater Portsmouth Community Foundation, 1984--. Claire, June 26, 1963, Alec, Sept. 10, 1964, Duncan, Sept. 7, 1967. Shaun (Kelley), Oct. 3, 1980. Deaglan, Aug. 5, 1983. Catholic. 70 Dennett St., Portsmouth.

Paul Michael McEachern

Duncan Scott McGowan

Duncan Scott McGowan

Architect, planner, developer. Trenton, N.J., Dec. 6, 1941, Donald and Helen (Schoeffel) McGowan. Lawrenceville (N.J.) School, 1960, Yale Univ., B.A., 1964, M.Arch., 1968. Planner, designer, Carter and Woodruff, Architects, Nashua, 1971-72, community planner, Nashua Regional Planning Commission, 1972-78, designer, co-developer, Bicentennial Square, Concord, 1975-78, originator, designer, co-developer, Eagle Square, Concord, 1978-83, president, Eagle Square Associates, 1979--, president, McGowan & Brook Architects Inc., 1986--. Trustee, Society for the Protection of N.H. Forests, 1982--, county vice president, 1978-82; president, N.H. Planners Association, 1976-78, director, Frontiers of Knowledge, 1982-84, Inherit N.H., 1984--, First Night N.H., 1986--, BankEast Regional Advisory Board, 1984--. Mary (Strayer), July 1, 1967. Molly, April 8, 1970, Abigail, Sept. 18, 1971. 11 Tahanto St., Concord.

Elizabeth Yates McGreal

Author. Buffalo, N.Y., Dec. 6, 1905, Harry and Mary (Duffy) Yates. Franklin School, Buffalo, 1924. Author, *High Holiday*, 1938, and 46 books since. Former staff member, writers conferences, Univ. of Conn., Ind., Colo., N.H., staff member, Christian Writers and Editors Conference, Green Lake, Wis., 1957-69, member, State Library commission, 1965-77, director, N.H. Association for the Blind, 1964--, president, 1976-84; trustee, Peterborough Town Library, 1959--, White Pines College, 1975-80, honorary, 1980--; Newbery Medal for distinguished biography, 1951, for the book *Amos Fortune, Free Man*, published in 1950. Seven honorary degrees. William McGreal, Nov. 6, 1929 (dec. Dec. 16, 1963). 381 Old Street Rd., Peterborough.

Elizabeth Yates McGreal

Ralph Aubrey McIninch

Ralph Aubrey McIninch

Banker, retired. Manchester, N.H., June 15, 1912, John and Gula (Ruiter) McIninch. Central High School, 1930, Harvard Univ., B.S., 1934, Rutgers Univ. Graduate School of Banking, 1938. Assistant trust officer, Merchants National Bank, Manchester, 1936-42, examiner, Federal Reserve Bank, Philadelphia, 1942-45, vice president, trust officer, Union Trust Co., Providence, 1945-48, president, Merchants National Bank, 1948-78, chairman, 1978-83; vice president, treasurer, Merchants Savings Bank, 1948-73. Director, treasurer, First Bancorp, 1977-84, honorary director, 1984--; president, N.H. Bankers Association, 1957-58, director, N.E. Council, 1954-61, trustee, Colby-Sawyer College, 1957-79, chairman, 1974-75, trustee emeritus, 1979--; member, *Union Leader* Advisory Board, 1961-83, trustee, New Hampton School, 1963-72, director, Federal Reserve Bank of Boston, 1971-73, president, director, Exeter Banking Co., 1969-73, chairman, Londonderry Bank and Trust Co., 1979-82, Professional Conduct Committee, N.H. Supreme Court, 1979-82. Two honorary degrees. Elizabeth (Farmer), Sept. 16, 1938. Richard, June 9, 1940, Douglas, July 8, 1944. Congregational. 847 Maple St., Manchester.

Thomas James McIntyre

Former United States senator. Laconia, N.H., Feb. 20, 1915, Thomas and Helen (Trask) McIntyre. Manlius (N.Y.) Military School, 1933, Dartmouth College, B.A., 1937, Boston Univ. School of Law, LL.B., 1940. U.S. Army, 1942-46, maj. Attorney, Laconia, 1946-62, mayor, Laconia, 1949-51, U.S. Senate, 1962-79, of counsel, Sullivan and Worcester, Boston and Washington D.C., 1979-81. City solicitor, Laconia, 1953, trustee, Taylor Home for the Aged, 1954-62, director, Laconia Industrial Development Corp., 1962, Community TV Corp., Laconia, 1952-53, president, Belknap County Bar Association, 1961-63, national board, Common Cause, 1980-81, consultant, Raytheon Corp., 1980-81, Tyco Laboratories, 1980-82. Author, *The Fear Brokers*, 1979. Six honorary degrees. Myrtle (Clement), May 3, 1941. Martha, June 15, 1947. Catholic. 250 South Rd., Rye.

John Roy McLane Jr.

John Roy McLane Jr.

Attorney. Manchester, N.H., Feb. 19, 1916, John and Elisabeth (Bancroft) McLane. St. Paul's School, 1934, Dartmouth College, A.B., 1938, Harvard Law School, LL.B., 1941. U.S. Naval Reserve, 1941-45, lieut. Attorney, Manchester, 1941--. Director, Manchester Savings Bank, 1962-80, Manchester Gas Co., 1970-83, N.H. Ball Bearings, 1970-77, N.H. Charitable Fund, 1962-70, Spaulding-Potter Charitable Fund, 1955-72, Norwin and Elizabeth Bean Foundation, 1967--, Palace Theatre Trust, 1974--, Council on Foundations, 1968-74, chairman, 1970-72; trustee, St. Paul's School, 1952-83, director, Child and Family Services, 1946-74, president, 1963-71; alderman, Manchester, 1952-53, trustee, N.H. Hospital, 1949-62, chairman, 1953-62; trustee, chairman, Advisory Commission on Health and Welfare, 1965-68. Blanche (Marshall), Feb. 15, 1935. John III, Sept. 20, 1935, Andrew, Nov. 2, 1936 (dec. Dec. 3, 1984), Lyn, Feb. 10, 1939, Blanche, Dec. 11, 1943, Angus, Dec. 1, 1947. Elisabeth (Deane), Dec. 30, 1960. Towner, Jan. 5, 1962, Virginia, Jan. 5, 1962, Kathryn, Aug. 2, 1964, Duncan, Nov. 10, 1965. Episcopal. 1595 North River Rd., Manchester.

Malcolm McLane

Attorney. Manchester, N.H., Oct. 3, 1924, John and Elisabeth (Bancroft) McLane. St. Paul's School, 1942, Dartmouth College, A.B., 1946, Rhodes scholar, Oxford Univ., 1948-50, Harvard Law School, J.D., 1952. U.S. Army Air Corps, 1942-45, 1st lt. Attorney, Concord, 1952--. Concord City Council, 1956-76, mayor, Concord, 1970-76, Concord Planning Board, 1976-80, N.H. Executive Council, 1977-83, former president, United Way of Greater Concord, director, U.S. Olympic Committee, 1957-72, U.S. Ski Association, 1957-68, N.E. Electric System, 1978--, trustee, Society for the Protection of N.H. Forests, 1984--, St. Paul's School, 1983--, director, founder, general counsel, Wildcat Mountain Corp., Pinkham Notch, 1955--, president, 1969-81, chairman, 1981--. Susan (Neidlinger), April 30, 1948. Susan, Dec. 17, 1948, Donald, Nov. 22, 1950, Deborah, Jan. 11, 1952, Alan, July 2, 1954, Ann, Sept. 5, 1956. Protestant. 205 Mountain Rd., Concord.

Malcolm McLane

Susan Neidlinger McLane

Susan Neidlinger McLane

State senator. Boston, Mass., Sept. 28, 1929, Lloyd and Marion (Walker) Neidlinger. Hanover High School, 1947, Mount Holyoke College, 1947-48. N.H. House of Rep., 1969-80, N.H. Senate, 1980,82--, trustee, Concord Hospital, 1979-84, director, N.H. Association for Mental Health, 1975-82, N.H. Audubon Society, 1981--, Kennedy fellow, Harvard Institute of Politics, 1979, Center for N.H.'s Future, 1981-83, N.E. Ski Museum, 1980--, Women's Campaign Fund, 1981--, co-chair, 1984--; Living Will Society, 1983--, board of visitors, Rockefeller Center, Dartmouth College, 1984--. One honorary degree. Malcolm McLane, April 30, 1948. (Ch. see Malcom McLane.) Protestant. 205 Mountain Rd., Concord.

Elisabeth McLane-Bradley

Former trustee, University System of New Hampshire. Manchester, N.H., July 2, 1921, John and Elisabeth (Bancroft) McLane. St. Mary's School, Littleton, 1938, Smith College, 1938-40, Univ. of Wis., B.A., 1943. Former trustee, White Mountain School, former member, Hanover School Board, chairman, 1964-67; former member, Dresden School Board, chairman, 1967-68; former director, N.H. School Boards Association, trustee, Mary Hitchcock Memorial Hospital, 1977-80, Hitchcock Foundation, 1979--, chairman, 1985--; Univ. System of N.H., 1979-84, director, N.H. Charitable Fund, 1980--, member, chair, board of governors, West Central N.H. Community Mental Health Services, 1977-82. David J. Bradley, April 26, 1941. (Ch. see David J. Bradley.) 30 Occom Ridge, Hanover.

David Thomas McLaughlin

David Thomas McLaughlin

President, Dartmouth College. Grand Rapids, Mich., March 16, 1932, Wilfred and Arlene (Sunderline) McLaughlin. Grand Rapids High School, 1950, Dartmouth College, B.A., 1954, M.B.A., 1955. U.S. Air Force, 1955-57, 1st lt. Vice president, general manager, Champion Papers, 1957-70, president, Toro Co., 1970, chief executive officer, 1972, chairman, 1977-81; president, Dartmouth College, 1981--. Trustee, Dartmouth College, 1971--, chairman, 1977-81; board of overseers, Tuck School, Dartmouth, 1968-74, chairman, 1970-72; director, Dayton-Hudson Corp., 1976--, Westinghouse, 1979--, Chase Manhattan Bank, 1980--, member, N.E. Council on Higher Education, N.H. College and Univ. Council, 1981--, trustee, Kimball Union Academy, 1985--, incorporator, N.H. Charitable Fund. Judith (Landauer), March 26, 1955. William, 1956, Wendy, 1957, Susan, 1959, Jay, 1962. Episcopal. Parkhurst Hall, Hanover.

Joseph Woodbury McQuaid

Editor in chief, *The Union Leader, New Hampshire Sunday News*. Candia, N.H., Feb. 12, 1949, Bernard and Margaret (Griffin) McQuaid. Manchester Memorial High School, 1967, Univ. of N.H., 1968-69. Reporter, *Manchester Union Leader*, 1969-70, reporter, photographer, *N.H. Sunday News*, 1971-72, editor, 1973-76; managing editor, *Manchester Union Leader* (name changed to *The Union Leader* in 1980), 1976-82, editor in chief, *The Union Leader, N.H. Sunday News*, 1982--. Director, Union Leader Corp., 1976--, secretary, Manchester Industrial Council, 1972-82, secretary, William Loeb Memorial Fund, 1981--. Signe (Anderson), Nov. 2, 1975. Katharine, Dec. 27, 1976, Brendan, April 22, 1979. Catholic. 7 West Appleton St., Manchester.

Joseph Woodbury McQuaid

Jack Earl Melton

Jack Earl Melton

Superintendent, New Hampshire Hospital. North Bend, Nebr., Aug. 6, 1941, John and Mabel (Tomasek) Melton. Fremont (Nebr.) High School, 1959, Hastings College, B.A., 1963, Univ. of Nebr., M.A., 1968, Ph.D., 1969. Psychologist, office of research and counseling, Dartmouth College, 1969-70, executive director, North Country Community Services, 1971-75, acting director, No. N.H. Mental Health System, 1975, superintendent, Laconia State School and Training Center, 1975-85, superintendent, N.H. Hospital, 1985--. Chairman, residential living section, Region X, American Association on Mental Deficiency, 1980-82, chairman, planning and policy committee, N.H. Division of Mental Health, 1973-75, director, Lakes Region YMCA, 1984-85, No. Counties Health Planning Council, 1972-75, trustee, Androscoggin Valley Hospital, 1972-75, Governor's Commission on Crime and Delinquency, Region III Planning Council, 1971-73. Linda Lee (Wright), Aug. 13, 1966. Jeffrey, Nov. 27, 1968, Christine, April 17, 1971. P.O. Box 153, Laconia.

Stephen Everett Merrill

Attorney general of New Hampshire. Norwich, Conn., June 21, 1946, Leslie and Muriel (Seeley) Merrill. Winnacunnet High School, Hampton, 1964, Univ. of N.H., B.A., 1969, Georgetown Univ. Law Center, J.D., 1972. U.S. Air Force, 1969-76, capt. Legal counsel, secretary of the Air Force, 1973-75, special assistant to the assistant secretary of the Air Force, 1975-76, attorney, Manchester, 1976-84, legal counsel, Gov. John Sununu, 1982-84, chief of staff, 1983-84; attorney general, N.H., 1985--. President, N.H. Task Force on Child Abuse and Neglect, 1978-86, legal counsel, 1978--; member, fellows of the American Bar Foundation, 1986--.

Stephen Everett Merrill

Jack Baer Middleton

Jack Baer Middleton

Attorney. Philadelphia, Pa., Jan. 13, 1929, Harry and Mildred (Baer) Middleton. Lower Merion High School, Ardmore, Pa., 1946, Lafayette College, A.B., 1950, Boston Univ. School of Law, J.D., 1956. U.S. Marine Corps, 1950-52, sgt. Attorney, Manchester, 1956--. Special justice, Merrimack District Court, 1962--, commissioner, Uniform State Laws, 1971-75, president, N.H. Bar Association, 1979-80, chairman, White Mountain School, 1976-79, trustee, N.E. Law Institute, 1977-80, member, N.H. Judicial Council, 1978-83, Mount Washington Commission, 1969--, advisory board, Merrimack Valley College, American College of Trial Lawyers, director, Greater Manchester Chamber of Commerce, 1967--, chairman, 1985-86; Bedford School Board, 1960-66. Ann (Dodge), Aug. 22, 1953. Susan, May 12, 1954, Jack Jr., March 31, 1957, Peter, March 7, 1959. Protestant. 40 Stark St., Manchester.

Joseph Allen Millimet

Attorney. West Orange, N.J., July 23, 1914, Morris and Dorothy (McBlain) Millimet. East Orange High School, 1932, Dartmouth College, B.A., 1936, Yale Law School, LL.B., 1939. U.S. Coast Guard, 1942-45, lt. sg. Attorney, Concord, 1939-41, board of war communications, Federal Communications Commission, 1941-42, attorney, Manchester, 1946--. President, N.H. Bar Association, 1962-63, member, State Board of Bar Examiners, 1953-61, director, various N.H. corporations, 1947-80, chairman, Commission to Study the N.H. Constitution, 1964,74,84, Democratic National Committeeman, 1967-68, commissioner, Uniform State Laws, 1963-71, vice chairman, Citizens Task Force, 1969-70, legal counsel, Democratic State Committee, 1955-75, Gov. John King, 1963-67. Elizabeth (Gingras), Jan. 10, 1942. Madlyn, May 27, 1943, Lisa, July 21, 1947, Rebecca, Nov. 10, 1950, Peter, March 3, 1953 (dec. 1976). 1850 Elm St., Manchester.

Marilyn Grace Monahan

Marilyn Grace Monahan

President, National Education Association - New Hampshire. Holyoke, Mass., Feb. 11, 1948, Michael and Grace (Ramondetta) Monahan. Holyoke Catholic High School, 1966, Westfield State College, B.Ed., 1970, Univ. of N.H., M.Ed., 1975. Elementary school teacher, Alton, 1970-72, Goffstown, 1972-83; president, National Education Association - N.H., 1983--. State executive board, NEA-NH, 1977--, vice president, 1981-83; member, National Council of State Education Associations, 1981--, N.H. Educators Political Action Committee, 1981--, Governor's Advisory Committee on Educational Block Grants, 1981--, State Council on Teacher Education, 1976-81, N.H. Constitutional Convention, 1984. Catholic. 233 Fieldcrest Rd., Manchester.

John Clarence Mongan
Federal government official. Manchester, N.H., April 17, 1925, John and Anne (Frain) Mongan. Manchester West High School, 1943, Boston Univ., B.S., 1950, Northeastern Univ., M.P.A., 1974. U.S. Navy, 1943-47,49-51, lieut. Communications consultant, N.E. Telephone, 1951-61, mayor, Manchester, 1962-64, town manager, Ipswich, Mass., 1964-65, city manager, Mount Prospect, Ill., 1965-67, mayor, Manchester, 1968-70, senior community planner, U.S. Department of Housing and Urban Development, Boston, 1970-80, director of city planning, Lynn, Mass., 1973-75, economic development director, N.E. Regional Commission, Boston, 1978-79, manager, Manchester office, U.S. Department of Housing and Urban Development, 1981-82, regional administrator, regional housing commissioner, U.S. Department of HUD, 1983--. Chairman, Manchester School Committee, trustee, Carpenter Memorial Library, member, Manchester Industrial Council, Manchester Planning Board, Manchester Water Board, all while serving as mayor, 1962-64,68-70. Margaret Mary (Mahoney), Sept. 27, 1947. Kathleen, March 18, 1950, John M., June 6, 1951. Catholic. 22 Elizabeth Ave., Manchester.

John Clarence Mongan

Margaret Mary Mongan

Margaret Mary Mongan
Commissioner, New Hampshire Department of Health and Human Services. Manchester, N.H., May 14, 1926, John and Ida (Bouchard) Mahoney. St. Joseph's High School for Girls, Manchester, 1943, St. Joseph's School of Nursing, Nashua, 1944-47, Univ. of Mich., 1969. Nurse, 1947-67, St. Margaret's Hospital, Dorchester, Mass., Stillman Infirmary, Harvard Univ., Elliot Hospital, Manchester, Holy Family Hospital, Des Plaines, Ill.; administrative assistant, mayor of Manchester, 1962-64,68-70, director of social services, Manchester Housing Authority, 1969-81, deputy director of housing, 1981-84; deputy commissioner, N.H. Department of Health and Human Services, 1984-85, acting commissioner, 1985-86, commissioner, 1986--. President, United Way of Greater Manchester, 1978-79, former president, Mid-Merrimack Health Planning Council, former chairman, Office of Youth Services, Manchester, director, Numerica Savings Bank, 1981--, trustee, Youth Development Center, 1974-84, St. Anselm College, 1983--, vice chairman, Havenwood Retirement Community, 1983--. John C. Mongan, Sept. 27, 1947. Kathleen, March 18, 1950, John M., June 6, 1951. Catholic. 22 Elizabeth Ave., Manchester.

Robert Burton Monier

Former president, New Hampshire Senate, college professor, retired. Binghamton, N.Y., March 5, 1922, Alexander and Abigail (Mantle) Monier (adopted). Cazenovia (N.Y.) Seminary, 1939, Syracuse Univ., B.A., 1946, M.A., 1947. U.S. Army, 1942-46, U.S. Air Force, 1948-58, capt. Assistant professor of social studies, Plymouth Teachers College, 1958-62, director of research and technical writing division, Sylvania Electric Corp., Waltham, Mass., 1962-63, chairman, assistant professor of geography, St. Anselm College, 1963-65, chairman, geography-urban studies program, 1965-82; director, comprehensive planning, N.H., 1973-74, senior executive officer, Gov. Meldrim Thomson Jr., 1973-74. N.H. House of Rep., 1971-73, N.H. Senate, 1975-82, president, 1979-82; Citizens Task Force, 1969-70, commissioner, N.H. Centralized Data Processing Commission, 1975-78, director, American Legislative Exchange Council, 1976--, St. Joseph Community Services, Nashua, 1984--, former affiliate member, American Institute for Planners. Gregory, Jan. 4, 1944, David, Sept. 13, 1945, Stephen, Sept. 5, 1952, Kenneth, Aug. 5, 1959. Claira (Pirozzi), March 23, 1966. Catholic. New Boston Rd., Goffstown.

Robert Burton Monier

Andrew Theodore Mooradian

Andrew Theodore Mooradian

Director of athletics, University of New Hampshire. Revere, Mass., Aug. 26, 1923, Theodore and Aroos (Vartenian) Mooradian. Revere High School, 1942, Univ. of N.H., B.S., 1948, Boston Univ., M.S., 1958. U.S. Army, 1942-44, pfc. Univ. of N.H., backfield coach, football, 1950-64, coach, freshmen baseball, basketball, 1950-60, head basketball coach, 1951-52, assistant athletic director, 1955, head baseball coach, 1960-64, head football coach,. 1965, director of athletics, 1965--. Durham School Committee, 1968, Portsmouth Rehabilitation Center, 1957-62, director, Dover Federal Savings and Loan, 1979--, president, National Association of College Directors of Athletics, 1985-86, executive director, Yankee Conference, 1969--, chairman, NCAA Division 1-AA Football Committee, 1982-83. Frances (Adams), June 22, 1952. Leslie, Dec. 27, 1954, Todd, May 14, 1957, Jody, May 14, 1959. Protestant. 31 Orchard Dr., Durham.

Thomas Holmes Moore

President, New Hampton School. Grafton, N.H., June 20, 1920, Thomas and Lillian (Thompson) Moore. New Hampton School, 1938, Middlebury College, A.B., 1946. U.S. Navy, 1941-45, lt. sg. New Hampton School, 1946--, instructor in English, director of summer session, admissions, 1946-54, executive headmaster, 1954-59, headmaster, 1959-72, president, 1972--. Member, Commission on Independent Schools, 1963-72, chairman, 1972-82; chairman, Nonpublic School Advisory Council, 1976--, president, N.H. Public Television, 1969, 1975-80, president, board of governors, 1980--; vice chairman, N.H. State Library Commission, 1972-76, trustee, Council for the Advancement of Support of Education, 1983-85, director, Bristol Bank, 1965--, chairman, 1982--; moderator, New Hampton, 1976-78,82--, moderator, Newfound Area School District, 1969-72,83--. One honorary degree. Norma Jean (Smith), Sept. 9, 1944. Thomas, Nov. 6, 1945, Andrew, July 19, 1947, Jamyn, Feb. 13, 1949, Robinson, June 23, 1955, Elibet, Feb. 11, 1957. Protestant. New Hampton School, New Hampton.

Thomas Holmes Moore

Elting Elmore Morison

Educator, historian. Milwaukee, Wis., Dec. 14, 1909, George and Amelia (Elmore) Morison. Loomis Institute, Windsor, Conn., 1928, Harvard Univ., A.B., 1932, M.A., 1937. U.S. Naval Reserve, 1942-46, lt. comdr. Teacher, St. Mark's School, Southborough, Mass., 1934-35, assistant dean of freshmen, Harvard, 1935-37, assistant professor, professor, MIT, 1946-67,72-80, professor, Yale Univ., 1967-72. Trustee, Hampshire College, 1966-74, Franklin Pierce College, 1978--, Peterborough Hospital, 1934-38, director, Corporate Council for Critical Skills, 1980-85, Hitchiner Manufacturing, 1970--, Forum on New Hampshire's Future, 1978-80, Center for N.H.'s Future, 1980--. Author of five books, including *New Hampshire, A Bicentennial History*, with Elizabeth Forbes Morison, editor, *The Letters of Theodore Roosevelt*, eight volumes, 1951-54. Two honorary degrees. Anne (Sims), June 26, 1935 (div. 1964). Mary, May 3, 1941, Nicholas, May 4, 1943, Sarah, June 17, 1947. Elizabeth (Forbes), Dec. 8, 1967. Unitarian. Old Sharon Rd., Peterborough.

John Hopkins Morison

Chairman, Hitchiner Manufacturing. Milwaukee, Wis., June 29, 1913, George and Amelia (Elmore) Morison. Milwaukee Univ. School, 1931, Harvard Univ., A.B., 1935. U.S. Navy, 1943-46, lt. jg. International division, Bucyrus-Erie Co., South Milwaukee, 1935-43, president, Hitchiner Manufacturing, 1949-73, chairman, 1973--. Director, Markem Corp., 1966--, Souhegan National Bank, 1966--, N.H. Charitable Fund, 1969-79, president, 1973-78; N.H. Commission on the Arts, 1967-77, trustee, Land Use Foundation, 1970-75, Currier Gallery of Art, 1969--, vice president, board of governors, N.H. Public Television, 1980--, member of the corporation, MacDowell Colony, 1972-84, incorporator, Forum on N.H.'s Future, 1979-81, trustee, Shaker Village, 1981--, vice chairman, Shaker Village Preservation Campaign, 1983-85, president, board of directors, Matthew Thornton Health Plan, 1972-82. One honorary degree. Olga (de Souza Dantas), July 29, 1944. Maria, April 14, 1951, John III, Oct. 30, 1954. Unitarian. Perham Corner, Lyndeboro.

John Hopkins Morison

Robert Stoning Morrell

Robert Stoning Morrell

President, The Morrell Corporation. Manchester, N.H., June 2, 1920, Nathan and Wiona (Foote) Morrell. Kennett High School, Conway, 1938, Bay Path Institute, 1939-41. U.S. Army, 1942-46,50-53, 1st lt. Owner, Eastern Slope Ice Cream Co., 1948-50, president, The Morrell Corp., Glen, 1954--. Director, Industrial Development Authority, 1984--, First N.H. Banks, 1981--, Memorial Hospital, North Conway, 1969-75, White Mountains Attractions Association, 1957--, Governor's Management Review, 1981-82, chairman, White Mountain National Bank, 1963--, vice chairman, Mount Washington Commission, 1973--, member, Conway School Board, 1950,53-57. Ruth (Taber), July 1, 1944. Nancy, April 16, 1947, R. Stoning Jr., Feb. 10, 1956. Protestant. Kearsarge Rd., North Conway.

Maxine Katz Morse

Director of community relations, Lake Shore Hospital. Manchester, N.H., June 9, 1924, Morris and Ethel (Lawrence) Katz. Choate School, Brookline, Mass., 1941, Cornell Univ., B.A., 1945. Assistant director, Neighborhood Youth Corps, Manchester, 1965-66, associate director, Community Action Program, Manchester, 1966-69, director, Greater Manchester Child Care Association, 1969-74, president, N.H. Gift Specialties, 1976-85, director of community relations, Lake Shore Hospital, Manchester, 1985--. Chairman, N.H. Commision on Laws Affecting Mental Health, 1974-75, member, Cornell Univ. Council, 1969--, N.H. Advisory Commission on Health and Welfare, 1971-77, Citizens Task Force, 1969-70, trustee, Greater Manchester Mental Health Center, 1976-84, president, 1977-79; director, N.H. Association for Mental Health, 1974--, N.H. Council of Community Health Centers, 1979-81, N.H. Social Welfare Council, 1979--, board of overseers, Franklin Pierce Law Center, 1981--, director, Odyssey House, 1984--. Beth, Aug. 12, 1949, Morris, June 15, 1951, Jane, May 22, 1953, Ellen, July 27, 1956. Richard Morse, Oct. 16, 1965. Jewish. RD 5, Box 98, Laconia.

Maxine Katz Morse

Richard Allen Morse

Richard Allen Morse

Attorney. Manchester, N.H., Oct. 7, 1929, Emilus and Rena (Philbrick) Morse. Manchester Central High School, 1947, Univ. of N.H., A.B., 1951, Harvard Law School, J.D., 1956. U.S. Air Force, 1951-53, 1st lt. Attorney, Manchester, 1956--. Trustee, Univ. System of N.H., 1971-86, chairman, 1977-85, interim chancellor, 1982-83; instructor in criminal law, St. Anselm College, 1965-69, president, Manchester Bar Association, 1971-72, vice chairman and general counsel, N.H. Republican State Committee, 1965-71, chairman, Manchester Charter Revision Commission, 1962-63, trustee, Tilton School, 1967--, Spaulding Youth Center, 1965-70. Maxine (Katz), Oct. 16, 1965. Methodist. RD 5, Box 98, Laconia.

Henry Willey Munroe

President, New Hampshire College and University Council. Milton, Mass., Jan. 26, 1928, Henry and Betty (Willey) Munroe. Pembroke Academy, 1946, N.E. College, B.A., 1952, Boston Univ., 1958-59, Notre Dame College, Ed.D., 1961. U.S. Army, 1945-48, cpl. History teacher, Pittsfield High School, 1952-56, Pembroke Academy, 1957-60, staff assistant, Sen. Styles Bridges, 1960-61, vice president, N.E. College, 1961-64, president, N.H. College and Univ. Council, 1964--. Secretary, N.H. Civil War Centennial Commission, 1959-66, member, N.H. Revolutionary War Centennial Commission, 1976-80, chairman, N.H. Fire Standard and Training Commission, 1979--, Governor's Commission on Higher Education, 1975, assistant fire chief, Pembroke, 1960--. Two honorary degrees. Myra (Palmer), Oct. 5, 1946. Nancy, Oct. 2, 1947, Terry, June 14, 1951, Mark, June 29, 1965. Protestant. 113 Perley Ave., Suncook.

Henry Willey Munroe

Joseph Peter Nadeau

Joseph Peter Nadeau

Associate justice, New Hampshire Superior Court. Rochester, N.H., June 30, 1938, James and Athena (Michael) Nadeau. Phillips Exeter Academy, 1955, Dartmouth College, B.A., 1959, Boston Univ. School of Law., LL.B., 1962. City attorney, Dover, 1966-67, justice, Durham District Court, 1968-81, associate justice, N.H. Superior Court, 1981--. N.H. Real Estate Commission, 1967-70, clerk, 1968, chairman, 1969; Dover Industrial Development Authority, 1971-75, chairman, City Charter Revision Committee, Dover, 1970, director, Dover Chamber of Commerce, 1974-80, president, 1977-78; faculty, American Academy of Judicial Education, 1972--, president, N.H. Judges Association, 1973-74, president, N.H. District and Municipal Court Judges Association, 1972-73, board of governors, American Judges Association, 1973, president, Strafford County Bar Association, 1972-73. Catherine (Lawlor), Sept. 27, 1975. Tina, Sept. 26, 1963, Diana, June 8, 1967, Brianna, Jan. 28, 1980. Catholic. P.O. Box 536, Durham.

Theodora Patricia Nardi

Former state representative. Warwick, R.I., Aug. 28, 1922, Alfred and Carlotta (Manente) McAlpine. Classical High School, Providence, 1940, Manhattanville College of the Sacred Heart, N.Y.C., 1940-43. Assistant to the superintendent, Catholic Schools, Diocese of Manchester, 1963-73. N.H. House of Rep., 1973-82, N.H. Order of Women Legislators, 1973--, president, 1979-80; charter member, Diocesan School Board, Manchester, director, Pine Haven Boys Center, 1966-71, N.H. Social Welfare Council, 1981--, president, 1983-86; chairman, Governor's Conference on Education, 1966, chairman, Merrimack Valley Regional Conference on Education, 1967, member, Governor's Commission on the Handicapped, 1979--, chairman, 1979-83; former president, N.H. Public Broadcasting Council. Bernard Nardi, June 7, 1943. Carlotta, Aug. 3, 1944, Vincent II, Feb. 28, 1946, Bernard Jr., Feb. 13, 1948, Josephine, Jan. 25, 1949. Catholic. 776 Chestnut St., Manchester.

Theodora Patricia Nardi

Gerald Quentin Nash

Gerald Quentin Nash

President, Nash Real Estate. Nashua, N.H., Oct. 6, 1923, Ralph and Lillian (Class) Nash. Detroit (Mich.) Northern High, 1943, Keene State College, 1946-47, Boston Univ., B.S., 1950. U.S. Army, 1943-46, pfc. Owner, treasurer, Nashua Paper Box Co., 1950-67, owner, president, Nash Real Estate, 1967--. President, Nashua Arts and Science Center, 1976, former president, Nashua Fresh Air Camp, director, BankEast Corp., 1978--, member, So. N.H. Association of Commerce and Industry, 1968--, clerk, 1974-75; director, N.E. Council, 1982-85, chairman, WNDS-TV, Derry, 1982--, vice chairman, Hudson Charter Commission, 1985--, member, Hudson Chamber of Commerce, 1969--, Business and Industry Association of N.H., 1979--, Nashua Board of Realtors, director, N.E. chapter, 10th Mountain Division. Lucille (Lafontaine) May 25, 1950. Quentin, April 18, 1951, Debra, July 16, 1952, Mark, Nov. 20, 1953, Priscilla, July 16, 1955, Jeffrey, Sept. 4, 1959, Rebecca, Oct. 19, 1961. Christian. Trigate Rd., Hudson.

Theodore Natti

Director, Division of Forests and Lands, retired. Gloucester, Mass., Aug. 22, 1922, Eric and Matilda (Sironen) Natti. Gloucester High School, 1940, Univ. of N.H., B.S., 1949, Yale Univ., M.S., 1950. U.S. Navy, lt. jg. Chief of forest management, N.H. Forestry and Recreation Commission, 1950-67, director, Division of Forest and Lands and state forester, 1967-86. Former chairman, Granite State chapter and N.E. section, Society of American Foresters, chairman, Pembroke Conservation Commission, 1972--, chairman, N.H. Pesticides Control Board, 1983-86, vice chairman, 1986; chairman, N.H. Forest Resources Committee, 1980-86, secretary, N.H. Current Use Advisory Board, 1973-86, member, Bulk Power Supply Site Evaluation Committee, 1974-86, Energy Facility Evaluation Committee, 1971-86, president, National Association of State Foresters, 1979. Elizabeth (Carlson), May 18, 1952. Wayne, March 3, 1953, Lisa, Sept. 29, 1954, Jon, Aug. 29, 1955. Protestant. Pembroke Hill Rd., Pembroke.

Jane Ellen (Bonnie) Newman

Jane Ellen (Bonnie) Newman

President, Business and Industry Association of New Hampshire. Lawrence, Mass., June 2, 1945, William and Louise (Casey) Newman. Nazareth Academy, Wakefield, Mass., 1963, St. Joseph's College, Standish, Maine, B.A., 1967, Pennsylvania State Univ., M.Ed., 1969. Assistant dean of students, Univ. of N.H., 1969-71, director of housing, Salem State College, 1971-72, dean of students, Univ. of N.H., 1972-78, executive director, Forum on N.H.'s Future, 1978-80, chief of staff, Rep. Judd Gregg, 1981-82, associate director, Office of Presidential Personnel, The White House, 1982-84, assistant secretary of commerce, Economic Development Administration, U.S. Department of Commerce, 1984-85, president, Business and Industry Association of N.H., 1985--. Director, Indian Head Banks Inc., 1978-82, board of overseers, St. Joseph's College, 1971-75, trustee, Granite State Public Radio, 1985--, member, Governor's High-Level Waste Task Force, 1985--, President's Export Council, 1985--, trustee, Society for the Protection of N.H. Forests, 1985--, director, Industrial Development Authority, 1986--. Catholic. Ocean Blvd., North Hampton.

Eddy Gene Nicholson

President, chief operating officer, Congoleum Corporation. Sherman, Texas, May 2, 1938, Voy and Doris (Dooley) Nicholson. Denison (Texas) High School, 1956, Harding College, 1956-58, Southeastern State Univ., 1958, Memphis State Univ., B.B.A., 1960. Financial analyst, controller, Alladdin Industries, Nashville, 1965-69, controller, Fuqua Industries, Atlanta, 1961-71, chairman, president, chief executive officer, Gable Industries, Atlanta, 1971-74, executive vice president, chief financial officer, Congoleum Corp., 1975, president, chief administrative officer, 1976, vice chairman, chief administrative officer, 1977, vice chairman, chief operating officer, 1979, president, chief operating officer, 1980--. Director, Congoleum Corp., 1975--, Scovill Inc., 1983--, trustee, Univ. System of N.H., 1983-85, member, Center for Strategic and International Studies, Georgetown Univ., research board of visitors, Memphis State Univ., 1982--, executive in residence, Univ. of Houston, 1983--. One honorary degree. Linda (Bennett), Aug. 15, 1958. Kevin, Feb. 17, 1960, Deidre, July 29, 1962, Steven, May 10, 1964. Church of Christ. Exeter Rd., Hampton Falls.

Eddy Gene Nicholson

Arthur Horton Nighswander

Arthur Horton Nighswander

Attorney. Haverhill, Mass., Oct. 2, 1908, Howard and Mildred (Chesley) Nighswander. Laconia High School, 1925, Dartmouth College, A.B., 1929, Columbia Univ. Law School, LL.B., 1932. U.S. Navy, 1945, seaman 1st class. Attorney, Laconia, 1933--. Vice president, N.H. Bar Association, 1954-55, president, 1955-56; member, N.H. Board of Bar Examiners, 1943-44,49-72, chairman, 1967-72; N.H. Constitutional Convention, 1974, director, N.H. Social Welfare Council, 1949-54, board of managers, National Conference of Bar Examiners, 1955-58, president, Belknap County Bar Association, 1955-56, chairman, Laconia Peoples National Bank and Trust, 1973-80, senior board member, 1980--; Laconia Board of Education, 1936-46, Gilford Planning Board, 1964-74, trustee, Golden Rule Farms and successor Spaulding Youth Center, 1936-70. Esther (Richardson), Aug. 14, 1933. Mildred, Feb. 11, 1936, Andrew, Dec. 15, 1938, Warren, June 5, 1941. Congregational. 38 Wildwood Rd., Laconia.

David Lee Nixon

Attorney. Concord, Mass., March 19, 1932, Louis and Alice (Williams) Nixon. Leominster (Mass.) High School, 1949, Wesleyan Univ., B.A., 1953, Univ. of Mich. Law School, LL.B., 1958. U.S. Army, 1953-55, pfc. Attorney, Manchester, 1958--. President, Manchester Bar Association, 1973-74, N.H. Bar Association, 1980-81, No. N.E. Bar Association, 1970-72, member, N.H. Judicial Council, 1980-84, director, American Judicature Society, 1972-74, Manchester Family Service Society, 1960-63, director, vice president, N.H. Social Welfare Council, 1960-63, corporator, Manchester Savings Bank, 1966-69, trustee, Colby-Sawyer College, 1972-79, moderator, New Boston, 1963--, N.H. House of Rep., 1969-71, N.H. Senate, 1971-75, president, 1973-75; N.H. Constitutional Convention, 1984, delegate, American Bar Association House of Delegates, 1970-72, lecturer, Franklin Pierce Law Center, 1980--, member, N.H. Supreme Court Committee on Court Accreditation, 1986--. Janet (Rich), July 10, 1954. Leslie, April 20, 1956, Melanie, Oct. 9, 1957, Wendy, Oct. 17, 1959, Amy, March 25, 1961, David Jr., April 25, 1964, Louis II, Dec. 25, 1965. Presbyterian. Old Coach Rd., New Boston.

David Lee Nixon

Karl Edgar Norwood

Karl Edgar Norwood

President, The Norwood Group Inc. Nashua, N.H., March 6, 1944, Edgar and Madeline (Oldfield) Norwood. Milford High School, 1962, Northeastern Univ., 1962-63, Univ. of N.H., 1963-64. Owner, Norwood's Dairy, 1965-68, president, The Norwood Group Inc., real estate development, Bedford, 1968--. Director, vice chairman, Amherst Bank and Trust, 1975-80, Nashua Board of Realtors, 1972-76, president, 1973; member, Society of Industrial Realtors, 1981--, secretary, treasurer, N.H. chapter, 1986; director, Greater Manchester Chamber of Commerce, 1982--, chairman, 1986--; Easter Seal Society of Manchester, 1978--, chairman, Easter Seal Telethon, N.H., 1985,86, finance chairman, Republican State Committee, 1985--, trustee, Notre Dame College, 1986--, director, Merchants National Bank, 1986--, N.E. Real Estate Directory, 1983--. Louise (Marchildon), Oct. 2, 1965. Todd, Feb. 22, 1976, Christopher, Dec. 28, 1980. Episcopal. Chestnut Hill Rd., Amherst.

Carl Bourneuf Noyes

Banker, retired. Haverhill, Mass., Feb. 4, 1916, Carl and M. Grace (Bourneuf) Noyes. Haverhill High School, 1933, Dartmouth College, A.B., 1937, M.B.A., 1938. U.S. Navy, 1942-46,51-53, comdr. Assistant treasurer, Chase Manhattan Bank, N.Y.C., 1953-58, first vice president, Merchants National Bank, Manchester, 1958-80, executive vice president, president, chairman, First N.H. Banks Inc., 1974-81. Trustee, treasurer, Catholic Medical Center, 1974--, member, Manchester Industrial Council, 1963-85, executive committee, Greater Manchester Development Corp., 1985--, director, Merchants National Bank, 1965--, First N.H. Banks Inc., 1977--, First N.H. Mortgage Corp., 1979--, Londonderry Bank and Trust, 1981-83, Manchester Chamber of Commerce, 1968-70, American Cancer Society, N.H. division, 1960-64, alderman, Manchester, 1963-65. Jean (Frye), June 8, 1946. David, Jan. 27, 1947, Deborah, March 16, 1949. Protestant. 989 Ray St., Manchester.

Paul Francis O'Leary

Paul Francis O'Leary

Director, New Hampshire State Police, retired. Boston, Mass., June 3, 1928, Daniel and Mary (Finnegan) O'Leary. Brewster Academy, Wolfeboro, 1949. U.S. Marine Corps, 1947-48,50-52, sgt. Trooper, N.H. State Police, progressed through the ranks to lt. col., 1972, appointed director, rank of col., 1982-86, deputy director, N.E. State Police Information System, 1986--. Instructor, police science, St. Anselm College, 1964--, president, FBI National Academy Associates of N.E., 1985--, vice chairman, N.E. State Police Information System Policy Board, 1983-86, former president, Strafford County Law Enforcement Association, associate in police science, Harvard Univ., 1955. Lucia (Jutras), June 25, 1949. Mary, Aug. 11, 1950, Kevin, April 25, 1952, Colleen, March 18, 1954, Daniel, April 14, 1957, Patricia, June 29, 1971. Catholic. Darrell St., Rochester.

Stanley Charles Olsen

Real estate developer. Bridgeport, Conn., Aug. 15, 1928, Oswald and Elizabeth (Nordling) Olsen. Stratford (Conn.) High School, 1946, Univ. of Bridgeport, 1947-49, Northeastern Univ., A.E.E., 1957, B.B.A., 1958. U.S. Army, 1952-54, cpl. Research engineer, MIT, 1954-57, co-founder, Digital Equipment Corp., 1957, vice president, 1969-71, vice president and group manager, commerical products group, 1971-78, vice president and group manager, computer products group, 1978-82; real estate developer, Citrus County, Fla., 1982--. Director, Light Machines Corp., 1982--, Cynosure Corp., 1983--, Codenoll Technology Corp., 1982-83, Gulf of Lakes Corp., 1982--, Meadowcrest Properties, 1984--, incorporator, Forum on N.H.'s Future, 1978-82, trustee emeritus, Worcester Polytechnic Institute, 1985--, trustee, Univ. of N.H., 1980-84, national council, Northeastern Univ. Two honorary degrees. Elizabeth (MacVicar), Dec. 6, 1952. Bruce, Jan. 5, 1956, Jon, Feb. 11, 1959, Beth, March 8, 1961. Protestant. 24 French Dr., Bedford.

Stanley Charles Olsen

Dudley Wainwright Orr

Attorney. Concord, N.H., June 9, 1907, Benjamin and Carolyn (Dudley) Orr. Phillips Exeter Academy, 1925, Dartmouth College, A.B., 1929, Harvard Law School, J.D., 1933. U.S. Naval Reserve, 1944-46, lieut., counsel, materials division, assistant secretary of the Navy, 1945-46. Assistant attorney general, N.H., 1935-37, commissioner, N.H. Tax Commission, 1937-42, attorney, Concord, 1937-42, state attorney, Office of Price Administration, 1942-43, attorney, Concord, 1946--. President, Northern Railroad, 1946-52, Peerless Insurance Co., 1955-59, Concord Natural Gas Corp., 1953-80, chairman, United Life and Accident Insurance Co., 1956-68, trust officer, Mechanicks National Bank, 1946-70, director, Merchants Mutual Insurance Co., 1946-82, N.E. Electric System, 1958-78, Spaulding Fibre Co., 1955-67, Merrimack County Savings Bank, 1935-82, trustee, Dartmouth College, 1941-71, Phillips Exeter Academy, 1945-65, N.H. Historical Society, 1946-80, honorary, 1980--, president, 1972-75; Concord Planning Board, 1937-67, N.H. Constitutional Convention, 1964, trustee, Concord Hospital 1938-58. Four honorary degrees. Florence-Gene (Ward), June 18, 1935. Marjorie, Nov. 13, 1939, Carolyn, Nov. 25, 1941. Congregational. 4 Bishopsgate, Concord.

Paul Donnelly Paganucci

Vice president-finance, Dartmouth College. Waterville, Maine, April 18, 1931, Romeo and Martha (Donnelly) Paganucci. Waterville High School, 1949, Dartmouth College, B.A., 1953, M.B.A., 1954, Harvard Law School, J.D., 1957. President's office staff, W.R. Grace & Co., 1958-61, investment banker and executive, New York City, 1961-72, Dartmouth College, associate dean, professor of business administration, Amos Tuck School, 1972-76, senior investment officer, professor of business administration, 1976-77, vice president-finance, 1977--. Overseer, Amos Tuck School, 1971-72, chairman of trustees, Catholic Student Center, Dartmouth, 1973--, director, Hanover Water Works, 1976--, president, Dartmouth Educational Loan Corp., 1982--, director, Home Insurance Co., 1976--, Dartmouth National Bank, 1973--, W.R. Grace & Co. Foundation, 1965--, trustee, N.H. Catholic Charities, 1985--, Colby College, 1975-85, member, Grace Commission, 1982-84, Two honorary degrees. Marilyn (McLean), Sept. 10, 1966. Thomas, April 23, 1970, Elizabeth, Aug. 7, 1971. Catholic. 33 Rope Ferry Rd., Hanover.

Paul Donnelly Paganucci

John Frederic Page

John Frederic Page

Historic preservationist. Ringoes, N.J. Aug. 3, 1935, Norman and Charlotte (Tunney) Page. Mount Hermon School, Northfield, Mass., 1954, Univ. of N.H., B.A., 1958, College of William and Mary, M.A., 1969. Teacher, Suffield (Conn.) Academy, 1959-63, curator, Old State House, Hartford, Conn., 1964-66, director, Litchfield (Conn.) Historical Society, 1966-69, director, N.H. Historical Society, 1969-84, assistant secretary of state, N.H., 1984-85, executive director, Inherit, N.H., 1985--. Board of advisors, Univ. of N.H. Art Galleries, 1975--, director, Committee for a N.E. Bibliography, 1970--, Inherit, N.H., 1985--, member, chairman, board of overseers, Strawbery Banke, 1970-74, member, N.H. Advisory Council on Libraries, 1985--, Task Force on Historic Preservation in N.H., 1983-84, N.H. Council for the Humanities, 1977-79, N.H. American Revolution Bicentennial Commission, 1972-83. Ruth (Cox), July 23, 1966. David, May 22, 1969, Christopher, July 24, 1973. Episcopal. 10 Wildemere Terrace, Concord.

William Dexter Paine II

Attorney. Cambridge, Mass., May 5, 1932, Dexter and Anna (Dennen) Paine. Proctor Academy, Andover, 1950, Univ. of N.H., B.S., 1956, Univ. of Mich., J.D., 1959. Attorney, North Conway, 1960--. County attorney, Carroll County, 1964-66,82--, instructor, School for Lifelong Learning, Univ. of N.H., 1978-85, member, Carroll County, N.H. Bar Associations, president, Carroll County Bar Association, 1962-63, president, N.H. Ski Racing Association, 1972-74, chairman, N.H. County Correctional Commission, 1968-70, North Conway Memorial Hospital Association, 1962-63, incorporator, N.H. Charitable Fund, 1973-83, director, No. N.H. Charitable Fund, 1984--, Bartlett Board of Adjustment, 1985--, moderator, Bartlett, 1974--, school moderator, Bartlett, 1975--. Gail (Foster), Dec. 28, 1957. Dexter, Dec. 14, 1960, Elizabeth, July 28, 1962, Stephanie, Feb. 4, 1965, Ellyn, Nov. 13, 1967. Protestant. Route 16A, Intervale.

Newell Joseph Paire

Commissioner, Department of Education, retired. Keene, N.H., July 3, 1913, John and Eva Mary (Castor) Paire. Keene High School, 1931, Keene State College, B.Ed., 1936, M.Ed., 1952. U.S. Naval Reserve, 1942-45, comdr. Teacher, principal, North Hampton, Concord, Wilton, 1936-42,46-47, superintendent of schools, Wilton, 1947-57, Claremont, 1957-63, deputy commissioner of education, Department of Education, 1963-68, commissioner, 1968-76. Hearing officer, Department of Education, 1979--, N.H. House of Rep., 1978-82, trustee, Univ. System of N.H., 1968-76,79--, supervisor of the checklist, Concord, 1977--, member, N.H. Education Association, 1936-63, National Education Association, 1936-63, American Association of School Administrators, 1947-76, American Association of Chief State School Officers, 1963-76. Two honorary degrees. Dorothy (Schurman), Sept. 4, 1937 (dec. Aug. 10, 1966). Newell Jr., Jan. 20, 1940. Patricia (Denning), April 16, 1967. St. ch., Deborah Seymour, May 26, 1940, Denning Smith, March 24, 1944, Tricia Smith, Oct. 12, 1950. Episcopal. 3 Tow Path Ln., Concord.

Christos Papoutsy

President, Papoutsy Participation Company. Haverhill, Mass., Dec. 10, 1936, Mikel and Helen (Demos) Papoutsy. Haverhill High School, 1954, N.H. College, A.A., 1959. U.S. Army, 1955-57, pvt. Accountant, Crompton & Knowles, Worcester, 1961-63, controller, Harrington Richardson Arms Manufacturer, Worcester, 1964-69, Hollis Engineering, Nashua, controller, 1969-71, sales manager, 1972-75, vice president, 1976-77, president, 1977-80, president, Cooper Electronics Division, 1980-83; president, Papoutsy Participation Co., (Papco), 1983--. Trustee, N.H. College, 1970-80, director, St. George Greek Orthodox Cathedral, 1970-81, chairman, Manchester Cancer Drive, 1980-82, director, Portsmouth Charitable Foundation, 1985--, founder, Christos Papoutsy Charitable Foundation, 1985--, board chairman, Advanced Systems Inc., Phoenix, 1985--, Automated Plasma Inc., Manchester, 1985--, Seacoast chairman, Liberty Centennial Campaign, 1985--. Muriel (Plante), 1959. Andrea, June 3, 1960, Angela, Feb. 13, 1964, Mikel, April 11, 1969. Greek Orthodox. 2234 Ocean Blvd., Rye Beach.

Christos Papoutsy

George Spiros Pappagianis

Associate justice, New Hampshire Superior Court. Nashua, N.H., April 23, 1924, Spiros and Spiridoula (Geoldasis) Pappagianis. Nashua High School, 1941, Harvard Univ., B.A., 1946 (class of 45), Boston Univ. School of Law, LL.B., 1949. U.S. Army, 1943-45, pfc. Deputy attorney general, N.H., 1964-66, attorney general, 1966-70, clerk, reporter of decisions, N.H. Supreme Court, 1970-80, associate justice, N.H. Superior Court, 1980--. Editor, *N.H. Bar Journal*, 1972-81. Helen (Hagibeys), Feb. 11, 1967. Maria, Feb. 9, 1975. Greek Orthodox. 29 Charlotte Ave., Nashua.

Denis Walter Parker

Executive director, New Hampshire State Employees Association. Manchester, N.H., April 22, 1943, John and Simonne (Caron) Parker. Bishop Bradley High School, Manchester, 1961, St. Anselm College, B.A., 1968. U.S. Army, 1961-64, spec. 4th. cl. Field representative, State Employees Association, 1969-70, director of employee services, 1970-72, executive director, 1972--. Director, Blue Cross and Blue Shield, 1973-80, United Health Systems Agency, 1980-81, commissioner, Manchester Transit Authority, 1980-83. Carole (Boulanger), July 16, 1966. Craig, Dec. 26, 1967, Susan, July 17, 1969, Ryan, Sept. 12, 1973. Catholic. 37 Coburn St., Manchester.

Denis Walter Parker

Jeanne Beatrice Perreault

Jeanne Beatrice Perreault

President, Rivier College. Providence, R.I., Dec. 13, 1929, Alphonse and Malvina (Chevalier) Perreault. Presentation of Mary High School, Hudson, 1947, Catholic Teachers College, B.S., 1959, Catholic Univ. of America, M.S., 1968. Professed, Sisters of the Presentation of Mary, Aug. 15, 1950. Teacher, 1950-65, instructor, assistant, associate professor, Rivier College, 1968-80, president, Rivier, 1980--. Director, So. N.H. Association of Commerce and Industry, 1982-84, N.H. College and Univ. Council, 1980--, Postsecondary Education Commission, 1984--, provincial council, Sisters of the Presentation of Mary, 1983--, provincial chapter, 1965,68,75,80. Catholic. Rivier College, Nashua.

Walter Rutherford Peterson Jr.

President, Franklin Pierce College, former governor. Nashua, N.H., Sept. 19, 1922, Walter and Helen (Reed) Peterson. New Hampton School, 1942, Dartmouth College, B.A., 1947. U.S. Naval Reserve, 1942-46, ensign. Partner, The Petersons Inc., real estate, Peterborough, 1949--, governor, N.H., 1969-73, president, Franklin Pierce College, 1975--. President, N.H. Realtors Association, 1960-61, director, National Association of Real Estate Boards, 1960-65, Monadnock Bank, 1961--, trustee, New Hampton School, 1968-74, N.H. House of Rep., 1961-69, speaker, 1965-69; president, N.H. Constitutional Convention, 1974, member, Postsecondary Education Commission, 1979--, chairman, 1981-82; director, N.H. Higher Education Assistance Foundation, 1985--, N.E. Education Loan Marketing Corp., 1983, N.H. College and Univ. Council, 1976--, chairman, 1985--; National Association of Independent Colleges and Universities, 1982-84, N.E. Board of Higher Education, 1982--, Inherit N.H. 1984--, incorporator, N.H. Charitable Fund, 1984--. Six honorary degrees. Dorothy (Donovan), Nov. 24, 1949. Margaret, Oct. 8, 1954, Andrew, Nov. 11, 1956. Episcopal. 19 East Mountain Rd., Peterborough.

Walter Rutherford Peterson Jr.

Milo Luther Pike

President, chairman, Pike Industries. Laconia, N.H., Aug. 15, 1930, Randolph and Beatrice (Towle) Pike. Laconia High School, 1948, Lawrence Academy, Groton, Mass., 1949. Pike Industries, Laconia, Tilton, 1949--, president, treasurer, 1957-80, president, chairman, 1980--. Treasurer, Pepi Herrmann Crystal, 1974-78, president, Green Apple Graphics, Laconia, 1974-77, president, Cooley Asphalt Paving, Barre, Vt., 1970--, vice president, Pike Realty, 1973--, partner, Autohaur, Vienna, Austria, 1972-82, partner, Gowdy Florida Broadcasting, 1974-78, director, Laconia Chamber of Commerce, 1956-74, trustee, Lakes Region General Hospital, 1960-78, chairman, 1966-74; director, Laconia Peoples National Bank, 1964-83, First Bancorp of N.H., 1976-83, State Prison Board of Trustees, 1980-82, Industrial Development Authority, 1966-82, member, Governor's Advisory Commttee on N.H.'s Future, 1977-78. Cecile (Morin), May 13, 1950 (div. Jan. 1959). Cynthia, Nov. 20, 1952, Randolph, May 28, 1955. Carol (Phelps), Nov. 28, 1959 (div. Jan. 1968). Miki, July 17, 1965. Penny (Pitou), Sept. 1, 1981. Windswept on Potter Hill, Gilford.

Penny Pitou-Pike

President, Penny Pitou Travel. Bay Side, Long Island, N.Y., Oct. 8,1938, Augustus and Eulalie (Shaefer) Pitou. Laconia High School, 1956, Middlebury College, 1957-58. Founder, co-director, Penny Pitou Ski School, Gilford, 1961-68, Milton, Mass., 1963-68, certified professional ski instructor, 1965--, International Ski and Winter Sports Shows, 1969-70, president, Penny Pitou Travel, 1974--. Director, Laconia Chamber of Commerce, 1983-84, Laconia Peoples National Bank, 1967-68, Lakes Region General Hospital, 1965-70, coach, girls ski team, Laconia High School, 1972-73, chair, board of directors, UNH Wildcat Winners Circle, 1984, National Ski Hall of Fame, 1976, member, U.S. Olympic team, 1956,60, two silver medals, 1960. Egon Zimmermann, Feb. 19, 1961 (div. Aug. 28, 1968). Christian, Aug. 16, 1962, Kim, Aug. 10, 1965. Milo Pike, Sept. 1, 1981. Unitarian. Windswept on Potter Hill, Gilford.

Penny Pitou-Pike

Ronald Felix Poltak

Executive director, New England Interstate Water Pollution Control Commission. Manchester, N.H., Nov. 3, 1946, Felix and Violet (Croteau) Poltak. Bishop Bradley High School, Manchester, 1964, Univ. of N.H., B.A., 1968. Office of State Planning, intern, 1968-70, planning technician, 1970-76, principal planner, 1976-79, planning director, 1979-82; director, Division of Parks and Recreation, 1982-83, executive director, N.E. Interstate Water Pollution Control Commission, Boston, 1983--. Chairman, State Council on Resources and Development, 1979-82, vice chairman, N.E. River Basins Commission, 1980-81, state representative, National Appalachian Trail Advisory Board, 1979-82, Water Supply and Pollution Control Commission, 1979-83, Water Resources Wetlands Board, 1979-82, member, N.H. Planners Association, 1980-83, American Society of Planning Officials, 1981-83. Anne Marie (Routhier), Nov. 23, 1968. Steffen, Aug. 7, 1980, Justin, March 16, 1982. Catholic. 125 Fairmount Ave., Manchester.

Peter Lawrence Pond

Minister. New Haven, Conn., Feb. 13, 1933, Joseph and Josephine (Clark) Pond. Pomfret (Conn.) School, 1951, Yale Univ., B.A., 1955, B.D., 1958, S.T.M., 1960. Ordained, United Church of Christ clergyman, 1982. Associate boys work secretary, YMCA, New Haven, 1955-59, executive director, YMCA, Milford, Conn., 1960-62, director of development, Federation of YMCA's, Puerto Rico, 1962-64, president, Indigenous Volunteers, Washington, D.C., 1968-69, director, Jefferson Center Foundation, 1970--, program developer, Community Action, Coos, Carroll and Grafton counties, 1975-78, organizer, incorporator, board member, Family Health Programs of Northern N.H., 1978, minister for refugees, Franconia Community Church, 1982--, president, Thai Friends Relief Foundation, Bangkok, 1979--, member, United Church of Christ State Refugee Task Force, 1984--. Karen (Morris), 1964 (div. 1976). Piper, May 9, 1965, Peter J., June 27, 1966, Anna, Oct. 17, 1968, Matthew, March 8, 1970. Shirley (Mason), May 9, 1982. Adopted ch., Sunthorn, Arn, Lakhana, Soneat, Thy, Kannarom, Dara, Meth. Congregational. Black Velvet Rd., RD 1, Box 123, Jefferson.

Harold Willard Pope

Harold Willard Pope

Chairman, Sanders Associates, retired. Boston, Mass., Dec. 14, 1917, Harold and Merinda (Mosher) Pope. Waltham (Mass.) High School, 1935, MIT, S.B., 1939. Dynamic analysis engineer, Wright Field, Dayton, U.S. Army Air Force, 1939-40, aerodynamics and structural engineer, Stinson and Vultee Aircraft Corp., 1940-45, project engineer, Vultee Aircraft, 1945-47, Consolidated-Vultee Aircraft Corp., 1947-50, chief engineer, Pomona division, General Dynamics Corp., 1950-53, Sanders Associates, vice president, operations, 1953-68, executive vice president, 1968-74, president, 1975-76, chairman, chief executive officer, 1976-78, chairman, 1978-82. Director, Sanders Associates, 1955--, Planning Research Corp., 1983--, N.H. chapter, American Cancer Society, 1979-83, trustee, Daniel Webster College, 1982--, Nashua Symphony Orchestra, 1984--, N.H. chairman, U.S. Savings Bond Program, 1978-80. Veronica (McLaughlin), Jan. 21, 1940. David, Nov. 24, 1940, Nancy, June 7, 1943, Christopher, Oct. 1, 1947, Lucy, Nov. 22, 1953, Harold, Feb. 15, 1958. Protestant. 22 Eaton Rd., Amherst.

Natalie Merriam Potter

Northumberland town manager, retired. Stratford, N.H., March 7, 1916, Harry and Henrietta (Thompson) Merriam. Stratford High School, 1933, Concord College of Business, 1936. Secretary, N.H. Liquor Commission, 1936-42, secretary, head of promotion department, Univ. of Tampa, 1943-47, secretary, Timberland Machines, Lancaster, 1967-77, town manager, Northumberland, 1977-80. N.H. House of Rep., 1961-65, State Council on Aging, 1961-69, Farm Bureau Board, 1963-66, Coos County Commission on Natural Beauty, 1966, member, secretary, town planning committee, Northumberland, 1966-80, member, clerk, Coos-Six Area Planning Committee, 1968-72, president, secretary-treasurer, Covered Bridge Association of N.H., 1962-68, selectwoman, Northumberland, 1974-77, N.H. Constitutional Convention, 1974, president, Lancaster Business and Professional Women's Club, 1974-76, co-chairman, Town Bicentennial Committee, 1976. Alton Potter, Nov. 2, 1949. Sally, Jan. 12, 1951, Risa Lynn, Sept. 16, 1953. Methodist. RFD 1, Box 91, Groveton.

J. Herman Pouliot

J. Herman Pouliot

Publisher, *Nashua Telegraph*. Sanford, Maine, Dec. 6, 1923, Henry and Alice (Brisson) Pouliot. Sanford High School, 1941, Univ. of N.H., B.A., 1954. U.S. Air Force, 1942-45, technical sgt. Manager, *Sanford* (Maine) *Tribune*, 1950-56, general manager, *Little Falls* (N.Y.) *Evening Times*, 1956-60, business manager, *Oneida* (N.Y.) *Daily Dispatch*, 1960-70, publisher, *Claremont Eagle*, 1970-71, publisher, *Nashua Telegraph*, 1971--. Board member, N.E. Newspaper Association, 1972-83, president, N.E. Newspaper Advertising Bureau, 1980, director, *Willimantic* (Conn.) *Chronicle*, 1980--, First Federal Bank, Nashua, 1974--, chairman, N.H. Association of Commerce and Industry, 1979-80, trustee, Univ. System of N.H., 1979-83, advisory board, Rivier College, 1973-81. Barbara (Joy), Feb. 17, 1949. Lisa, March 6, 1955, Jacqueline, Sept. 18, 1962. Catholic. 133 Peele Rd., Nashua.

Henry Martin Powers Jr.

President, C.H. Sprague and Son Co. Bath, Maine, July 18, 1932, Henry and Eva (Saunders) Powers. Morse High School, Bath, 1951, Maine Maritime Academy, B.S., 1954. U.S. Navy, 1957-59, lieut. Engineer, American Export Lines, 1954-57, staff engineer, Bull & Roberts, N.Y.C., 1959-60, staff, Moran Towing and Transportation, Portland, 1960-61, sales department, C.H. Sprague and Son., 1961-68, vice president, marketing, 1968-71, president, chief executive officer, 1971--. Director, C.H. Sprague and Son., 1972--, Petroleum Heat and Power of R.I., 1970--, Portsmouth Trust Co., 1972-81, First N.H. Banks, 1981--, Seaward Construction Co., 1983--, Shanley Corp., 1979--, Governor's Management Review, 1981-82, board of visitors, Maine Maritime Academy, 1963-76. Hepzibah (Reed), June 20, 1959. Henry III, Sept. 23, 1960, Carlton, July 3, 1963. Protestant. 68 River Rd., Stratham.

Henry Martin Powers Jr.

Faith Preston

Faith Preston

President, White Pines College. Boston, Mass., Sept. 14, 1921, Howard and Edith (Wilson) Preston. Beverly (Mass.) High School, 1939, Boston Univ., B.A., 1944, M.A., 1945, Columbia Univ., Ed.D., 1963. Teacher, Perley High School, Georgetown, Mass., 1945-47, teacher, Stoneham (Mass.) High School, 1947-50, teacher, Endicott Junior College, Beverly, 1950-53, Puerto Rico Junior College, director of research, 1953-55, dean of administration, 1955-63, vice president, 1963-65; founding president, White Pines College, Chester, 1965--. Trustee, White Pines College, 1965--, incoporator, Catholic Medical Center, 1978--, director, Swift Water Girl Scout Council, member, American Association of University Women, N.H. Steering Committee for Career Education. Author of three children's books. Winthrop Wadleigh, Dec. 19, 1970 (dec. March 3, 1986). Baptist. P.O. Box 25, Chester.

Robert Francis Preston

State senator. Lowell, Mass., May 11, 1929, Richard and Margaret (Burke) Preston. Keith Academy, Lowell, 1946, Salem State College, B.S., 1962. U.S. Army, 1946-47,50-51, sgt. Owner, operator, Preston Real Estate, 1967--. N.H. Senate, 1973--, co-founder, director, Seabrook Bank, 1972--, corporator, Exeter Hospital, 1978--, president, Hampton Chamber of Commerce, 1968-70, former member, Governor's Commission on Public Disturbances, advisor, N.H. Small Business Council. Charlotte (Keefe), Oct. 4, 1952. Robert Jr., July 30, 1953, Charles, Feb. 7, 1955, Martha, Nov. 7, 1956, James, May 25, 1959, Mary Rae, Dec. 13, 1961. Catholic. 226 Winnacunnet Rd., Hampton.

Lloyd Mortimer Price

Lloyd Mortimer Price

Adjutant general, New Hampshire National Guard. Portsmouth, N.H., Oct. 24, 1931, Arnold and Viola (Noble) Price. Concord High School, 1949, Univ. of N.H., B.S., 1958. U.S. Army, 1953-55, 1st lt., N.H. National Guard, 1949--, rank of major general. Manager, Internal Revenue Service, Portsmouth, 1958-73, commissioner, Department of Revenue Administration, 1973-84, adjutant general, N.H. National Guard, 1984--. President, N.E. Tax Officials, 1979-80, director, Northeast Tax Officials Association, 1981-84, personnel committee, Adjutant General's Association, 1984--, member, Army Reserve Forces Policy Committee, 1984--, instructor, accounting and taxation, N.E. College, 1963-64, N.H. College, 1964-78, finance committee, National Guard Association of the U.S., 1984--. Joan (Lufkin), March 16, 1955. James, Oct. 31, 1959, Susan, April 28, 1962, Linda, Dec. 6, 1964. Protestant. 285 South St., Concord.

David Frederick Putnam

Chairman emeritus, Markem Corporation. Melrose, Mass., April 28, 1914, Claude and Louise (Adams) Putnam. Phillips Andover (Mass.) Academy, 1932, Dartmouth College, B.A., 1936. Research chemist, F.A. Putnam Manufacturing, Keene, 1936-39, Markem Corp., Keene, sales department, 1939-42, sales manager, 1942, vice president-marketing, 1945, president, 1956, chairman, 1973, chairman emeritus, 1979--. Director, Markem Corp., 1945--, First National Bank of Boston, 1970-79, honorary, 1979--; N.H. Charitable Fund, 1973-83, chairman, 1982-83; Center for N.H.'s Future, 1980--, Keene Clinic, 1959-66, trustee, Society for the Protection of N.H. Forests, 1980-83, senior trustee, Putnam Foundation, 1952--, trustee, Cheshire County Savings Bank, 1944-73, Foundation for the Preservation of Historic Keene, 1967--, Elliot Community Hospital, Keene, 1945-65, N.H. Historical Society, 1966-68,75-80, Historic Harrisville, 1972-78, chairman, 1972-73; Keene City Council, 1938-40,45-47,66-69, Keene Planning Board, 1968-74, chairman, 1972; Keene Conservation Commission, 1975-78, Keene Architectural Review Board, 1979-82, president, Forum on N.H.'s Future, 1978-82. Two honorary degrees. Rosamond (Page), March 17, 1938. David Jr., Sept. 22, 1941, Thomas, Feb. 14, 1943, James, April 1, 1945, Rosamond, May 31, 1946, Frederick, July 4, 1947, Louise, June 29, 1948. Episcopal. 150 Court St., Keene.

David Frederick Putnam

Hamilton Staples Putnam

Hamilton Staples Putnam

Former chief executive officer, New Hampshire Medical Society. Wilton, N.H., Nov. 1, 1910, Henry and Alice (Staples) Putnam. Wilton High School, 1929. U.S. Navy, 1943-46, comdr. Newspaper reporter, 1930-42, chief of staff, Sen. Styles Bridges, 1942-43, Gov. Sherman Adams, 1948-49, owner, public relations firm, Concord, 1948-75, chief executive officer, N.H. Medical Society, 1948-85, consulting partner, Dawson Advertising Agency, Concord, 1985--, director, John P. Bowler Memorial Library, 1985--. Director, Blue Cross and Blue Shield, 1950-81, corporator, Concord Savings Bank, 1968--, advisory council, National Institutes of Health, 1950-75, chairman, N.H. Mental Health Advisory Council, 1975-78, treasurer, Republican State Committee, 1947-53, honorary member, N.H. Medical Society, 1978--, member, Indigent Care Task Force, 1985--, Author of five books, including the *History of Wilton*, 1939. Ruth (Perley), June 24, 1933. Virginia, Dec. 28, 1934. Congregational. 34 Ridge Rd., Concord.

Thomas Page Putnam

President, treasurer, Markem Corporation. Keene, N.H., Feb. 14, 1943, David and Rosamond (Page) Putnam. Keene High School, 1961, Univ. of Denver, B.S.B.A., 1967. U.S. Army, 1962-64, spec. 4th cl. Markem Corp., manufacturing and marketing positions, 1968-73, treasurer, vice president, 1973-79, president, treasurer, director, 1979--. Director, Indian Head National Bank, Keene, 1973-86, Indian Head Banks Inc., 1980-86, Monadnock United Way, 1979-86, president, 1984; Greater Keene Chamber of Commerce, 1972-78, president, 1978; incorporator, Wentworth Institute, 1978--, Cheshire County Savings Bank, 1972--, Cheshire Hospital, 1972--, advisory board, Crotched Mountain Center, 1976--. Barbara (Brown), Aug. 13, 1966. Alexandra, July 26, 1970, George, Sept. 10, 1981. Episcopal. Peg Shop Rd., Keene.

Thomas Page Putnam

Conrad Llewellyn Quimby

Conrad Llewellyn Quimby

Newspaper publisher, state representative. Cleveland, Ohio, April 17, 1925, Arthur and Marguerite (Lewin) Quimby. Windsor (Vt.) High School, 1943, Univ. of Conn., B.A., 1950, Western Reserve Univ., M.A., 1951. U.S. Navy, 1943-46, electrician 2nd cl. Community services director, Cleveland Council on World Affairs, 1952-53, regional representative, Great Lakes Foreign Policy Association, 1953-55, executive director, N.H. Council on World Affairs, 1955-62, publisher, *Derry News*, 1963--. President, N.H. Press Association, 1979-83, director, N.E. Press Association, 1976-79, N.H. House of Rep., 1976--, founder, director, Derry Chamber of Commerce, 1964-70, founder, chairman, Derry Housing and Redevelopment Authority, 1977--, chairman, N.H. Office of Economic Opportunity, 1972-74, chairman, Rockingham County Community Action Program, 1966-72. Lillian (Mattson), April 13, 1946. Gay Cameron, Aug. 9, 1953, Elsbeth, May 13, 1955, Curtis, May 8, 1957. Protestant. 76 English Range Rd., Derry.

Byron C. Radaker

Chairman, chief executive officer, Congoleum Corporation. West Freedom, Pa., March 19, 1934, Ralph and Mary (Kilgore) Radaker. Meadville (Pa.) High School, 1952, Kent State Univ., B.S., 1959. U.S. Army, 1954-56, spec. 4th cl. Sales, marketing research, Gillette Safety Razor Co., 1951-61, sales management, marketing, Allied Chemical Corp., 1961-66, management, Certain-Teed Products Corp., 1966-74, Congoleum Corp., executive vice president, planning, 1975-76, deputy chairman, chief operating officer, 1976-77, president, chief executive officer, 1977-79, chairman, chief executive officer, 1979--. Director, Public Service Co. of N.H., 1980-82, national chairman, business council, Democratic National Committee, 1981-84, trustee, Portsmouth Hospital, 1980-81, director, Center for N.H.'s Future, 1980-81, Bath Iron Works Corp., 1979--, incorporator, N.H. Charitable Fund, 1981-85, executive committee, Greater Portsmouth Community Foundation, 1984-86. Shirley Ann (Hotchkiss), Nov. 28, 1953. Keith, Jan. 26, 1955, Kelly, May 27, 1958, Kirsten, Aug. 22, 1962, Kyle, Sept. 20, 1964. Baptist. 179 Pleasant St., Portsmouth.

Byron C. Radaker

Lawrence Ingram Radway

Professor, Dartmouth College. Staten Island, N.Y., Feb. 2, 1919, Frederick and Dorothy (Segall) Radway. Greenbrier Military Academy, Lewisburg, W. Va., 1935, Harvard Univ., B.S., 1940, Univ. of Minn., M.P.A., 1943, Harvard, M.A., 1948, Ph.D., 1950. U.S. Army, 1943-46, capt. Tutor, teaching fellow, Harvard, 1946-50, government department, Dartmouth College, instructor, 1950-52, assistant professor, 1952-57, associate professor, 1957-58, professor, 1958--. Professor of national security affairs, National War College, 1962-63, visiting professor, Karl Marx Univ., Budapest, 1986, board of advisors, Industrial College of the Armed Forces, 1958-62, civilian aide, secretary of the Army, 1962-70, director, N.H. Council on World Affairs, 1955-81, member, International Institute of Strategic Studies, London, 1982--, N.H. House of Rep., 1969-73, chairman, Democratic State Committee, 1975-77, member, Democratic National Committee, 1975-77, Winograd Commission, 1977-78, Council on Foreign Relations, 1965--, Royal Institute of International Affairs, 1981--, president, N.E. Political Science Association, 1963-65. Author, *Foreign Policy and National Defense*, 1969. One honorary degree. Robert, Nov. 25, 1943. Patricia (Headland), Aug. 20, 1949. Carol, Oct. 16, 1951, Michael, Dec. 14, 1953, Deborah, Nov. 5, 1956. Protestant. 22 Occom Ridge, Hanover.

Robert Edward Raiche

Attorney. Manchester, N.H., Feb. 18, 1937, Edward and Lucienne (Harris) Raiche. Bishop Bradley High School, Manchester, 1955, Nathaniel Hawthorne College, B.A., 1967, Univ. of N.H., M.A., 1970, Franklin Pierce Law Center, J.D., 1980. U.S. Marine Corps, 1955-61, sgt. Instructor, administrator, Nathaniel Hawthorne College, 1968-72, dean of admissions, 1972-75, assistant to the president for external affairs and vice president for external affairs, 1975-77; U.S. marshall, N.H., 1977-81, attorney, Manchester, 1981--. Chairman, N.H. Ceara Partners of the Americas, 1968-70,73-77, chairman, Partners of the Americas, 1971-75, chairman, National Association of the Partners of the Americas, 1984--, commissioner, Education Commission of the States, 1970-71, corporator, N.H. Savings Bank, 1971-80, director, N.H. Social Welfare Council, 1982-83. Mary (Duval), Oct. 4, 1958. Robert Jr., Sept. 4, 1959, Denise, Aug. 13, 1960, Maureen, Sept. 12, 1961, Donna, Dec. 22, 1962, Kathleen, Nov. 22, 1968. Catholic. 957 Somerville St., Manchester.

Robert Edward Raiche

Margaret Ann Ramsay

State representative. Houlton, Maine, Jan. 4, 1935, Eugene and Barbara (Adams) Russell. Houlton High School, 1952, Keene State College, B.Ed., 1956, M.Ed., 1964. Teacher, Marlborough Elementary School, 1956-62, Keene Junior High School, 1962-65. Trustee, Univ. System of N.H., 1971-79, Keene Endowment Association, 1977--, Keene State College Campus Ministry, 1972-80, director, Monadnock Credit Union, 1979-83, N.H. Constitutional Convention, 1974,84, N.H. House of Rep., 1977--, delegate, National Association of State Legislators, 1981--, president, Keene State College Alumni Association, 1969-71, chairman, Keene State College Alumni Distinguished Teacher Award Committee, 1971-79. Murray Ramsay, Aug. 18, 1956. Heather, June 29, 1965, Jonathan, July 31, 1967. Episcopal. Matthews Rd., Swanzey Center.

Peter Evans Randall

Author, publisher, photographer. Newburyport, Mass., Nov. 12, 1940, Carlyle and Virginia (Chase) Randall. Amesbury (Mass.) High School, 1959, Univ. of N.H., B.A., 1964. Reporter, *Foster's Daily Democrat*, 1963, sports editor, *Manchester Free Press*, 1963-64, editor, *Hampton Union* , 1966-68, editorial assistant, *N.H. Profiles*, 1968-70, editor, 1971-76; owner, Peter E. Randall Publisher, 1976--, professional photographer, 1964--. Founder, board member, former president, Seacoast Anti-Pollution League, 1968-81, member, former chairman, Hampton Conservation Commission, 1970-74,79-85, director, vice president, N.H. Association of Conservation Commissions, 1980-84, director, Portsmouth Athenaeum, 1983--, library committee, Strawbery Banke, 1979--. Author of eight books, including *Mount Washington, A Short History and Guide* , 1974, publisher of more than 100 titles since 1976. Judith (Davis), Feb. 21, 1964. Deidre, Dec. 12, 1964, Davis, March 14, 1966, Katelyn, Oct. 12, 1970. Protestant. 36 Mace Rd., Hampton.

Peter Evans Randall

Thomas David Rath

Thomas David Rath

Attorney. East Orange, N.J., June 1, 1945, Harvey and Helen (Feeley) Rath. Old Saybrook (Conn.) High School, 1963, Dartmouth College, A.B., 1967, Georgetown Univ. Law Center, J.D., 1971. Law clerk, U.S. District Court, N.J., 1971-72, office of attorney general, N.H., criminal division, 1972-73, assistant attorney general, criminal division, 1973-76, deputy attorney general, 1976-78, attorney general, 1978-80; attorney, Concord, 1980--. Trustee, Concord Hospital, 1981--, Daniel Webster College, 1981--, chairman, 1982--; member, N.H. Crime Commission, 1978-83, chairman, 1979-83; treasurer, Republican State Committee, 1981--, vice chairman, Eastern Association of Attorneys General, 1979-80, member, N.H. Judicial Council, 1978-80, National Association of Attorneys General, 1978-80, director, Concord Chamber of Commerce, 1981--, member, Police Standards and Training Council, 1978-80, Judicial Planning Committee, 1979-80, national director, The Baker Committee, 1986--. Christine (Casey), Dec. 18, 1971. Timothy, Aug. 29, 1975, Erin, Aug. 29, 1975. Catholic. 120 Franklin St., Concord.

Carroll Purinton Reed

President, Carroll Reed Ski Shops, retired. West Roxbury, Mass., Oct. 9, 1905, Frank and Bertha (Fay) Reed. Mechanic Arts High School, Boston, 1924. President, Eastern Slope Ski School, 1936-38, president, Carroll Reed Ski Shops, 1936-69, president, Carroll County Hardware, 1944-69. Vice president, Conway Scenic Railroad, 1974--, director, Memorial Hospital, 1945-59, president, 1957-59; director, White Mountain National Bank, 1965-74, North Conway Chamber of Commerce, 1938-43, president, Eastern Slope Region, 1944-46, member, Mount Washington Valley Association, 1946-59, White Mountain Region, 1948-52, North Conway Rotary Club, 1950-76, president, 1959-60; honorary member, Mount Washington Valley Chamber of Commerce, 1979--. Katharine (Damon), Dec. 18, 1937. Carol, 1938 (dec. 1985), Damon, 1940, Stephanie, 1943. Episcopal. Kearsarge Rd., North Conway.

Carroll Purinton Reed

Donald Bruce Reed

Donald Bruce Reed

Former New Hampshire vice president, New England Telephone. Winthrop, Mass., June 19, 1944. Frank and Dorothy (Daly) Reed. Georgetown (Mass.) High School, 1962, Va. Military Institute, B.A., 1966. U.S. Army, 1967-69, capt. N.E. Telephone, supervisory assistant, manager, business officer, Providence, 1966-67, district manager, Bangor, 1973, financial planning supervisor, Portland, Boston, 1977, division manager, Northeast, 1979, vice president, N.H., 1983-86; vice president, federal relations, NYNEX Corp., Washington, D.C., 1986--. Chairman, N.H. Job Training Private Industry Council, 1983--, director, Business and Industry Association of N.H., 1983--, Blue Cross and Blue Shield, 1984--, Indian Head Banks Inc., 1984--, Federated Arts of Manchester, 1984--, Palace Theatre Trust, 1983--, N.H. Commission on the Arts, 1984--, board of governors, N.H. Public Television, 1985--, incorporator, N.H. Charitable Fund, 1984--, founder, director, N.H. Business Committee for the Arts, 1984--, chairman, Excellence in Education Project, 1985--. Karmyn, May 22, 1968. Corrine (Swett), Dec. 24, 1973. Kristyn, Nov. 9, 1976, Ryan, June 6, 1978. Catholic. 1828 L. St., N.W., Washington, D.C.

Dorothea Morrell Reed

Senior citizen advocate. Lakewood, N.J., April 22, 1905, Henry and Joanne (Wolters) Morrell. Assistant public relations director, Planned Parenthood Federation, N.Y.C., 1936-41, freelance public relations, 1941-48, public relations director, Pearl S. Buck East and West Association, 1948-53, public relations director, Caledonian Hospital, Brooklyn, 1953-55, co-founder, president, director, Community Council of Senior Citizens, Portsmouth, 1971-84, consultant to the board, 1984--. Advisory board, ombudsman, State Council on Aging, 1984-85, board member, Community Health Services, Portsmouth, 1979-85, member, City Charter Amendment Study Committee, Portsmouth, 1985, Portsmouth Hospital Foundation Advisory Committee on the Elderly, 1986--. Alfred Reed, Oct. 1, 1955 (dec. June, 1977). Baha'i. 15 Van Buren Ave., Portsmouth.

John Joseph Reilly Jr.

John Joseph Reilly Jr.

President, treasurer, John J. Reilly Inc. Manchester, N.H., Nov. 5, 1928, John and Marguerite (Farmer) Reilly. St. Joseph's High School, Manchester, 1946, Tilton School, 1949, Tufts Univ., B.S., 1955. U.S. Marine Corps, 1946-48,50-52, 1st lt. Treasurer, John J. Reilly Inc., electrical contractors and engineers, Manchester, 1956--, president, 1962--. President, Manchester Historical Association, 1974-77, director, Public Service Co. of N.H., 1980-84, founder, trustee, Derryfield School, 1964-69,76-85, trustee, St. Anselm College, 1977--, chairman, 1979--; incorporator, Catholic Medical Center, 1978--, chairman, Bedford Zoning Board of Appeals, 1980--, corporator, Merchants Savings Bank, 1965-83, president, 1971-73, chairman, 1973-83; director, chairman, Numerica Savings Bank, 1983--, director, chairman, Numerica Financial Corp., 1985--. One honorary degree. June (Bray), Sept. 11, 1951. Robin, Sept. 17, 1952, Cynthia, Nov. 17, 1953, Jennifer, Nov. 15, 1959, Allison, Nov. 9, 1965, Kimberly, Nov. 16, 1966, Peter, Sept. 26, 1969, Mark, June 8, 1971. Catholic. 22 Laurel Dr., Bedford.

Robert Henkle Reno

Attorney. Macomb, Ill., March 24, 1917, Jay and Gertrude (Henkle) Reno. Western Academy, Macomb, 1934, Dartmouth College, A.B., 1938, Yale Law School, LL.B., 1941. U.S. Marine Corps, 1944-46, capt. Special agent, Federal Bureau of Investigation, 1941-43, attorney, Concord, 1946--. Trustee, Merrimack County Savings Bank, 1964--, Concord Hospital, 1962-80, director, United Life and Accident Insurance Co., 1956--, Chubb LifeAmerica, 1982--, Chubb Corporation, 1981--, N.H. Charitable Fund, 1981--, Concord Chamber of Commerce, 1953-56, Concord Boys Club, 1960-72, N.H. Council on World Affairs, 1955--, Concord United Way, 1950-55, president, 1955; Concord School Board, 1957-62, president, 1961-62; Grenville Clark Fund, 1968--, Ballot Law Commission, 1951-59, chairman, 1954-59; N.H. Constitutional Convention, 1964,74, director, treasurer, president, Family Services of Concord, 1951-57, managing committee, World Law Fund, 1960-72. Marion (Stickney), April 30, 1949. Robert S., May 1, 1950, Rebecca, July 29, 1952, Richard, April 10, 1956. Episcopal. 12 Spaulding St., Concord.

Tudor Richards

Executive director, Audubon Society of New Hampshire, retired. Groton, Mass., Feb. 16, 1915, Henry and Julia (Coolidge) Richards. Groton School, 1934, Harvard Univ., A.B., 1938, Yale Univ., 1938-39, Univ. of Mich., B.S., 1941, master of wildlife management, 1952. U.S. Naval Reserve, 1941-45, lieut. Forester, U.S. Forest Service, 1946-47, game biologist, N.H. Fish and Game Department, 1948-51, faculty, St. Paul's School, 1952-54, county forester, Cheshire County, 1954-65, executive director, Beaver Brook Association, Hollis, 1965-68, executive director, Audubon Society of N.H., 1968-82, consultant, 1982-85. Trustee, Beaver Brook Association, 1967--, president, Audubon Society of N.H., 1953-68, council member, Nuttall Ornithological Club, Cambridge, 1965-70, former president, N.H. Academy of Science, advisor to the trustees, William P. Wharton Trust, Boston, 1976--. Barbara (Day), Aug. 10, 1949. Francis, Feb. 15, 1952, Victoria, Nov. 18, 1956, Robert, Nov. 7, 1960. Protestant. Henniker Rd., Hopkinton.

Placidus Harry Riley

Priest, professor, former president, Saint Anselm College. Concord, N.H., July 28, 1921, William and Eldya (Maclean) Riley. Saint John High School, Concord, 1938, Saint Anselm College, B.A., 1942, Univ. of Ottawa, S.T.L., 1949, S.T.D., 1953. Professed as a monk, Saint Anselm Abbey, July 2, 1943, ordained a Roman Catholic priest, Sept. 7, 1946. Saint Anselm College, assistant professor, 1949-52,53-56, assistant to the president, 1957, dean, 1958-64, president, 1964-72, dean, 1972-77, professor of theology, 1978-83,85--; treasurer, Woodside Priory School, Portola Valley, Calif., 1983-85. Trustee, Notre Dame College, 1974--, N.H. College, 1982--, Saint Anselm College, 1985--, member, N.H. Coordinating Board of Advanced Education and Accreditation, 1966-79, Commission on Institutions of Higher Education, N.E. Association of Schools and Colleges, 1972-78. Four honorary degrees. Catholic. Saint Anselm Abbey, Goffstown.

A. Roland Roberge

Commissioner, New Hampshire Banking Department. North Battleford, Saskatchewan, Canada, May 13, 1933, Albert and Marianna (Trottier) Roberge. Bishop Bradley High School, Manchester, 1953, St. Anselm College, B.A., 1957, Columbia Univ., M.S., 1959. Financial analyst trainee, institutional salesman, Merrill Lynch, New York City, 1959-66, instructor, N.H. College, 1966-68, officer, branch manager, Smith, Barney, Harris, Upham & Co., Manchester, 1968-74, instructor, Franklin Pierce College, 1974-76, coordinator of federal funds, N.H., 1976, commissioner, N.H. Banking Department, 1977--. Ex-officio director, N.H. Municipal Bond Bank, 1977-86, ex-officio chairman of the board, Trust Company Incorporation, 1977--, director, N.H. Insurance Board of Approval, 1977--, chairman, investment committee, N.H. Retirement System, 1977--, treasurer, Republican State Committee, 1973, Manchester chairman, N.H. Easter Seal Society, 1973, advisor, city of Manchester Pension Trust, 1975, board of advisors, Manchester Bank, 1972-76, director, Conference of State Bank Supervisors, 1986--, chairman, northeast, 1986--. Sheila (Skeffington), Sept. 7, 1957. Carolyn, Feb. 10, 1961, John, Aug. 5, 1966. Catholic. Olde Lantern Rd., Bedford.

A. Roland Roberge

George Bernard Roberts Jr.

George Bernard Roberts Jr.

Former speaker, New Hampshire House of Representatives, consultant. Andover, Mass., June 13, 1939, George and Helene (Eversen) Roberts. Laconia High School, 1957, Univ. of N.H., B.S., 1964, M.P.A., 1967. U.S. Coast Guard, 1957-58, petty officer, 2nd cl. Partner, Roberts Associates, real estate, 1963--, lobbyist, consultant, Concord, 1981--. N.H. House of Rep., 1967-80, speaker, 1975-80, president, National Conference of State Legislatures, 1980-81, founding member, National Republican Legislators Association, president, 1979; director, Lakes Region Clean Waters Association, 1967-81, Lakes Region Mental Health Clinic, 1967-78, N.E. Legislative Leaders Caucus, 1971-81, member, Centralized Data Processing Commission, 1970-73, town, school moderator, Gilmanton, 1973--, N.H. Constitutional Convention, 1974,84, president, Gilmanton Historical Society, 1978-79, president, Concord Coach Society, 1985--. Margaret (Edmunds), Aug. 26, 1967. Abigail, Dec. 30, 1975, Jessica, Nov. 28, 1977. Congregational. Meeting House Rd., Gilmanton.

Sam Rosen

Professor emeritus of economics, University of New Hampshire. Baltimore, Md., April 1, 1920, Louis and Belle (Kurtz) Rosen. Baltimore City College High School, 1936, Univ. of Wis., A.B., 1942, Harvard Univ., M.A., 1948, Ph.D., 1952. U.S. Navy, 1942-45, lt. sg. Assistant professor of economics, Univ. of Wyo., 1949-51, Univ. of Del., 1952-57, associate professor of economics, Univ. of N.H., 1957-63, professor, 1963-74, Nashua Corp. Professor of Economics, 1974-85, professor emeritus, 1985--. Member, American Economic Association, International Association for Research in Income and Wealth, American Finance Association, American Association of Univ. Professors, president, Univ. of N.H., chapter, 1962-63,72-73. Author, *National Income*, 1963, *National Income and Other Social Accounts*, 1972. Mary (Berman), March 5, 1943. Michael, March 8, 1948, Laura, Oct. 22, 1950, Jonathan, June 7, 1954. Jewish. 17 Oyster River Rd., Durham.

William Boylston Rotch

William Boylston Rotch

Publisher, *Milford Cabinet and Wilton Journal*. Milford, N.H., March 28, 1916, Arthur and Serena (Elliman) Rotch. Milford High School, 1933, Dartmouth College, B.A., 1937. U.S. Naval Reserve, 1944-46, lt. jg. Secretary, Eastern Slope Ski Club, North Conway, 1937-38, editor, *Milford Cabinet*, 1938-42, state information executive, Office of Price Administration, 1942-44, *Milford Cabinet and Wilton Journal*, 1946--, editor, editorial page editor, publisher. Director, Souhegan National Bank, 1955--, former president, N.H. Press Association, N.E. Press Association, Milford Rotary Club. Martha (McLane), Sept. 7, 1940. Peter, June 6, 1941, Martha, Dec. 12, 1942, Elizabeth, Nov. 4, 1946, Malcolm, June 11, 1950 (dec. June 12, 1966), John, June 26, 1955. Mont Vernon St., Milford.

Bruce Colby Rounds

State representative. Hill, N.H., June 29, 1928, Floyd and Pauline (Colby) Rounds. Franklin High School, 1946, Univ. of N.H., 1949-50. U.S. Army, 1946-49, sgt. Operations officer, Central Intelligence Agency, 1950-75. President, BCR Associates, 1975--, director, Charles A. Carr Co., 1977-84, N.H. House of Rep., 1976-, director, Franklin Regional Hospital, 1979-83, Newfound Area Nursing Association, 1982--, Upper Valley Senior Citizens Council, 1976--, member, Rotary, American Legion. Mary Therese (Gillgannon), May 8, 1952 (dec. Jan. 13, 1979). Judith, April 6, 1953, Michael, April 25, 1955, Therese, Feb. 4, 1957, Timothy, Jan. 20, 1958. Protestant. 41 South Main St., Bristol.

Bruce Colby Rounds

Warren Bruce Rudman

Warren Bruce Rudman

United States senator. Boston, Mass., May 18, 1930, Edward and Theresa (Levenson) Rudman. Valley Forge Military Academy, Wayne, Pa., 1948, Syracuse Univ., B.S., 1952, Boston College Law School, LL.B., 1960. U.S. Army, 1952-54, capt. Attorney, Nashua, 1960-69, counsel, Gov. Walter Peterson, 1969-70, attorney general, N.H., 1970-76, attorney, Manchester, 1976-80, U.S. Senate, 1980--. Founder, board chairman, Daniel Webster College and N.E. Aeronautical Institute, 1965-81, president, National Association of Attorneys General, 1975, chairman, Citizens Alliance Against Casinos, 1977, member, Ballot Law Commission, 1970-76, senior advisory committee, John F. Kennedy School of Government, Harvard Univ. Five honorary degrees. Shirley (Wahl), July 9, 1952. Laura, Alan, Debra. Jewish. 41 Indian Rock Rd., Nashua.

Thomas Walker Rush

Musician. Portsmouth, N.H., Feb. 8, 1941, Richard and Mary (Conover) Rush. Groton (Mass.) School, 1959, Harvard Univ., B.A., 1963. Performer, 1960--, founder, Night Light Recordings, record label, 1982--, founder, Maple Hill Productions, artist management and media production company, 1984--. Deering Planning Board, 1985--, member, Harvard Faculty Club, Harvard Club of N.Y. Beverly (Mundy), Oct. 4, 1974. Benjamin, June 20, 1975, Richard, March 9, 1983. Christian. Box 16, Hillsboro.

Thomas Walker Rush

Susan Ellen Salls

Comptroller, Energy Publications. Rutland, Vt., Nov. 19, 1946, Allie and Margaret (Foley) Salls. Mary A. Burnham School, Northampton, Mass., 1964, State Univ. of N.Y., Potsdam, B.A., 1969. Teacher, Laconia, 1969-71, office manager, *N.H. Times and Flea Market*, 1971-73, publisher, *N.H. Times*, 1973-81, comptroller, Energy Publications, 1981--. Director, *N.H. Times* 1974-81, Energy Publications, 1981--. Kenneth Daggett, June 16, 1979. Danielle, Feb. 19, 1980, Alexander, April 14, 1982. Episcopal. Beacon Hill Dr., Gilford.

Royden Coe Sanders Jr.

Founder, Sanders Associates. Camden, N.J., Aug. 27, 1917, Royden and Fannie (Harris) Sanders. Audubon (N.J.) High School, 1934, Rensselaer Polytechnic Institute, 1934-37. Engineer, RCA Laboratories, 1938-45, division manager, missile and radar division, Raytheon, 1945-51, founder, chief executive officer, Sanders Associates, 1951-75, founder, chief executive officer, Sanders Technology, 1975-82, owner, SDI, Wilton, 1982--. Director, Sanders Associates, 1951-75, Sanders Technology, 1975-82, Superior Electric, 1970-79, trustee, Memorial Hospital, 1956-65, Monadnock Community Hospital, 1983--, chairman, Citizens Task Force, 1969-70. Three honorary degrees. Betty (Petersen), Aug. 4, 1939 (div. 1975). Barbara, June 9, 1941, John, Oct. 10, 1943, Dorothy, Nov. 3, 1944, William, July 23, 1946. Janice (Ferguson), Nov. 27, 1976. Wade, May 7, 1979, Jillian, May 20, 1982. Protestant. Burton Highway, RR 2, Wilton.

Royden Coe Sanders Jr.

Wilfred Leroy Sanders Jr.

Wilfred Leroy Sanders Jr.

Attorney. Marlboro, Mass., Nov. 20, 1935, Wilfred and Rose (Harpin) Sanders. Shrewsbury (Mass.) High School, 1953, Univ. of N.H., B.A., 1959, Boston College Law School, J.D., 1962. Attorney, Hampton, 1962--. Lecturer, Univ. of N.H., 1968--, trustee, legal advisor, Univ. System of N.H., 1979--, director, chairman, Seabrook Bank and Trust Co., 1974--, president, 1974-75; owner, Hampton Mall Shopping Center, 1979--, director, Odyssey House, 1970-75, chairman, Hampton Industrial Development Committee, 1971-75, president, Seacoast Region Child and Family Services, 1970-72, trustee, U.S. Skiing Foundation, 1984--, N.H. Constitutional Convention, 1964,74. Mary Jo (Price), Aug. 22, 1959. Elizabeth, Nov. 2, 1965, Jonathan, March 14, 1967, Steven, Dec. 3, 1969. Catholic. 21 Exeter Rd., Hampton.

Eugene Arnold Savage

Vice chancellor for university system relations, University System of New Hampshire. Stratford, N.H., Aug. 29, 1934, Raymond and Harriet (Kennedy) Savage. Stratford High School, 1952, Plymouth State College, B.Ed., 1958, Boston Univ., M.Ed., 1963. U.S. Navy, 1952-54, seaman 1st cl. Teacher, coach, guidance director, acting principal, high schools in N.H. and Vt., 1958-67, Univ. of N.H., associate director of admissions, 1967-68, director of admissions, 1968-78, dean of admissions, 1978-80, vice president for university relations, 1980-81, vice chancellor for university system relations, Univ. System of N.H., 1981--. Trustee, Berwick Academy, 1982--, advisory council, regional student program, N.E. Board of Higher Education, 1978--, president, N.H. Admissions Consortium, 1974-75, president, N.E. Association of College Registrars and Admissions Officers, 1973, Oyster River School Board, 1972-73, incorporator, Wentworth-Douglass Hospital, Dover, 1983--, trustee, The College Board, 1977-81. Joan (Doyon), June 21, 1957. Suzanne, Aug. 23, 1958, Deborah, June 13, 1964, Kathleen, June 11, 1968. Catholic. 14 Garden Ln., Durham.

Eugene Arnold Savage

W. Douglas Scamman Jr.

State representative. Concord, N.H., Nov. 26, 1941, W. Douglas and Frances (Gile) Scamman. Exeter High School, 1959, Univ. of N.H., B.A., 1964. Owner, operator, dairy farm, Stratham, 1964--. School auditor, Stratham, 1964-65, town auditor, 1964-66, Stratham School Board, 1966-72, Stratham Budget Committee, 1969,70,72, N.H. House of Rep., 1969--, director, Easter Seals Society, 1984--, advisory board, Vocational-Technical College, Stratham, 1979--, member, Univ. of N.H. Alumni Association. Stella (Emanuel), April 13, 1963. Karl, June 13, 1964, Kirk, June 13, 1964, Kimberly, July 11, 1969, Bruce, Dec. 11, 1972. Protestant. Bittersweet Farm, Stratham.

Herbert Schneider

President, general manager, Herbert Schneider Corp. St. Anton am Arlberg, Tirol, Austria, May 20, 1920, Hannes and Ludwina (Seeberger) Schneider. L'Ecole Superior de Commerce, Neuchatel, Switz., 1938. U.S. Army, 1943-46, pfc. Certified ski instructor, 1940, examiner of certification, 1952, director, Hannes Schneider Ski School, Mt. Cranmore, 1955, president, general manager, Herbert Schneider Corp., 1963-84. Founder, Mt. Cranmore Ski Educational Foundation, director, Professional Ski Instructors Association, 1963-72, Eastern Slope Ski Club, 1947-62, Carroll County Trust Co. (now Indian Head Bank North), 1963--, secretary, treasurer, vice president, president, White Mountains Recreation Association, 1963-72, founder, director, Mount Washington Valley Association (now Mount Washington Valley Chamber of Commerce), 1960-85. Author, *Let's Go Skiing*, 1967. Doris (Beaudet), Feb. 8, 1966. Hannes, May 26, 1967, Christoph, Aug. 18, 1968. Catholic. Grove St., North Conway.

Herbert Schneider

Andrea Abbott Scranton

Andrea Abbott Scranton

State representative. Cambridge, Mass., Nov. 7, 1919, William and Andrea (Mahan) Abbott. Walnut Hill School, Natick, Mass., 1937, Smith College, B.A., 1941. U.S. Coast Guard Women's Reserve, 1943-46, lt. jg. Teacher, physical education, Pembroke College, Brown Univ., 1946-48, chairman, department of physical education, Walnut Hill School, 1948-49. N.H. House of Rep., 1973--, Keene Board of Education, 1970-73, arts, tourism and cultural resources committee, National Council of State Legislatures, 1983--, director, N.H. Council for Better Schools, 1975-80, incorporator, Cheshire Hospital, 1977--, director, Monadnock Family and Mental Health Service, 1982--, vice chairman, Swift Water Girl Scout Council, 1957-65. William Scranton, Sept. 24, 1949. John, Jan. 4, 1954, Nancy, Jan. 4, 1954, James, April 10, 1956, Sarah, Feb. 4, 1957. Episcopal. Box 288, RFD 2, Hurricane Rd., Keene.

William Maxwell Scranton

General management consultant. Scranton, Pa., March 1, 1921, William H. and Dorothy (Bessell) Scranton. Central High School, Scranton, 1938, Princeton Univ., B.S., 1942, Harvard Univ., M.B.A., 1948. U.S. Air Force, 1947-48, pvt. Pratt & Whitney Aircraft, East Hartford, Conn., 1942-46,48-50, MPB Corp., Keene, 1950-77, executive vice president, 1953-62, president, 1962-77; president, Beede Electrical Instrument Co., Penacook, 1977-82, general management consultant, 1983--, senior vice president, First Financial Management Corp., Boston, 1983--. Director, MPB Corp., 1959-76, Indian Head National Bank, Keene, 1966--, IPC Limited Partnership, 1967--, Public Service Co. of N.H., 1971--, O.K. Tool Co., 1977--, EMF Inc., 1984--, N.H. Business Development Corp., 1982, vice president, 1984--; trustee, executive committee, N.H. Historical Society, 1983--, Keene Planning Board, 1984--, director, Beede Electrical Instrument Co., 1977-82. Andrea (Abbott), Sept. 24, 1949. (Ch. see Andrea Scranton.) Episcopal. Box 288, RFD 2, Hurricane Rd., Keene.

William Maxwell Scranton

Barbara Jane Seelye

Barbara Jane Seelye

Former president, Keene State College. Manito, Ill., Nov. 29, 1930, John and Mayme (Dwyer) Seelye. Manito High School, 1948, Eureka College, B.S., 1952, Univ. of Denver, M.A., 1955, Ph.D., 1967. Teacher, 1952-55, instructor, Wash. Univ. School of Medicine, St. Louis, 1957-59, instructor, assistant, associate professor of speech, St. Louis Univ., 1959-68, associate professor, chair, department of communication disorders, 1968-72, professor, 1972-73; fellowship, American Council on Education, 1973-74, dean, College of Professional Studies, professor, Northern Ill. Univ., 1974-80, president, Keene State College, 1980-86. Board of advisors, Colony House Museum, 1981--, incorporator, Harrisville Center for Conservation, 1981--, purposes and policies committee, American Association of State Colleges and Universities, 1984--, Postsecondary Education Commission, 1980--, trustee, Univ. System of N.H., 1980--, executive committee, Keene Endowment Association, 1980--, incorporator, Cheshire County Savings Bank, 1981--, president's commission, chair, division II, NCAA, 1984--. 251 Main St., Keene.

Cynthia Jeanne Shaheen

Campaign director. St. Charles, Mo., Jan. 28, 1947, Ivan and Belle (Stillings) Bowers. Selinsgrove (Pa.) High School, 1965, Shippensburg Univ., B.A., 1969, Univ. of Miss., M.S.S., 1973. High school teacher, 1969-71, administrative assistant, University Senate, Univ. of N.H., 1973-74, manager, owner, seasonal retail business, 1973-76, state coordinator, N.H. primary, President Jimmy Carter, 1979-80, co-director, Somersworth International Children's Festival, 1981-82, program coordinator, Univ. of N.H. Parents Association, 1982--, campaign director, N.H. primary, Sen. Gary Hart, 1983-84. Vice chairman, N.H. Commission on the Status of Women, 1980-83, vice chairman, N.H. Women's Lobby, 1982-83, Madbury Zoning Board, 1983--, N.H. Civil Liberties Union Foundation Board of Trustees, 1981--. William Shaheen, Oct. 15, 1969. Stefany, Sept. 1, 1974, Stacey, Jan. 16, 1978, Molly, Dec. 19, 1985. Protestant. Perkins Rd., Madbury.

William Henry Shaheen

William Henry Shaheen

Attorney, judge. Dover, N.H., Dec. 30, 1943, William N. and Josephine (Skiep) Shaheen. Dover High School, 1961, Univ. of N.H. B.A., 1965, Univ. of Miss., J.D., 1973. U.S. Army, 1965-69, capt. Attorney, Dover, 1973-77, city attorney, Somersworth, 1974-77, U.S. attorney, District of N.H., 1977-81, attorney, Dover, 1981--, justice, Durham District Court, 1981--. First Circuit Judicial Nominating Committee, 1977, state chairman, N.H. Heart Fund, 1978-79, director, 1979-80. Cynthia Jeanne (Bowers), Oct. 15, 1969. Stefany, Sept. 1, 1974, Stacey, Jan. 16, 1978, Molly, Dec. 19, 1985. Catholic. Perkins Rd., Madbury.

Robert Arthur Shaines

Attorney. Newburyport, Mass., Nov. 24, 1929, Edward and Ruth (Diamond) Shaines. Portsmouth High School, 1947, Univ. of N.H., 1947-49, Boston Univ. School of Law., LL.B., 1952. U.S. Air Force, 1952-53, 1st lt. Attorney, Portsmouth, 1954--. Member, national panel of arbitrators, American Arbitration Association, 1965--, chairman, N.H. State Board of Conciliation and Arbitration, 1957-80, president, Portsmouth Bar Association, 1963, Rockingham County Bar Association, 1972, Portsmouth City Council, 1958-62,64-66, mayor, Portsmouth, 1960-62, Portsmouth Police Commission, 1980-81, president, Strawbery Banke, 1977-80, Portsmouth Planning Board, 1958-59, secretary, N.H. Bar Association, 1974-78. Gladys (Berger), Dec. 5, 1954 (div. 1984). Stephanie, March 9, 1961, Pamela, March 4, 1965, Kate, March 4, 1966. Denise (Kelly), Dec. 30, 1984. Jewish. Garland Rd., Rye.

Robert Arthur Shaines

Edward Mark Shapiro

Edward Mark Shapiro

President, New Hampshire College. Manchester, N.H., Nov. 25, 1933, Harry and Gertrude (Crockett) Shapiro. Manchester Central High School, 1951, Univ. of N.H., B.S., 1955, Boston Univ., 1958-59. U.S. Army, 1955-57, sgt. maj. N.H. College, director of admissions, 1957-62, vice president, 1962-69, executive vice president, 1969-71, president, 1971--. Director, N.H. Performing Arts Center, 1975-77, president, N.E. Business College Association, 1969-71, member, United Business School Association, 1969-71, commissioner, Association of Independent Colleges and Schools, 1974--, chairman, 1984--; vice president, Business Education Research of America, 1975, president, 1976-77; Postsecondary Education Commission, 1976--, president, N.H. College and Univ. Council, 1981--, trustee, Elliot Hospital, 1982--, director, Public Service Co. of N.H., 1983--. One honorary degree. Judith (Cohen), July 5, 1959. Harry, July 10, 1962, Elizabeth, Sept. 1, 1965, Sharon, April 5, 1967. Jewish. 276 North Bay St., Manchester.

Milton Shapiro

Real estate developer. Nashua, N.H., Sept. 9, 1902, Harry and Hattie (Simon) Shapiro. Concord High School, 1920, Univ. of N.H., 1920-21. Basement manager, The Boston Store, department store, Concord, 1921-23, treasurer, 1924-41; president, Harry Shapiro and Sons, real estate developers, 1941--. Member, N.H. Water Resources Board, 1938-44, chairman, advisory commission, Department of Resources and Economic Development Authority, 1963-84, chairman emeritus, 1984--; president, Temple Beth Jacob, 1943-49. One honorary degree. Blanche (Sherman), Dec. 31, 1934. R. Peter, March 13, 1937. Jewish. 207 Mountain Rd., Concord.

Milton Shapiro

Robert Francis Shaw

Robert Francis Shaw

Mayor of Manchester. Portland, Maine, May 29, 1934, Elmer and Dorothy (McDonough) Shaw. Deering High School, Portland, 1952. U.S. Army, 1953-57, pvt. 1st cl. Assistant manager, F.W. Woolworth, Brunswick, Maine, 1952-53, repaired and installed x-ray and dental equipment, Russell Alternberg Co., Portland, 1956-60, Smith-Holden Co., Manchester, 1960-63; owner, Shaw's Mobil Station, Manchester, 1963--, mayor, Manchester, 1984--. Chairman, Manchester Crimeline, 1983-84, former president, N.H.-Vt. Gasoline Retail Association, vice president, Greater Manchester Chamber of Commerce, 1976-78, board member, United Way of Manchester, 1976-77, corporator, Amoskeag Savings Bank, 1970-83. Lorraine (Moreau), Aug. 12, 1954. Robert E., May 31, 1955, Diane, Sept. 13, 1956, Linda Ann, Feb. 1, 1958, Donald, Aug. 12, 1968. Catholic. 117 Webster St., Manchester.

John Joseph Sheehan

Attorney. Manchester, N.H., April 28, 1899, Daniel and Mary (Sullivan) Sheehan. U.S. Army Air Force, 1942-45, maj. Attorney, Manchester, 1923--. N.H. House of Rep., 1925-29, N.H. Senate, 1931-33, county attorney, Hillsborough County, 1933-37, U.S. attorney, District of N.H., 1949-53, N.H. Constitutional Convention, 1930,38,41,48,56,64, trustee, Carpenter Memorial City Library, 1947--, chairman, 1965--; Shaker Village, 1969--, president, N.H. Bar Association, 1966-67, Manchester Bar Association, 1940-41, member, American Bar Association. Ellinor (Nielsen), Jan. 8, 1943. Karen, Susan, Mary. Catholic. 525 Concord St., Manchester.

Mary Shaw Shirley

Mary Shaw Shirley

Trustee emerita, Currier Gallery of Art. Braintree, Mass., Oct. 7, 1909, Winfield and Lois (Warren) Shaw. Manchester Central High School, 1928, Vassar College, B.A., 1932. Trustee, Currier Gallery of Art, Manchester, 1961-84, vice president, 1979-84, trustee emerita, 1984--; fund chairman, Vassar College '32, 1967-72, director, Women's Aid Home, Manchester, 1956--, president, 1971--; member, The National Society of the Colonial Dames of America, N.H., 1956--, president, 1983-85; director, Manchester YWCA, 1952-66, president, 1963-64, trustee, 1978-82; corporator, Shaker Village, 1985--, chairman, heritage committee, Goffstown Bicentennial, 1976-83. Lawrence Shirley, June 17, 1933. Mary, Feb. 12, 1936, Constance, May 22, 1937 (dec. May 10, 1981), James, May 26, 1942. Protestant. RFD 5, Shirley Hill Rd., Goffstown.

Allan Bruce Silber

Business consultant, real estate broker. Nashua, N.H., Sept. 12, 1943, Max and Edith (Kamenske) Silber. Nashua High School, 1961, Colo. School of Mines, 1961-63, Boston Univ., B.S., 1966. Production manager, spectrochemist, N. Kamenske and Co., 1966-72, vice president, 1974--; vice president, treasurer, Hot Tops Inc., 1983--, vice president, Double-Oh-Seven Ltd., 1978--, owner, On-The-Move, real estate referral agency, 1979--, owner, Silber and Associates, business consultants, 1984--. Director, Association of Brass and Bronze Ingot Manufacturers, 1976--, vice president, 1984--; N.H. Association of Commerce and Industry, 1976-85, vice chairman, 1982-85; Chamber of Commerce, 1978-82, president, 1980-81; member, Nashua Park and Recreation Commission, 1968-72, chairman, 1970-71; alderman, Nashua, 1972-76, chairman, Nashua Growth Study Commission, 1978-79, chairman, Nashua Long Range Planning Committee, 1984-85, director, incorporator, Boys Club of Nashua, 1972-80, regional board of directors, BankEast, Nashua, 1981--. Dorothy (Andler), Dec. 20, 1964. Shari, Jan. 28, 1967, Kenneth, Sept. 4, 1968, Andrew, Sept. 27, 1970. Jewish. 19 Fairhaven Rd., Nashua.

Allan Bruce Silber

Arthur Joseph Singer

Arthur Joseph Singer

General manager, New Hampshire Public Television. Boston, Mass., March 24, 1939, Samuel and Gertrude (Weiner) Singer. Roxbury (Mass.) Memorial High School, 1956, Boston Univ., B.S., 1960, M.S., 1961. Copywriter, Allied Advertising Agency, Boston, 1961-62, producer-director, Connecticut Public TV, Hartford, 1962-63, director, alumni affairs, Boston Univ. College of Communications, 1963-67, director of development, WETA-TV, Washington, D.C., 1967-69, chief executive officer, Arthur J. Singer Associates, Boston, 1969-72, director of development and public information, WMHT-TV-FM, Schenectady, N.Y., 1972-81, consultant, Corporation for Public Broadcasting, 1978--, general manager, N.H. Public Television, 1981--. Trustee, Eastern Educational Television Network, 1981--, director, Theatre by the Sea, 1982--. Donna (Levin). Michael, Marjorie. 46 Woodridge Rd., Durham.

James Barker Smith

Owner, Wentworth by the Sea, retired. Pittsburg, Kans., June 4, 1908, Victor and Mary Louise (Barker) Smith. South Denver (Colo.) High School, 1926, Univ. of Colo., 1926-27, Cornell Univ., B.S., 1931. U.S. Army Air Force, 1941-45, maj. Manager, Broadmoor Hotel, Colorado Springs, 1934-39, senior manager, Plaza Hotel, Houston, 1939-41, owner, Wentworth by the Sea, 1946-81. Vice president, Seacoast Recreation, 1981--, vice president, Flamingo Hotel, Miami Beach, 1948-54, president, N.H. Hotel Association, 1949-50, president, Portsmouth Chamber of Commerce, 1955-57, president, N.E. Innkeepers, 1966, board member, Salvation Army, Seacoast Family Y, Portsmouth Tourism Council, N.H. Hospitality Association, N.E. Innkeepers. Margaret (Tasher), Oct. 5, 1934. James II, Nov. 5, 1943. Episcopal. 2 Wentworth Rd., Rye.

James Barker Smith

Margaret Tasher Smith

Margaret Tasher Smith

Vice president, Wentworth by the Sea, retired. Denver, Colo., Oct. 16, 1907, Clarence and Louise (Neil) Tasher. East Denver High School, 1925, Univ. of Colo., B.S., 1929. General manager, Plaza Hotel, Houston, 1942-46, vice president, treasurer, Wentworth by the Sea, 1946-80. President, Wentworth Fairways, 1950-80, board chairman, Seacoast Recreation Inc., 1980--, president, Texas Hotelman's Association, 1943-44, board member, YWCA, Portsmouth, 1948-78, president, Seacoast Family Y, 1984--, co-founder, Guild of Strawbery Banke, 1960, overseer, Strawbery Banke, 1960--, director, Greater Portsmouth Community Fund, 1982--, president, Seacoast Community Concert Association, 1965, incorporator, Portsmouth Hospital, 1979. James Barker Smith, Oct. 5, 1934. James II, Nov. 5, 1943. Episcopal. 2 Wentworth Rd., Rye.

Philip Alan Smith

Episcopal bishop of New Hampshire. Cambridge, Mass., April 2, 1920, Herbert and Elizabeth (MacDonald) Smith. Belmont (Mass.) High School, 1938, Harvard Univ., B.A., 1942, Va. Theological Seminary, M.Div., 1949, St. Augustine's College, Canterbury, Eng., 1957-58. Ordained, Episcopal priest, Dec. 1949. U.S. Army Air Force, 1942-46, capt. Assistant rector, All Saints Church, Atlanta, 1949-52, rector, Christ Church, Exeter, 1952-59, faculty, Va. Theological Seminary, assistant professor, chaplain, associate dean for student affairs, 1959-70, suffragan bishop, Diocese of Va., 1970-73, bishop, Diocese of N.H., 1973-87. Executive council, Episcopal Church, 1974-82, board member, Presiding Bishops Fund for World Relief, 1976-82, Board of Theological Education, 1980--, Evangelical Education Society, 1982--, president, Exeter Community Services Association, 1957, board president, White Mountain School, 1973--, Holderness School, 1973--. One honorary degree. Barbara Ann (Taylor), June 19, 1949. Sarah, Sept. 13, 1951, Ann, March 30, 1954, Jeremy, May 13, 1957. 122 School St., Concord.

Philip Alan Smith

Robert Clinton Smith

Robert Clinton Smith

United States congressman. Trenton, N.J., March 30, 1941, Donald and Margaret (Eldridge) Smith. Hamilton High East, Trenton, 1959, Rutgers Univ., 1959-60, Trenton Junior College, A.A., 1963, Lafayette College, B.A., 1965, Calif. State College at Long Beach, 1967-68. U.S. Navy, 1965-67, E-4. Teacher, Kingswood Regional High School, Wolfeboro, 1970-73, owner, manager, Yankee Pedlar Realtors, Wolfeboro, 1975-85, U.S. Congress, First District, 1985--. Governor Wentworth Regional School Board, 1978-84, chairman, 1979,81-82; member, N.H. Association of Realtors, National Association of Realtors, 1978-85, member, ethics committee, Lakes Region Board of Realtors, 1979-83, Wolfeboro Zoning Board, 1972-74, National Rifle Association, 1983--. Mary Jo (Hutchinson), July 2, 1966. Jennifer, Nov. 29, 1974, Bobby, Oct. 19, 1979, Jason, Aug. 29, 1982. Congregational. Box 658, Wolfeboro.

Bernard Irwin Snierson

Attorney, judge, retired. Laconia, N.H., Feb. 7, 1913, David and Yetta (Trachtenburg) Snierson. Laconia High School, 1930, Cornell Univ., 1931-33, Univ. of N.H., A.B., 1935, Harvard Law School, J.D., 1938. U.S. Army Air Force, 1942-46, capt. Attorney, Laconia, 1938-85. Justice, Laconia District Court, 1956-79, special master, N.H. Superior Courts, 1979-84, chairman, administrative committee, N.H. District and Municipal Courts, 1964-71, trustee, Univ. System of N.H., 1963-75, vice chairman, 1975; director, vice president, secretary, Keewaydin Shores Inc., judge advocate, American Legion. Richard, Sept. 4, 1944. Muriel (Goldberg), Aug. 6, 1950. Lynne, Feb. 28, 1952. Jewish. 5361 Stonybrook Dr., Boynton Beach, Fla.

Bernard Irwin Snierson

Ronald Louis Snow

Ronald Louis Snow

Attorney. Franklin, N.H., Aug. 3, 1935, Louis and Evangeline (Pinard) Snow. Laconia High School, 1954, Dartmouth College, B.A., 1958, Yale Univ. Law School, LL.D., 1961. Attorney, Concord, 1961--. Chairman, committee on drug abuse, N.H. Bar Association, 1972, fellow, American College of Trial Lawyers, 1982--, chairman, committee on public defender expansion to Rockingham County, N.H. Bar Association, 1975, member, Governor's Commission on Laws Affecting Children, 1970-72, chairman, Ballot Law Commission, 1972-76,77-81, member, Governor's Commission for Study of Halfway House Regulations, 1969, president, Concord YMCA, 1974-76, member, Concord Board of Family Service, 1965-74. Mary Ellen (Holopainen), July 8, 1960. Mark, Dec. 5, 1961, Lisa, June 5, 1963, Ronald Jr., April 25, 1965. Catholic. 87 Mountain Rd., Concord.

Martha Stern Solow

Executive director, Healthcare Utilization Board. Boston, Mass., July 20, 1933, I. Henry and Janet (Frank) Stern. Brookline (Mass.) High School, 1950, Wellesley College, B.A., 1954. Executive director, Common Cause N.H./Vt., 1980-82, Common Cause/Vt., 1982-85, executive director, Healthcare Utilization Board, 1985--. Adjunct instructor in community and family medicine, Dartmouth Medical School, 1986--, trustee, Granite State Public Radio, 1980-81, Howe Library, 1975-81, member, Mary Hitchcock Memorial Hospital Corp., 1979--, director, N.H. Environmental Coalition, 1979-82, Upper Valley Sierra Club, 1978-84, N.H. League of Women Voters, 1977-82, Hanover Conservation Council, 1978--, selectman, Hanover, 1975-81, N.H. Constitutional Convention, 1984, Hanover Conservation Commission, 1985--, Hanover Planning Board, 1975-81, Hanover Health Council, 1975-78, Citizens Advisory Committee for Lebanon Airport, 1981--, charter officer, director, Women's Network of the Upper Valley, 1980--. Charles Solow, June 12, 1955. Barbara, Nov. 28, 1958, Marjorie, April, 26, 1960, Nancy, March 1, 1964. 11 Rayton Rd., Hanover.

Martha Stern Solow

David Hackett Souter

Associate justice, New Hampshire Supreme Court. Melrose, Mass., Sept. 17, 1939, Joseph and Helen (Hackett) Souter. Concord High School, 1957, Harvard Univ., B.A., 1961, Rhodes scholar, Oxford Univ., 1961-63, Harvard Law School, LL.B., 1966. Attorney, Concord, 1966-68, assistant attorney general, N.H., 1968-71, deputy attorney general, 1971-76, attorney general, 1976-78; associate justice, N.H. Superior Court, 1978-83, associate justice, N.H. Supreme Court, 1983--. Trustee, Concord Hospital, 1973-85, president, 1978-84; N.H. Historical Society, 1976-85, vice president, 1980-85; overseer, Dartmouth Medical School, 1981--. Episcopal. Weare.

Harry Vaios Spanos

Attorney, judge. Newport, N.H., May 8, 1926, Vaios and Mary (Stassos) Spanos. Towle High School, Newport, 1944, Harvard Univ., B.A., 1948, LL.B., 1951. Attorney, Newport, 1952--, associate justice, Newport District Court, 1968-72, judge of probate, Sullivan County, 1980--. N.H. House of Rep., 1963-67,78-80, N.H. Senate, 1967-75, town counsel, Newport, 1954-60,72--, moderator, Newport, 1960-76,78--, moderator, Newport School District, 1973--, member, Newport Planning Board, 1955-58, N.H. Constitutional Convention, 1964, president, Newport Chamber of Commerce, 1953, trustee, Sugar River Savings Bank, 1971--, Newport Hospital, 1970-71, Richards Free Library, 1969-79, member, National Probate Judges Association, 1980--, N.H. Bar Association, 1951--, Sullivan County Bar Association, 1952--. Eve (Whittaker), Aug. 1, 1945. William, July 11, 1946, Timothy, Nov. 26, 1959, Peter, June 28, 1965. Greek Orthodox. 1 Hatch Ave., Newport.

Christos Costa Spirou

Christos Costa Spirou

Former state representative. Porti, Thessalias, Greece, Sept. 14, 1942, Constantine and Aphrodite (Plentzas) Spirou. Manchester Central High School, St. Anselm College, Goddard Graduate School for Urban Studies and Social Change, Cambridge, Mass., M.A., 1972. Shoe factory worker, labor organizer, 1958-67, president, chairman, Northeast Model Cities Citizens Union, 1968-71, neighborhood representative, Manchester Model Cities Program, 1968-71, chairman, Career Opportunities Advisory Council, Manchester school system, 1970, chairman, Manchester Neighborhood Information and Referral Office, 1970, alderman, Manchester, 1972-76, N.H. House of Rep., 1971-84, president, Chris Spirou Consultants, 1975--, member, Manchester Highway Commission, 1976-86, chairman, 1979-80; president, partner, Alpha Travel Agency, 1978-84. Director, N.H. Social Welfare Council, 1972-74, Community Action Program, Manchester, 1969-71, member, Mid-Merrimack Health Planning Council, 1971-76. Marika (Rammeas), Sept. 16, 1962. Aphrodite, Jan. 22, 1964, Stavroula, Nov. 25, 1966. Greek Orthodox. 129 Spruce St., Manchester.

James Wood Squires

Surgeon. New London, N.H., Sept. 14, 1937, James Duane and Catherine (Tuttle) Squires. New London High School, 1955, U.S. Naval Academy, 1955-57, Williams College, B.A., 1959, McGill Univ. Medical School, M.D., 1963. U.S. Air Force, 1964-66, capt. Founder, Medical Services Research Foundation, 1968-71, Matthew Thornton Health Plan, staff surgeon, 1971--, medical director, 1971-75, general director, 1975--. Associate clinical professor of surgery, Tufts Univ. School of Medicine, 1970--, fellow, American College of Surgeons, 1974--, director, Matthew Thornton Health Plan, 1985--, school district moderator, Hollis, 1982--, incorporator, Forum on N.H.'s Future, 1979-82, N.H. Charitable Fund, 1983--, member, N.E. Society for Vascular Surgery, 1979--, N.E. Surgical Society, 1984--, moderator, Hollis, 1986--. Jessica (Austin), July 23, 1960. James, Sept. 6, 1961, Anne, Dec. 10, 1964, Martha, Nov. 10, 1969, Marc, Oct. 21, 1974. Protestant. 58 Pepperell Rd., Hollis.

James Wood Squires

David G. Stahl

David G. Stahl

Dentist. Manchester, N.H., Nov. 1, 1926, Samuel and Sadie (Flaxman) Stahl. Manchester Central High School, 1943, Dartmouth College, A.B., 1947, Tufts Dental School, D.M.D., 1951. U.S. Naval Reserve, 1945-46, seaman 1st cl. General dentistry, 1951--. Instructor, Boston Univ. School of Graduate Dentistry, 1962-70, assistant professor of stomatology, 1970-74; president, Manchester Dental Society, 1963-64, president, N.H. Dental Society, 1978-79, staff, Catholic Medical Center, 1962--, N.H. Constitutional Convention, 1964, Advisory Commission on Health and Welfare, 1962-68,73-78, N.H. Council on World Affairs, 1964--, president, 1979-83; vice president, N.H. Symphony, 1975-80, president, 1980-82; trustee, N.H. Historical Society, 1975-83,84--, vice president, 85--; board member, Manchester Jewish Community Center, 1956-69, Manchester Institute of Arts and Sciences, 1959-68,73-78, Manchester Historical Association, 1968-71. Barbara (Jaffe), July 7, 1951. Susan, Jan. 29, 1953, Nancy, Jan. 24, 1956, Sarah Anne, Sept. 12, 1959, John, June 12, 1961. 100 Magnolia Rd., Manchester.

Bernard Albra Streeter Jr.

Executive councilor. Keene, N.H., Feb. 6, 1935, Bernard and Isabella (Crane) Streeter. Keene High School, 1953, Boston Univ., B.S., 1957. U.S. Army, 1957-58, pfc. Public relations positions, N.H. and Mass., 1958-66, director, community relations, development, Somerville (Mass.) Hospital, 1966-68, vice president, St. John's Hospital, Lowell, 1968--. N.H. Executive Council, 1969-79,81--, member, national advisory commission, National Health Service Corps., 1983--, National Health Care Planning Council, 1973-76, trustee, New London Hospital, 1960-62, St. John's Hospital, 1985--, president, board member, Merrimack Valley Region Association, 1964-66, founding member, N.E. Hospital Public Relations Association, 1966--, president's council, Franklin Pierce College, 1972-78, N.H. State Prison Board of Trustees, 1969-78, executive committee, N.H. Commission on Crime and Delinquency, 1972-78, director, N.H. Council on World Affairs, 1970-80. Janice (Bowman), Aug. 31, 1958. Shannon, May 24, 1959, Christopher, Aug. 9, 1960, Stephanie, Oct. 24, 1972. Methodist. 26 Indiana Dr., Nashua.

Bernard Albra Streeter Jr.

John Henry Sununu

Governor of New Hampshire. Havana, Cuba, July 2, 1939, John and Victoria (Dada) Sununu. LaSalle Military Academy, Oakdale, N.Y., 1957, MIT, B.S.M.E., 1961, M.S.M.E., 1962, Ph.D., 1966. Founder, chief engineer, Astro Dynamics Inc., 1960-65, president, JHS Engineering Co., and Thermal Research Inc., 1965-82, associate professor of mechanical engineering, Tufts Univ., 1966-82, associate dean, College of Engineering, Tufts, 1968-73, governor, N.H., 1983--. Nancy (Hayes), Sept. 5, 1958. Catherine, Feb. 16, 1960, Elizabeth, June 5, 1961, Christina, April 5, 1963, John, Sept. 10, 1964, Michael, Oct. 21, 1967, James, Jan. 7, 1969, Christopher, Nov. 5, 1974, Peter, Oct. 8, 1979. Catholic. 24 Samoset Dr., Salem. Biography has not been verified by the biographee.

John Franklin Swope

President, Chubb Life Insurance Company. Mt. Kisco, N.Y., June 21, 1938, Gerard Jr. and Marjorie (Park) Swope. Tabor Academy, Marion, Mass., 1956, Amherst College, B.A., 1960, Yale Law School, LL.B., 1963. United Life and Accident Insurance Co., Concord, attorney, 1963-67, assistant counsel, 1967-69, corporate secretary, counsel, 1969-70, vice president, corporate secretary, 1970-74, senior vice president, corporate secretary, 1974-77, president, director, 1977--, president, director, Chubb Life Insurance Co. of America, 1981--, Colonial Life Insurance Co. of America, 1981--, Chubb America Service Corp., 1982--, senior vice president, Chubb Corp., 1985--. Trustee, N.H. Higher Education Assistance Foundation, 1969-80, president, Greater Concord Chamber of Commerce, 1974-75, director, Concord Regional Development Corp., 1975-82, Concord Zoning Board, 1973-82, chairman, Channel 11 Capital Fund Drive, 1985--, incorporator, N.H. Charitable Fund, 1984--, member, N.H. Commission on the Arts, 1985--, director, Bank of N.H., 1981--, Business Committee on the Arts, 1986--, chairman, Merrimack County United Way Drive, 1983, board of governors, N.H. Public Television, 1985--. Marjory (Mason), June 9, 1962. Kristen, Nov. 4, 1963, Kevin, Sept. 19, 1967, John G., Aug. 10, 1970. Long Pond Rd., Concord.

John Franklin Swope

Geraldine Flora Sylvester

Geraldine Flora Sylvester

Director, New Hampshire Office of Alcohol and Drug Abuse Prevention. Biddeford, Maine, Aug. 16, 1931, Ford and Janet (Columbus) Steeves. Nute Academy, Milton, 1948, Univ. of N.H., B.S., 1969. Co-owner, vice president, director, GFS Manufacturing, Dover, 1971--, director, N.H. Office of Alcohol and Drug Abuse Prevention, 1983--. Dover City Council, 1970-84, mayor, Dover, 1974-75, trustee, N.H. Youth Development Center, 1976-83, vice president, National Conference of Republican Mayors and Municipal Officers, 1983, volunteer foster mother to troubled youths, 1969-82, executive committee, N.H. Municipal Association, 1972-83, president, 1977-78; director, Strafford County Homemakers Home Health Association, 1976-83, president, Dover Business and Professional Women's Club, 1981-82, member, National Alcohol Drug Abuse and Mental Health Advisory Board, 1985--. Two honorary degrees. Robert Sylvester, June 15, 1968. (Combined family.) Bonny, Jan. 9, 1950, Paula, Aug. 23, 1952, Linda, Aug. 4, 1953, Robert, Sept. 19, 1955, Scott, May 30, 1956, Janet, Dec. 14, 1957, Lisa, Nov. 10, 1960. Protestant. 115 Cocheco St., Dover.

William Chester Tallman

Chairman, Public Service Company of New Hampshire, retired. Newton, Mass., May 25, 1920, Vernon and Phyllis (Thayer) Tallman. Weston (Mass.) High School, 1937, Williams College, A.B., 1941, MIT, B.S., 1942, M.S., 1943. Research assistant, MIT, 1942-46, Public Service Co. of N.H., technical assistant, research engineer, 1946-61, manager, research department, 1961-65, vice president, 1964-65, president, 1965-80, chief executive officer, 1969-83, chairman, 1980-84. Director, Public Service Co. of N.H., 1965--, Amoskeag National Bank and Trust Co., 1964-86, Amoskeag Industries, 1973--, Federated Arts of Manchester, 1975--, Forum on N.H.'s Future, 1978-82, Industrial Development Authority, 1972-78, executive committee, N.E. Power Pool, 1970-84, chairman, 1970-73; former chairman, Electric Power Council on Environment. One honorary degree. Jean (Gysan), Dec. 19, 1943. Elizabeth, July 31, 1957. Protestant. 12 Ministerial Rd., Bedford.

William Chester Tallman

Samuel Augustus Tamposi

Real estate developer. Nashua, N.H., Aug. 31, 1924, Nasi and Aspasia (Pattatolica) Tamposi. Nashua Senior High School, 1941, Nashua Business College. Salesman, insurance agent, founder, The Tamposi Co., real estate, commercial and industrial development, 1959--. Limited partner, Boston Red Sox, 1978--, trustee, Franklin Pierce College, 1978-81, director, Nashua Trust Co., 1961--, N.H. Business Development Corp., 1979-83, former trustee, Nashua Memorial Hospital, Nashua Arts and Science Center, finance chairman, N.H. Republican State Committee, 1968-69, former director, So. N.H. Association of Commerce and Industry, chairman, 1977-78. Samuel Jr., Sept. 4, 1952, Michael, Aug. 27, 1953, Betty, Feb. 13, 1955, Nicholas, Feb. 18, 1957, Celina, April 5, 1958, Stephen, Dec. 31, 1960. 402 Amherst St., Nashua.

John Andrew Taylor

President, The Morley Company. Lowell, Mass., Aug. 3, 1917, John and Edith (Barnes) Taylor. Lowell High School, 1935. Machine designer, Moore Corp., Dover, 1935-42, The Morley Co., methods engineer, 1942, plant superintendent, 1946, executive vice president, 1951, president, 1962--. President, Data Card Manufacturers Association, 1962-64, N.H. Manufacturers Association, 1966-69, director, Business and Industry Assn. of N.H., 1982--, president, 1982-84; director, National Manufacturers Association, 1964-68, North Utilities, 1972-79, Portsmouth Regional Development Corp., 1971-80, N.H. Business Development Corp., 1965-68,71-74,76-79, trustee, Chase Home for Children, 1980--, director, First National Bank, Portsmouth, 1970--, First Coastal Banks, 1984--, advisory board, American Mutual Insurance Co., 1970--. Virginia (Rugg), Feb. 22, 1939 (dec. 1978). Marcia, Dec. 29, 1939, John B., July 20, 1943. Baptist. One Meadow Ln., Dover.

John Andrew Taylor

Malcolm Tink Taylor

Journalist, conservationist. Rochester, N.Y., July 18, 1936, Malcolm and Helen (Moorhouse) Taylor. Allendale School, Pittsford, N.Y., 1955. Plymouth State College, B.Ed., 1965, Mich. State Univ., M.S., 1970. N.H. state trooper, 1958-62, Squam Lakes map survey, Boston Museum of Science, 1962-65, teacher, Inter-Lakes High School, Meredith, 1965-66, associate editor, *Plymouth Record*, 1966-69, founder, executive secretary, N.H. Association of Conservation Commissions, 1970-80, correspondent, *Evening Citizen*, Laconia, 1983--. N.H. House of Rep., 1975-78, chairman, Holderness Conservation Commission, 1968--, member, Current Use Advisory Board, 1973-80, chairman, Natural Resources Council of N.H., 1973-81, policy advisory committee, N.H. Municipal Association, 1974-80, N.H. Constitutional Convention, 1974, moderator, Holderness School District, 1979--, co-founder, trustee, Granite State Public Radio, 1979-84, president, Squam Lakes Association, 1982-84, adjunct lecturer, Plymouth State College, 1982--. Frances (Howe), July 14, 1984. Congregational. Greenleaf Hill Farm, Holderness.

Stephen Howard Taylor

Commissioner, Department of Agriculture. Hanover, N.H., June 13, 1939, Lawrence and Edith (Howard) Taylor. Hanover High School, 1956, Univ. of N.H., A.B., 1962. Reporter, *Portsmouth Herald*, 1963-65, managing editor, *Valley News*, Lebanon, 1965-72, executive director, N.H. Council for the Humanities, 1972-77, freelance writer, editor, dairy farmer, 1977-82, commissioner, Department of Agriculture, 1982--. Director, vice president, Northern Farms Cooperative, 1977-81, partner, N.H. Blanket Association, 1975--, member, Advisory Commission on Health and Welfare, 1967-71, selectman, Plainfield, 1966-78, moderator, town of Plainfield, Plainfield School District, 1980--, trustee, Society for the Protection of N.H. Forests, 1972-75, supervisor, Sullivan County Conservation District, 1980-82, director, West Central Community Mental Health Services, 1979-82, manager, Meriden Bird Club, 1970-75, incorporator, N.H. Charitable Fund, 1976-85. Gretchen (Schnare), Aug. 17, 1963. James, Sept. 14, 1965, William, Dec. 8, 1966, Robert, June 21, 1971. Congregational. West Main St., Meriden Village.

Stephen Howard Taylor

Bert Teague

Bert Teague

State director, Small Business Administration, retired. Newport, N.H., Aug. 16, 1917, Fred and Adeline (Rowe) Teague. Sunapee High School, 1933, Kimball Union Academy, 1935, Univ. of N.H., A.B., 1939. U.S. Army, 1941-46, maj. Aide, Sen. Styles Bridges, 1946-52, administrative assistant, Gov. Hugh Gregg, 1953-54, sales manager, Gregg and Son, Nashua, 1955-63, executive director, N.H. primary, Rockefeller for President, 1963-64, manager, vice president, Anderson Nichols and Co., Concord, 1965-73, state director, Small Business Administration, Concord, 1973-84, director of business development, N.H. Savings Bank, 1984--. Chairman, N.H. Republican Party, 1953, director, Univ. of N.H. Alumni Association, 1963-69, president, 1969; director, N.E. Council, 1972-75. Joanne (Condon), Aug. 29, 1942. Virginia, Oct. 26, 1943, John, Nov. 14, 1946, Calista, July 27, 1948, Beverly, Nov. 15, 1950, Thomas, June 23, 1954. 123 Franklin Street, Concord.

Costas S. Tentas

Chairman, New Hampshire Liquor Commission. Winchendon, Mass., Sept. 28, 1921, Stergios and Vasilike (Karagianis) Tentas. Manchester Central High School, 1940. Manager, shoe store, owner, operator, foodstore, Manchester, 1947-61, commissioner, N.H. Liquor Commission, 1961--, chairman, 1969-80,85--. Director, National Alcoholic Beverage Control Association, 1966--, president, 1970-71, honorary life member; member, Masons, N.H. Consistory, Shriners, Elks, Navy League, Social and Fraternal Associations of N.H. Licensed Clubs, director, life member, Hundred Club. Greek Orthodox. 1490 Elm St., Manchester.

Costas S. Tentas

Meldrim Thomson Jr.

Meldrim Thomson Jr.

Former governor of New Hampshire. Pittsburgh, Pa., March 8, 1912, Meldrim and Marion (Booth) Thomson. Miami (Fla.) High School, 1930, Univ. of Miami, 1930-32, Miami College of Law, 1932-33, Mercer Univ. Law School, 1933-34, Univ of Ga., LL.B., 1935. Managing editor, Edward Thompson Co., Brooklyn, 1936-42, editor in chief, 1942-51; founder, president, Equity Publishing, 1952--, owner, Mount Cube Farm, 1954--, governor, N.H., 1973-79. Orford School Board, 1957-66, chairman, 1960-66; N.H. Constitutional Convention, 1964, chairman, Tax Relief Inc., 1980-84, president, Public Schools Association, 1962-68. Four honorary degrees. Gale (Kelly), Oct. 29, 1938. Peter, Nov. 7, 1941, David, July 31, 1943, Thomas, Nov. 5, 1945, Marion, March 21, 1948, Janet, May 19, 1950, Robb, June 5, 1952. Protestant. Mount Cube Farm, Orford.

A. Robert Thoresen

Planning and development consultant. Claremont, N.H., March 13, 1943, Alfred and Eleanor (Billings) Thoresen. Stevens High School, Claremont, 1961, Syracuse Univ., A.B., 1965, M.R.P., 1969, Univ. of N.H., M.P.A., 1976. U.S. Army, 1967-70, E-5. Planner, The Planning Services Group, Cambridge, 1967, director of community affairs, Neighborhood Information and Referral Services, Manchester, 1970-71, planning director, Portsmouth, 1971-77, principal, owner, The Thoresen Group, Portsmouth, 1977--. Director, N.H. Planners Association, 1972-77, president, 1975-76; legislative policy committee, N.H. Municipal Association, 1976-77, proprietor, Portsmouth Athenaeum, 1982--, Mayor's Blue Ribbon Committee on Tax Assessment, 1984--, trustee, Strawbery Banke, 1984--, N.H. Public Radio, 1984--, director, Preservation Action, 1979-85, Portsmouth Community Health Services, 1975-77, Seacoast United Way, 1975-81, president, 1979-80; trustee, Theatre by the Sea, 1978-81. Susan (Werner), Aug. 19, 1967. Kristin, Oct. 1, 1970, Erik, June 30, 1972. Unitarian. 100 Kensington Rd., Portsmouth.

A. Robert Thoresen

Susan Werner Thoresen

Planning and management consultant. Syracuse, N.Y., Nov. 5, 1944, Clemens and Jane (Ellithorp) Werner. St. Katherine's School, Davenport, Iowa, 1962, Smith College, A.B., 1966, Syracuse Univ., M.P.A., 1967. Junior planner, Metropolitan Area Planning Council, Boston, 1967-68, associate planner, Columbus-Muscogee County (Ga.) Planning Commission, 1968-70, consultant, N.H. and Ga., 1970-77, principal, owner, The Thoresen Group, Portsmouth, 1977--. Portsmouth Board of Education, 1984--, N.H. Constitutional Convention, 1974, director, N.H. Planners Association, 1973-81, president, 1979-80; Greater Portsmouth Community Foundation, 1984--, Portsmouth-Seacoast YWCA, 1973-77, president, 1974-75; trustee, Society for the Protection of N.H. Forests, 1976-82, clerk, 1982-84; chair, state issues committee, Greater Portsmouth Chamber of Commerce, 1982-85, moderator, "Inside the Issues," cable TV program, 1982--, board member, Portsmouth League of Women Voters, 1975-78,85--, president, N.H. Smith College Club, 1980-82. A. Robert Thoresen, Aug. 19, 1967. Kristin, Oct. 1, 1970, Erik, June 30, 1972. Unitarian. 100 Kensington Rd., Portsmouth.

Davis Peabody Thurber

President, chairman, Bank of New Hampshire. Nashua, N.H., May 20, 1925, George and Muriel (Davis) Thurber. Phillips Academy, Andover, Mass., 1943, Holy Cross College, B.Naval Science, 1945, MIT, M.S., 1948. U.S. Naval Reserve, 1943-46, lt. jg. Sales engineer, Amos Thompson Corp., Edinburg, Ind., 1950-55, assistant to the president, White Mountain Freezer Co., Nashua, 1955-56, assistant cashier to president, Second National Bank of Nashua, 1956-69, president, chairman, Bank of N.H., N.A., 1969--. Chairman, president, Bank of N.H. Corp., 1980--, underwriting member, Lloyd's of London, 1973--, director, Energy North, Pennichuck Corp., Whitney Screw, N.H. Bankers Association, 1964-65,84--, trustee, Currier Gallery, 1973--, Squam Lakes Science Center, 1967-78, president, Squam Lakes Association, 1965-67. Shirley (Amos), July 14, 1946 (dec. Jan. 1970). Shelley, Nov. 20, 1949, Steven, April 3, 1952, George, April 12, 1955, Matthew, May 18, 1959. Patricia (Martin), April 25, 1971. 25 Swart Terrace, Nashua.

Donn Edward Tibbetts

Donn Edward Tibbetts

Newspaper reporter. Manchester, N.H., Nov. 29, 1930, Joseph and Yvonne (Tardiff) Tibbetts. LaSalle Military Academy, Oakdale, N.Y., 1948, Univ. of N.H., 1948-49. Radio disk jockey, 1949-56, news director, assistant general manager, WGIR Radio, Manchester, 1956-72, reporter, *Manchester Union Leader*, 1972--, State House bureau chief, 1974--. Director, Greater Manchester Chamber of Commerce, 1972-73, N.H. Lung Association, 1961-73, director, national vice president, National Association of Sportswriters and Sportscasters, 1960-72, member, Small Business Advisory Council, 1968-75, state chairman, 1969. Author, *The Closest U.S. Senate Race in History*, 1976. Jane (Savage), Jan. 20, 1951. Donald, Nov, 11, 1951, Gary, June 7, 1954, Amy, July 26, 1958, Cindy, Nov. 17, 1959. Catholic. 293 Harrison St., Manchester.

Gordon MacLean Tiffany

Attorney, retired, artist. Port Chester, N.Y., Dec. 13, 1912, Henry and Eleanor (Gordon) Tiffany. St. Paul's School, 1931, Yale Univ., B.A., 1935, Columbia Univ. Law School, LL.B., 1942, graduated, School of the Museum of Fine Arts, Boston, 1979. U.S. Naval Reserve, 1942-45, lt. sg. *N.Y. Herald Tribune* , 1935-39, attorney, N.Y.C., 1942-43, Concord, 1953-56,55-58, assistant attorney general, N.H., 1946-49, legislative counsel, Gov. Sherman Adams, 1949-50, attorney general, N.H., 1950-53, staff director, U.S. Commission on Civil Rights, Washington, D.C., 1958-60, chancellor, Episcopal Diocese of N.H., 1961-74. City solicitor, Concord, 1953-54, N.H. House of Rep., 1957-59, N.H. Constitutional Convention, 1956, chairman, Commission on Interstate Cooperation, 1950-53, moderator, Weare, 1972-79, trustee, Society for the Protection of N.H. Forests, 1964-74, treasurer, 1971-74; artist, 1967--. Ellen (Auchincloss), June 12, 1940. William, June 8, 1946, Jean, Aug. 15, 1948. Episcopal. Tiffany Hill Farm, P.O. Box 200, Weare.

Thomas Neil Tillotson

General manager, Tillotson Rubber Company. Boston, Mass., Feb. 1, 1945, Neil and Alma (Eastin) Tillotson. Pompano Beach (Fla.) Senior High School, 1963, Princeton Univ., B.S., 1967. U.S. Army Corps of Engineers, 1968-70, spec. 5th cl. Tillotson Rubber Co., sales manager, 1970-73, partner, 1970--, general manager, 1973--. Director, Business and Industry Association of N.H., 1976-82,84--, Center for N.H.'s Future, 1980--, N.H. Social Welfare Council, 1984--, board of visitors, Whittemore School of Business, 1984--, member, Governor's High-Level Waste Task Force, 1985--, Citizens Energy Policy Advisory Group, 1980-82, N.E. Energy Congress, 1978-79, incorporator, N.H. Charitable Fund, 1983--. Deborah (Tucker), Nov. 22, 1980. Protestant. Dixville Notch.

Howard Canfield Townsend

State representative. Lebanon, N.H., June 21, 1917, Harry and Bessie (Canfield) Townsend. Lebanon High School, 1935. Tomapo Farm, operator, 1935--, owner, 1952--; commissioner, Department of Agriculture, 1972-82. Lebanon City Council, 1956-66, N.H. Senate, 1967-73, N.H. House of Rep., 1984--, director, Grafton County Farm Bureau, 1938-48, president, 1946-48; N.H. Maple Producers, 1941-51, president, 1948-50; N.H.-Vt. Breeding Association, 1960-66, Concord Group Insurance Co., 1946--, Putnam Agricultural Foundation, 1978--, Rural Rehabilitation Foundation, 1976--, trustee, Univ. System of N.H., 1972-82, Eastern States Exposition, 1972-82. Madeline (Townsend), Oct. 31, 1937. Bruce, Aug. 23, 1938, Marilyn, March 19, 1941, Rebecca, March 20, 1944, Faith, Aug. 25, 1946. Protestant. Storrs Hill, Lebanon.

Sara Martenis Townsend

State representative. Putney, Vt., Dec. 30, 1919, George and Katherine (Booth) Martenis. Stevens High School, Claremont, 1937, Middlebury College, A.B., 1941. Instructor, Kimball Union Academy, Meriden, 1941-70, coordinator, Elderworks, N.H., 1984--. N.H. House of Rep., 1971--, Plainfield School Board, 1961-64, Plainfield Conservation Commission, 1971-74, director, National Council on Aging, 1984--, founder, chairman, Friends of the Meriden Library, 1965-69, advisory council, Norris Cotton Cancer Center, 1981-83, representative from the N.H. House, State Council on Aging, 1973-81, executive committee, National Conference of State Legislatures, 1984--, public relations consultant, 1984--, member, Meriden Bird Club, 1952--, advisory committee on the future of public health, National Academy of Sciences, Institute of Medicine, 1985--. Ira Townsend, July 14, 1943. James, Feb. 25, 1946, Patricia, Feb. 21, 1949. Congregational. Box 65, Columbus Jordan Rd., Meriden.

Howard Canfield Townsend

William Wardwell Treat

William Wardwell Treat

Banker, retired judge. Boston, Mass., May 23, 1918, Joshua II and Clara (Atwood) Treat. Winterport (Maine) High School, 1936, Univ. of Maine, A.B., 1940, Boston Univ. School of Law, 1944-46, Harvard Univ., M.B.A., 1947. Attorney, Hampton, 1949--, president, Hampton National Bank (name changed to Bank Meridian in 1983), 1958-84, chairman, 1958--; justice, Seabrook Municipal Court, 1952-73, judge of probate, Rockingham County, 1958-83. Member, N.H. Judicial Council, 1970-83, chairman, 1976-83; president, National College of Probate Judges, 1968-77, president emeritus, 1977--; director, Towle Manufacturing Co., 1963--, chairman, 1985--; Exeter and Hampton Electric Co., 1974--, Federal Reserve Bank of Boston, 1982-85, advisory board, N.E. Law Institute, 1969-76, chairman, Republican State Committee, 1954-58, Republican National Committeeman, 1954-58,60-64, faculty, National Center for State Judiciary, 1975-78, Phillips Exeter Academy, 1965-66, trustee, Franklin Pierce College, 1985--. Author, *Local Justice in the Granite State*, 1961, *Treat on Probate*, three volumes, 1968. Vivian (Baker), Feb. 22, 1947. Mary Esther, March 2, 1950, Jonathan, June 2, 1951. Episcopal. P.O. Box 498, Hampton.

Cornelius Robertson Trowbridge

President, publisher, Yankee Publishing. Salem, Mass., March 31, 1932, Cornelius P. and Margaret (Laird) Trowbridge. Phillips Exeter Academy, 1950, Princeton Univ., A.B., 1954, Harvard Univ., LL.B., 1957. Vice president, Yankee Publishing, Dublin, 1964-70, president, publisher, 1970--. N.H. House of Rep., 1967-73, N.H. Senate, 1973-78, moderator, Dublin, 1970--, director, First National Bank, Peterborough, 1979-86, N.H. Charitable Fund, 1979-86, Chewonki Foundation, 1982--, member, regional board of advisors, N.E. Congressional Institute, 1981-84, trustee, Phillips Exeter Academy, 1977--, Franklin Pierce College, 1979-83, Society for the Protection of N.H. Forests, 1978--, secretary, 1985--. Two honorary degrees. Lorna (Sagendorph), July 7, 1956. James, March 19, 1960, Cornelia, Aug. 31, 1962, Beatrix, July 16, 1965, Philip, March 28, 1969. Episcopal. Old Marlborough Rd., Dublin.

John Bartlett Tucker

John Bartlett Tucker

Speaker, New Hampshire House of Representatives. Claremont, N.H., Nov. 14, 1937, Bernard and Blanche (Bartlett) Tucker. Stevens High School, Claremont, 1955, Keene State College, B.Ed., 1959, Northeastern Univ., M.Ed., 1963. Radio broadcasting and sales, 1954-67, teacher, 1959-66, executive director, N.H. Education Association, 1966-77, advertising, public relations consultant, 1977--. N.H. House of Rep., 1971--, speaker, 1981--; N.H. Constitutional Convention, 1964,74, director, Claremont Chamber of Commerce, 1977-82, United Way of Sullivan County, 1977-79, incorporator, Claremont General Hospital (now Valley Regional Hospital), 1978--, corporator, Claremont Savings Bank, 1978--, member, National Conference of State Legislatures, 1976--, chairman, assembly on the legislature, NCSL, 1985--. Katherine, Sept. 9, 1956, Kim, Aug. 10, 1957, Jay, July 26, 1958, Maryellen, March 26, 1959, Lynn, Dec. 17, 1960, James, Oct. 8, 1961, Beth, May 10, 1966. Carol (O'Brien), June 20, 1971. Sarah, May 26, 1972. Congregational. 14 East St., Claremont.

J. Arthur Tufts

State representative. Lowell, Mass., Dec. 28, 1921, James and Hazel (Weinbeck) Tufts. Exeter High School, 1939, Univ. of N.H., B.S., 1948, Boston Univ., M.Ed., 1961. U.S. Army, 1942-46, 1st lt. Owner, Granite State Nurseries, Exeter, 1948--. Ice hockey coaching, officiating, Phillips Exeter Academy, 1948--, science teacher, Pentucket Regional High School, Newbury, Mass., 1967-68, N.H. Senate, 1965-73, president, 1969-70; N.H. House of Rep., 1961-63,78--, commissioner, Rockingham County, 1970-72, trustee, Univ. System of N.H., 1962-66, director, Seacoast Regional Counsel Center, 1971-74, president, 1974; Rockingham County School for Special Children, 1960-63, First Unitarian Society of Exeter, 1984--, vice president, Tufts Family Association, 1984--. Jean (Staples), Aug. 20, 1950 (dec. Feb. 13, 1983). James, July 17, 1951, Anne, Dec. 10, 1953, Peter, Feb. 17, 1956, Thomas, Dec. 4, 1959. Dorothy (Giles), Aug. 25, 1984. Unitarian. 200 High St., Exeter.

J. Arthur Tufts

Frederic Kendall Upton

Frederic Kendall Upton

Attorney. Concord, N.H., Dec. 21, 1918, Robert and Martha (Burroughs) Upton. Concord High School, 1935, Dartmouth College, A.B., 1939, Harvard Law School, LL.B., 1942. U.S. Navy, 1942-45, lieut. Attorney, Concord, 1946--. President, N.H. Bar Association, 1970-71, member, N.H. Judicial Council, 1971-75, Supreme Court Committee on Judicial Conduct, 1978--, trustee, director, N.H. Savings Bank, 1959-86, director, D.D. Bean and Sons, 1958--, Concord School Board, 1948-56, chairman, 1953-56; trustee, Mary Hitchcock Memorial Hospital, 1977--. Jean (Thornton), Feb. 21, 1943. Robert, March 16, 1944, Mark, Jan. 9, 1947, Katherine, March 7, 1950, John, Aug. 9, 1953, Evelyn, June 12, 1957. Episcopal. 32 Dunklee St., Concord.

Richard Francis Upton

Attorney. Bow, N.H., Sept. 3, 1914, Robert and Martha (Burroughs) Upton. Concord High School, 1930, Phillips Exeter Academy, 1931, Dartmouth College, A.B., 1935, Harvard Law School, LL.B., 1938. U.S. Army, 1942-46, capt. Attorney, Concord, 1938-42,46--. President, N.H. Bar Association, 1964-65, trustee, N.H. Historical Society, 1966--, president, 1976-80; director, Concord National Bank, 1958--, Concord Group Insurance Companies, 1971--, N.H. House of Rep., 1941,1947-51, speaker, 1949-51; trustee, N.H. Hospital, 1946-48, member, N.H. Commission on Alcoholism, 1951-63, chairman, N.H. Civil Rights Advisory Committee, 1958-62, member, N.H. Historical Commission, 1963-68, chairman, 1965-68; chairman, N.H. Fish and Game Commission, 1968-74, chairman, N.H. Environmental Council, 1970-71, member, N.H. Interstate Boundary Commission, 1971-73, president, N.H. Constitutional Convention, 1964,84. Author, *Revolutionary New Hampshire*, 1936. Marie (Audibert), Sept. 23, 1950 (dec. 1970). William, Jan. 4, 1955, Matthew, March 13, 1958. Shirley (Knowland), May 17, 1975. Episcopal. 110 Centre St., Concord.

Richard Francis Upton

James William Varnum

James William Varnum

President, Mary Hitchcock Memorial Hospital. Grand Rapids, Mich, May 29, 1940, Robert and Jeannette (Badger) Varnum. Birmingham (Mich.) High School, 1958, Dartmouth College, A.B., 1962, Univ. of Mich., M.H.A., 1964. University Hospitals, Madison, Wis., administrative assistant, 1964-66, assistant superintendent, 1966-68, associate superintendent, 1968-69, superintendent, 1969-73; administrator, University Hospital, Seattle, 1973-78, president, Mary Hitchcock Memorial Hospital, 1978--, The Hitchcock Alliance, 1983--. Trustee, Mary Hitchcock Memorial Hospital, 1978--, Dartmouth-Hitchcock Medical Center, 1983--, director, First N.H. Bank of Lebanon, 1983--, N.H. Hospital Association, 1981--, chairman, 1984--; director, chairman, Voluntary Hospitals of America, N.E., 1985--, United Health Systems Agency, 1978-84, president, 1982-84; Society of Hospital Planning and Marketing, 1984--, president-elect. Lucinda (Hotchkiss), June 6, 1964. Kenneth, May 24, 1967, Susan, May 23, 1970. Protestant. Woodcock Ln., Etna.

Dorothy Mansfield Vaughan

Librarian emeritus, Portsmouth Public Library. Penacook, N.H., Sept. 20, 1904, Raymon and Mary (Smith) Vaughan. Portsmouth High School, 1922, Univ. of N.H., 1931, Univ. of Chicago Graduate Library School, 1946. Portsmouth Public Library, children's reference, assistant librarian, 1922-46, librarian, 1946-74, librarian emeritus, 1976--. N.H. State Library Commission, 1946-49, founder, president, Strawbery Banke, 1960-65, honorary chairman, 1985--; State Historical Commission, 1965-82, member, N.H. Historical Society, 1922--, life member, N.H. Library Association, president, 1954-57; honorary trustee, Portsmouth Historical Society, honorary governor of the board, Warner House Association, proprietor, Portsmouth Athenaeum, member, Portsmouth Historic District, 1981--. One honorary degree. Episcopal. 202 Summer St., Portsmouth.

Dorothy Mansfield Vaughan

Richard Greville Verney

Richard Greville Verney

Chairman, chief executive officer, Monadnock Paper Mills Inc. Providence, R.I., Aug. 24, 1946. Gilbert and Virginia (Piggott) Verney. St. George's School, Newport, R.I., 1964, Brown Univ., A.B., 1968. Monadnock Paper Mills, Bennington, management trainee, 1969, assistant general manager, 1970, executive vice president, 1970-77, president, 1977-85, chairman, chief executive officer, 1978--. Director, American Paper Institute, 1980-82, Boston Paper Trade Association, 1980--, president, 1985-86; Center for N.H.'s Future, 1981--, member, Sales Association of the Paper Industry, 1969--, Paper Industry Management Association, 1969--, trustee, Crotched Mountain Foundation, 1974--, executive committee, 1975--, chairman, development committee, 1980-82; trustee, St. George's School, 1978--, chairman, 1985--. Dorothy (Howard), Aug. 26, 1967. Virginia, Dec. 29, 1969, Elizabeth, March 5, 1972, Heather, Dec. 7, 1973, Eric, March 23, 1976. Episcopal. The Verney Farm, Bennington.

Jeannette Eva Vezeau

Former president, Notre Dame College. Rochester, N.H., May 11, 1913, Edward and Laura (Richey) Vezeau. Our Lady of Angels Academy, Montreal, 1930, Boston Univ., B.S., 1948, M.Ed., 1955, Ed.D., 1960. Entered, Sisters of Holy Cross, Feb. 16, 1933. High school teacher, Manchester, New Bedford, Mass., Grosvenor Dale, Conn., 1937-57, principal, St. George High School, Manchester, 1960-64, supervisor of schools, Sisters of Holy Cross, N.E., 1964-67, president, Notre Dame College, Manchester, 1967-84, superior, St. Anthony Convent, Manchester, 1985--. Diocesan School Board and Commission for Christian Unity, Manchester, 1965-71, advisory board, Elliot School of Nursing, 1968-71, executive board, N.H. College and Univ. Council, 1967-84, member, Postsecondary Education Commission, 1973-84, vice chairman, 1976-78; incorporator, Catholic Medical Center, 1979--, corporator, Amoskeag Savings Bank, 1981-84, executive board, Council for Better Schools, 1975-77. Co-author, *10,000 Legal Words*, 1971. One honorary degree. Catholic. 181 Hall St., Manchester.

Jeannette Eva Vezeau

Winthrop Wadleigh

Winthrop Wadleigh

Attorney. Milford, N.H., Jan. 23, 1902, Fred and Alice (Conant) Wadleigh. Milford High School, 1919, Dartmouth College, A.B., 1923, Harvard Law School, J.D., 1927. School teacher, Honolulu, 1923-24, attorney, Concord, 1927-29, assistant attorney general, N.H., 1929-31, attorney, Manchester, 1931--. Director, Merchants National Bank, 1938-74, N.H. Constitutional Convention, 1930, member, Committee to Revise Corporation Laws of N.H., 1932, moderator, Ward I, Manchester, 1944-46, secretary, Amoskeag Co., 1957-68, chairman, investment committee, N.H. Conference United Church of Christ, 1967--, member, N.H. Commission for Human Rights, 1967-70, vice chairman, board of directors, N.H. Civil Liberties Union, 1967--, treasurer, American Civil Liberties Union, N.Y.C., 1969-75, director, 1967-73; trustee, White Pines College, 1970--, Cogswell Benevolent Trust, 1945--, life member, Audubon Society of N.H., Society for the Protection of N.H. Forests. Sylvia (Leach), June 11, 1932 (dec. Sept. 1967). Theodore, April 17, 1934, James, Feb. 4, 1936. Faith (Preston), Dec. 19, 1970. Congregational. Walnut Hill, Chester. Winthrop Wadleigh died on March 3, 1986.

Ralph Stuart Wallace

Director, New Hampshire Historical Society. Plainfield, N.J., Dec. 26, 1944, Ralph and Helen (Harris) Wallace. Westfield (N.J.) Senior High School, 1963, Lehigh Univ., B.A., 1968, Univ. of N.H., M.A., 1973, Ph.D., 1984. U.S. Army, 1968-71, sgt. Editor, *Historical New Hampshire*, 1974-84, assistant director, N.H. Historical Society, 1979-84, director, 1985--. Trustee, N.H. Coordinating Committee for the Promotion of History, 1980--, Inherit N.H., 1984--, advisory council, Merrimack Retired Senior Volunteer Program, 1983-84, tourism committee, Greater Concord Chamber of Commerce, 1984--. Ruth (Weeden), Nov. 1, 1980. Ethan, Jan. 19, 1984. Presbyterian. 10 Albin St., Concord.

Ralph Stuart Wallace

Jean Rogers Wallin

Jean Rogers Wallin

Former chairman, New Hampshire Liquor Commission. Hibbing, Minn., Jan. 13, 1934, William and Rhea (Madison) Rogers. Roosevelt High School, Virginia, Minn., 1951, Virginia (Minn.) Junior College, 1951-52, Univ. of Minn., 1952-54. Director, women's program office, N.H. Social Welfare Council, 1974, real estate broker, Merrimack, Nashua, 1975-80, chairman, N.H. Liquor Commission, 1980-85, consultant, Nashua, 1985--. N.H. House of Rep., 1967-71,1975-80, Nashua Board of Education, 1968-75, president, 1974-75; N.H. Constitutional Convention, 1974, Democratic National Committeewoman, 1968-72, member, National Alcoholic Beverage Control Association, 1980-85, N.H. chapter, Order of Women Legislators, 1967--. Donald Wallin, June 12, 1954. Rikka, March, 16, 1957, Amy, Feb. 1, 1959. Unitarian. 3 Durham St. Nashua.

Kathleen Whelpley Ward

State representative. Brooklyn, N.Y., Aug. 9, 1928, William and Margaret (McAllister) Whelpley. St. Bartholomew's School for Girls, Elmhurst, N.Y., 1946. Assistant, board of selectmen, Whitefield, 1960-64, co-owner, treasurer, office manager, Ward Mechanical Contractors, Littleton, 1964-83, owner, developer, Ward's Emporium, Littleton, 1979-83. President, N.H. Federated Republican Women, 1978-79, executive board, N.H. Federated Women's Clubs, 1974-78, Interstate Association of Status of Women, 1974-76, director, Blue Cross and Blue Shield, 1981--, member, N.H. Advisory Council, Small Business Administration, 1970-78, National Small Business Advisory Council, 1969-79, N.H. House of Rep., 1975--, vice chairman, N.H. Commission on the Status of Women, 1971-75, member, N.E. Telephone Consumers Panel, 1982--, chairman, 1983--. John Ward, March 9, 1947 (dec. Nov. 2, 1980). M. Candice, April 17, 1948, Mary Lee, Aug. 7, 1950, Brien, April 10, 1952. Catholic. 61 Pleasant St., Littleton.

Kathleen Whelpley Ward

John Fremont Weeks Jr.

John Fremont Weeks Jr.

President, Weeks Dairy Foods. Laconia, N.H., Dec. 7, 1932, John and Esther (Smith) Weeks. Laconia High School, 1950, Univ. of N.H., B.S., 1955. Employee, Weeks Dairy Foods, 1956--, president, chief executive officer, 1969--. Trustee, Laconia Savings Bank, 1973--, Taylor Home for the Aged, Laconia, 1975-82, director, Dow Oil Co., Laconia, 1973--, Milk Industry Foundation, 1977--, N.E. Association of Milk Dealers, 1972--, Northeast Ice Cream Association, 1982--, Univ. of N.H. Alumni Association, 1982--, Concord Rotary Club, 1985--, Concord Chamber of Commerce, 1984--, secretary, International Association of Ice Cream Manufacturers, 1979-81. Patricia (Foley), Sept. 20, 1958. Sheryl, May 27, 1959, Jane, April 27, 1960, John III, May 17, 1961, Michael, July 16, 1963. Congregational. 165 School St., Concord.

James Campbell Wemyss Jr.

Paper company executive. Stamford, Conn., Nov. 25, 1925, James and Dorothy (Beaver) Wemyss. Fishburn Military School, Waynesboro, Va., 1944, Babson Institute, B.A., 1948. U.S. Army, 1944-45, sgt. Executive vice president, Groveton Papers Co., 1956-68, president, 1968-83; corporate vice president, Diamond International Corp., 1969-71, group vice president, 1971-86; president, Groveton Paper Board Inc., 1967-86. Director, Groveton Papers Co., 1956-83, Diamond International Corp., 1971-83, Groveton Paper Board Inc., 1967-86, selectman, Northumberland, 1973-86, Industrial Development Authority, 1980-84. Zelma (Robinson), Sept. 9, 1949. James III, June 13, 1950, Heather, Aug. 6, 1951. Protestant. Red Dam Rd., Groveton.

Katherine Wells Wheeler

Katherine Wells Wheeler

St. Louis, Mo., Feb. 8, 1940, Benjamin and Katherine (Gladney) Wells. John Burroughs School, St. Louis, 1957, Smith College, B.A., 1961, Washington Univ., St. Louis, M.A., 1966. Board of governors, N.H. Public Television, 1980--, trustee, Berwick Academy, 1983--, incorporator, N.H. Charitable Fund, 1983--, advisory council, Currier Gallery, 1983--, coordinator, short-term visitor program, N.H. Council of World Affairs, 1981--, president, League of Women Voters, Durham, 1970-71, chairman, N.H. Public Television Auction, 1973-76, president, Friends Advisory Board, N.H. Public Television, 1976-84, member, budget committee, Durham, 1974-76, president, N.H. Smith College Club, 1984-86, deacon, Durham Community Church, 1980-84. Douglas Wheeler, June 13, 1964. Katherine, Sept. 8, 1967, Lucille, May 16, 1970. Protestant. 27 Mill Rd., Durham.

Major William Wheelock

Vice president, treasurer, Franklin Pierce College. Fall River, Mass., Dec. 12, 1936, Major and Mildred (Rogers) Wheelock. Durfee High School, Fall River, 1954, Providence College, B.S., 1958. U.S. Army, 1959-61, 1st lt. Legislative analyst, budget examiner, Bureau of the Budget, Washington, D.C., 1966-71, executive assistant, Gov. Walter Peterson, 1971-73, superintendent, N.H. Hospital, 1973-77, executive director, N.H. Charitable Fund, 1977-78, president, Rumford Press, 1978-82, senior vice president, N.H. Savings Bank, 1982-85, vice president, treasurer, Franklin Pierce College, 1985--. Director, Industrial Development Authority, 1972-75, N.H. Association for Mental Health, 1979-85, president, 1980-82; N.H. Social Welfare Council, 1983--, president, 1986--; Crotched Mountain Rehabilitation Center, 1980--, member, N.H. Council for the Humanities, 1981--, chairman, 1984--; corporator, trustee, N.H. Savings Bank, 1981-83. Rita (Gauthier), Feb. 22, 1962. Major III, Sept. 3, 1963, Nancy, March 20, 1967. Windmill Hill Rd., Dublin.

Major William Wheelock

Arthur Knowlton Whitcomb

Arthur Knowlton Whitcomb

President, Arthur Whitcomb Inc., retired. Greenfield, N.H., Nov. 5, 1906, Frank and Lucy (Knowlton) Whitcomb. Marlboro High School, 1924, Vermont Academy, Saxtons River, 1925, Univ. of N.H., B.S., 1931. Founder, president, Arthur Whitcomb Inc., Keene, 1931-71. Charter member, president, director, Keene Regional Industrial Foundation, president, N.H. Good Roads Association, 1952-53, former director, Associated General Contractors of N.H., president, 1956; former director, N.E. Industrial Council, member, Governor's Industrial Advisory Council, 1950-60, former president, director, Keene Chamber of Commerce, former chairman, Keene Planning Board, former incorporator, Cheshire County Savings Bank, chairman, Univ. of N.H. Fund Drive, 1966. Lena (McConnell), Aug. 5, 1933. Robert, July 3, 1937, Barbara, Sept. 1, 1939. Protestant. Arthur Whitcomb died on June 11, 1986.

Robert Allen Whitcomb

President, Arthur Whitcomb Inc. Keene, N.H., July 3, 1937, Arthur and Lena (McConnell) Whitcomb. Keene High School, 1954, Mount Hermon School, Northfield, Mass., 1956, Univ. of Miami, 1956-58, Univ. of N.H., B.S., 1961. Arthur Whitcomb Inc., personnel manager, 1961, assistant to the president, 1963, president, 1971--. Director, Cheshire National Bank, 1975--, incorporator, Cheshire Hospital, 1972--, trustee, 1978-82; member, National Association of General Contractors, 1980--, president, N.H. Good Roads Association, 1969-70, director, Industrial Development Authority, 1975-85, Governor's Industrial Advisory Council, 1975-85, Keene Chamber of Commerce, 1970-83, president, 1971-72; Cheshire Fair Association, 1968-70, director, chairman, Keene Air Show, 1975, incorporator, Cheshire County Savings Bank, 1970-85. Ciona (Martell), Aug. 23, 1958. Gwen, May 20, 1959, Gregory, Feb. 21, 1966, Melanie, July 17, 1970, Michael, Aug. 25, 1974. Catholic. 45 Greenwood Ave., Keene.

Robert Allen Whitcomb

Ralph Paul White

Ralph Paul White

President, chief executive officer, Troy Mills Inc. Watertown, Mass., Aug. 1, 1926, Irving and Margaret (McGowan) White. Westboro (Mass.) High School, 1944, Columbia Univ., B.S., 1951. Industrial engineer, Chase Brass & Copper Co., 1951-53, production control manager, Sperry Rand Co., 1953-55, data processing manager, B.F. Goodrich, 1955-61, management consulting, Bavier, Bulger & Goodyear, 1961-66, Davidson Rubber Co., vice president, 1966, president, 1969-80, group vice president, Ex-Cell-O (parent co.), 1980-83; president, chief executive officer, Troy Mills Inc., 1983--. Director, Business and Industry Association of N.H., 1970-80,84--, president, 1972-73; Troy Mills, 1972--, International Packings, 1984--, J.A. Wright Co., 1985--, J.D. Cahill Co., 1985--, Industrial Development Authority, 1973-80,85--, member, American Institute of Industrial Engineers, 1959--, Society of Automotive Engineers, 1970--, Dover Development Authority, 1969-70. Shirley (Christie), Nov. 22, 1947. Karin Ann, Dec. 18, 1952, Eric, Aug. 9, 1955. Catholic. Spring Hill Rd., Hancock.

Charles Fulford Whittemore

President, Catholic Medical Center. Concord, N.H., May 28, 1927, Laurence and Evelyn (Fulford) Whittemore. Pembroke Academy, 1944, Univ. of N.H., B.A., 1949, Harvard Law School, 1949-51, Univ. of Colo., 1951-54. U.S. Army, 1944-46, pvt. N.H. director, Federal Housing Administration, 1962-64, director, N.H. Office of Economic Opportunity, 1964-67, commissioner, N.H. Department of Health and Welfare, 1967-70, consultant, Concord, 1971-83, president, Catholic Medical Center, Manchester, 1983--. Vice president, Merrimack Valley Realty, 1960-66, director, Philbrook Children's Foundation, 1967--, chairman, 1967-74; N.H. Lung Association, 1965-80, president, 1977-79; N.H. Social Welfare Council, 1968-70, trustee, Concord Hospital, 1963-66, moderator, Pembroke, 1972--, chairman, N.E. Conference of State Welfare Commissioners, 1968-69, Pembroke Town Budget Committee, 1962-72, chairman, 1969-72. Nancy (Jones), 1950. Aaron, Jan. 21, 1956. Shirley (Feather), Aug. 13, 1959. Mary, June 11, 1960, Laura, April 7, 1962, Jesse, Feb. 27, 1967. United Church of Christ. 279 Pembroke St., Pembroke.

Charles Fulford Whittemore

Frederick Gerald Williams

Potter. Asansol, Bengal, India, Jan. 5, 1926, Frederick and Irene (Hays) Williams. Woodstock High School, Mussoorie, India, 1942, Cornell College, Mount Vernon, Iowa, 1943-44. Professional potter, 1949--, instructor, sculptor, Currier Gallery School of Art, 1952-72. Founder, editor, *Studio Potter Magazine*, 1972--, executive director, Studio Potter Foundation, 1976--, president, National Apprenticeship Council, 1979--, trustee, Boston Society of Arts and Crafts, 1974-78, Haystack School of Crafts, 1974-83, trustee, advisor, Appalachian Craft Center, 1978-80, fellow, American Craft Council, 1979, honorary member, National Council on Education for the Ceramic Arts, 1984. One honorary degree. Lillian (Blake), Sept. 3, 1955. Jennifer, Aug. 16, 1956, Shelley, July 8, 1959. Dunbarton.

George William Wilson

Publisher, *Concord Monitor*. Norfolk, Va., April 17, 1937, Jack and Elsie (Hausser) Wilson. Aiken (S.C.) High School, 1955, Harvard Univ., B.A., 1962. *Concord Monitor*, advertising salesman, reporter, photographer, news editor, editorial writer, 1962-64, assistant general manager, 1964, general manager, 1968, publisher, 1974--. Director, *Catskill* (N.Y.) *Daily Mail*, 1980-86, Continental Cablevision of N.H., 1973-77, Washington Post Co., 1985--, American Newspaper Publishers Association, 1982--, Newspapers of N.E., 1978--, president, 1978--; president, N.E. Newspaper Association, 1981-82, former director, Greater Concord Mental Health Center, Merrimack Valley Day Care Center, Greater Concord Chamber of Commerce, Concord Red Cross, director, *Greenfield* (Mass.) *Recorder*, 1964--, vice president, American Newspaper Publishers Association, 1986--. Marily (Dwight), Feb. 4, 1961. Abigail, Oct. 5, 1961, George D., May 2, 1963, Elizabeth, May 5, 1967. 125 Centre St., Concord.

George William Wilson

Robert Omer Wilson

Robert Omer Wilson

Oral surgeon. Syracuse, N.Y., March 30, 1937, Robert and Isabel (Sandford) Wilson. William Nottingham High School, Syracuse, 1955, Syracuse Univ., A.B., 1959, Univ. of Buffalo School of Dentistry, D.D.S., 1962, Millard Fillmore Hospital, 1962-65. Oral surgeon, Concord, 1965--, chief of dental department, Concord Hospital, 1968-84, clinical instructor, Harvard Univ. School of Dental Medicine, 1969-75, professor of oral pathology, N.H. Technical Institute, Concord, 1970--. President, Concord Dental Society, 1975, N.H. Dental Society, 1981-82, N.H. Society of Oral Surgeons, 1973, director, American Heart Association, N.H. affiliate of A.H.A., 1979-84, president, 1975-77; advisory board, N.H. Technical Institute, 1983--, director, N.H.-Vt. Blue Shield, 1975-84, Indian Head National Bank, Concord, 1974-84, N.H. Savings Bank, 1985--, trustee, Tilton School, 1984--, N.H. Historical Society, 1981--, president, 1985--; member, Advisory Commission on Health and Welfare, 1968-73, chairman, 1970-73; Concord Zoning Board, 1968--, chairman, 1974--; president, Rotary Club of Concord, 1977-78, Greater Concord Chamber of Commerce, 1970-71, campaign chair, United Way of Merrimack County, 1985. Jill (Coldren), July 21, 1962. Andrew, July 25, 1964. Benjamin, Jan. 27, 1968, Abigail, May 23, 1971. Methodist. 10 Kensington Rd., Concord.

Stephen White Winship

Editor, publisher, writer. Concord, N.H., Aug. 29, 1919, Kendall and Rose (White) Winship. Concord High School, 1937, Dartmouth College, A.B., 1941, Columbia Univ., 1945-46. U.S. Navy, 1941-45, lieut. *Herald Tribune*, New York and Paris, copy boy, reporter, correspondent, assistant city editor, 1946-51, freelance European correspondent, 1952-55, co-editor, *N.H. Notables*, 1955-56, Stephen W. Winship & Co., magazine, book publisher, (founded *N.E. Guide*, 1957), Concord, 1956-80, editor, *Forest Notes*, Society for the Protection of N.H. Forests, 1981-83, columnist, *Concord Monitor*, 1983--. Publications committee, Society for the Protection of N.H. Forests, 1961-65, co-founder, director, Regional Publishers Association, 1963-68, president, 1963-64; Citizens Task Force, 1969-70, chairman, N.E. Winter Sports Conference, 1971-72, co-founder, director, N.H. Travel Council, 1973--, alumni trustee, *Daily Dartmouth*, 1978--, Concord Bicentennial Commission, 1975-76, president, Concord Community Concerts, 1964-68, chairman, Hopkinton History Committee, 1984--, co-founder, director, Everett Arena, 1964-80, chairman, Common Cause-N.H., 1983. Author, *At the Bend in the River*, 1965. Lucy (Hawkes), Nov. 28, 1971. St. ch., Fay, June 7, 1945, Betsey, April 26, 1947, Peter, June 20, 1949. Protestant. Jewett Rd., Hopkinton.

Stephen White Winship

Richard Whittier Withington

Auctioneer. Jamaica Plain, Boston, Mass., March 31, 1918, Frank and Edith (Nelson) Withington. Kimball Union Academy, Meriden, 1937, Univ. of N.H., 1937-39. U.S. Army, 1942-46, sgt. Auctioneer, 1934--, president, treasurer, Richard W. Withington Inc., Hillsboro, 1949--. Founder, Valley Bank, Hillsboro, 1973, president, chairman, 1973--; trustee, Concord Hospital, 1979-84, Monadnock Community Hospital, 1966--, N.H. House of Rep., 1971-76, Hillsboro School Board, 1948-51, trustee of trust funds, Hillsboro, 1965--, president, Hillsboro Businessman's Association, 1948-49, founder, Hillsboro Medical Center, 1978. Mary (McClure), Jan. 13, 1942 (dec. Sept. 19, 1980). Nancy, Feb. 6, 1946, Janet, Oct. 6, 1948, Richard Jr., Oct. 7, 1952, Robert, April 27, 1955. Joan (Oak), Jan. 4, 1981. Protestant. RD 2, Box 440, Hillsboro.

Rawson Lyman Wood

Conservationist. New York, N.Y., Sept. 16, 1908, Rawson and Teresa (Schwab) Wood. St. George's School, Newport, R.I., 1926, Harvard Univ., A.B., 1930. President, Arwood Corp., Rockleigh, N.J., 1945-70, chairman, 1970-76; president, ArtCarved Inc., N.Y.C., 1960-64, chairman, 1964-70. Director, Lenox Inc., 1970-80, advisory council, Columbia Univ. School of Social Work, 1964-69, director, N.Y. Urban League, 1967-72, member, Merrimack River Flood Control Commission, 1981-85, Governor's Council on Environment, 1980-82, director, National Audubon Society, 1967-73,83--, president's council, 1980-83; trustee, Audubon Society of N.H., 1975--, chairman, Loon Committee, 1976--; Lakes Region Planning Commission, 1975-84, chairman, North American Loon Fund, 1978--, trustee, N.H. Association of Conservation Commissions, 1974-78, Marlboro School of Music, 1974--, Boston Ballet, 1980-84. Three honorary degrees. Elizabeth (Ford), Oct. 10, 1931. Sheila, Feb. 1, 1933, Ellen, Jan. 20, 1936, Lyman, June 24, 1937, Carolyn, Jan. 23, 1943, Hilary, April 15, 1950. Catholic. High Haith Rd., Center Harbor.

Rawson Lyman Wood

Marian Davis Woodruff

Marian Davis Woodruff

Education director, Currier Gallery of Art. Boston, Mass., Dec. 15, 1922, Harvey and Alice (Rohde) Davis. Milton (Mass.) Academy, 1941, Smith College, A.B., 1945, Institute of Fine Arts, N.Y.C., 1945-46. Lecturer, Museum of Art, Rhode Island School of Design, 1946-51, supervisor of education, Currier Gallery of Art, Manchester, 1962-66, program director, Nashua Arts and Science Center, 1968-69, director of education, Currier Gallery, 1970--. Adjunct instructor in fine arts, White Pines College, 1979-81, state council, League of N.H. Craftsmen, 1978-84, executive committee, N.H. Alliance for Arts Education, 1976-81, state board, United Health Systems Agency, 1971-81, director, Nashua Youth Council, 1974-80, League of N.H. Craftsmen Foundation, 1984--, Nashua Conservation Commission, 1978-80, N.H. House of Rep., 1973-76, president, Randolph Mountain Club, 1975-76, grants reviewer, Institute of Museum Services, Washington, D.C., 1985--. Bliss Woodruff, Sept. 21, 1952. N. Rohde, Sept. 5, 1953, William, June 7, 1955, Davis, Aug. 10, 1958 (dec. July 7, 1980), Charlotte, March 25, 1960. Unitarian-Universalist. 587 Maple St., Manchester.

Brinton Webb Woodward

Headmaster, Holderness School. Topeka, Kans., Jan. 16, 1940, Webb and Agnes (Robert) Woodward. Topeka High School, 1958, Univ. of Kans., B.A., 1962, General Theological Seminary, M.Div., 1965. Ordained, Episcopal priest, Dec. 21, 1965. Curate, St. David's Episcopal Church, Topeka, 1965-67, assistant chaplain, chaplain, chairman, theology department, Kent (Conn.) School, 1967-76, headmaster, Holderness School, Plymouth, 1977--. Governing board, Associated Alumni of General Theological Seminary, N.Y.C., 1975-79, National Association of Episcopal Schools, 1971-81, trustee, Squam Lakes Science Center, 1980-85, Sceva Speare Memorial Hospital, 1978-79, incorporator, Spaulding Youth Center, 1978--, director, Nor-East Outdoor Education Centre, 1984--. Brinton III, April 23, 1971, Peter, Dec. 9, 1973. Kathleen (Roberts), July 5, 1985. Episcopal. Holderness School, Plymouth.

Brinton Webb Woodward

Richard Charles Wright

Richard Charles Wright

Magazine publisher. Boston, Mass., April 20, 1942, Charles and Florence (Bourgault) Wright. Laconia High School, 1960, Boston College, B.A., 1969. U.S. Army, 1965-68, 1st lt. Founder, editor, *N.H. Times*, 1971-81, founder, executive editor, *Wood 'n Energy* magazine, 1980-81, publisher, 1981--; publisher, *WoodHeat*, 1984--, founder, publisher, *New Home*, 1985--. Wright Way, Barnstead.

Louis Crosby Wyman

Associate justice, New Hampshire Superior Court. Manchester, N.H., March 16, 1917, Louis E. and Alice (Crosby) Wyman. Brookline (Mass.) High School, 1935, Univ. of N.H., B.S., 1938, Harvard Law School, J.D., 1941. U.S. Naval Reserve, 1942-46, lieut. General counsel, U.S. Senate Committee on Campaign Expenditures, 1946-47, secretary, Sen. Styles Bridges, 1947, counsel, Joint Congressional Committee on Foreign Economic Cooperation, 1948-49, attorney, Manchester, 1949-52, attorney general, N.H., 1953-61, U.S. Congress, First District, 1963-65,67-74, U.S. Senate, 1974-75 (appointed by Gov. Meldrim Thomson Jr. on Dec. 30, 1974 to fill the final three days of the term of retiring Sen. Norris Cotton), associate justice, N.H. Superior Court, 1978--. Chairman, N.H. Commission on Interstate Cooperation, 1953-61, president, National Association of Attorneys General, 1957, member, Ballot Law Commission, 1953-61, N.H. Judicial Council, 1953-61, former chairman, American Bar Association Standing Committee on Jurisprudence and Law Reform. Virginia (Markley), Aug. 20, 1938. Jo Ann, May 27, 1943, Louis E. II, Feb. 4, 1951. Congregational. 121 Shaw Street, Manchester.

Louis Crosby Wyman

Joseph Michael Yukica

Joseph Michael Yukica

Football coach, Dartmouth College, Aliquippa, Pa., May 27, 1931, Joseph and Elizabeth (Holava) Yukica. Lincoln High School, Midland, Pa., 1949, Penn State Univ., B.S., 1954, M.Ed., 1958. Head football coach, teacher, State College (Pa.) High School, 1954-55, Central Dauphin High School, Harrisburg, Pa., 1955-60, teacher, assistant coach, West Chester State College, 1960-61, assistant football coach, Dartmouth College, 1961-65, head football coach, Univ. of N.H., 1966-67, Boston College, 1968-77, Dartmouth College, 1978--. Advisory staff, Wilson Sporting Goods, 1970--, chairman, Muscular Dystrophy Drive, Greater Boston, 1971, head coach, East-West Shrine Classic, 1974, Blue-Gray Classic, 1979. Betty (Rine), Dec. 26, 1959. Joseph, Oct. 19, 1960, James, April 26, 1963, Jackson, Oct. 15, 1964. 19 Lyme Rd., Hanover.

Kimon Stephen Zachos

Attorney. Concord, N.H., Nov. 20, 1930, Stephen and Sophia (Bacogiannis) Zachos. Concord High School, 1948, Wesleyan Univ., B.A., 1952, N.Y.U. School of Law, LL.B., 1955, Boston Univ., LL.M., 1969. U.S. Army, 1955-57, spec. 3rd cl. Attorney, Manchester, 1957--. Director, Merchants National Bank, 1967--, First N.H. Banks, 1974--, N.E. Telephone, 1980--, Havenwood Retirement Community, 1977-83, trustee, Currier Gallery of Art, 1967--, president, 1976--; trustee, N.H. College, 1968--, director, N.H. Charitable Fund, 1982--, chairman, 1985--; member, presidential search committee, Univ. of N.H., 1971-72, vice chairman, Manchester Model City Agency, 1967-72, N.H. Constitutional Convention, 1964, N.H. House of Rep., 1969-75. Anne (Colby), July 5, 1959. Ellen, Jan. 17, 1960, Elizabeth, Dec. 23, 1961, Sarah, July 18, 1963. Greek Orthodox. 2093 Elm St., Manchester.

Kimon Stephen Zachos

Victoria Zachos

Former Republican National Committeewoman. Bennington, N.H., July 6, 1929, Stephen and Sophia (Bacogiannis) Zachos. Concord High School, 1947, Concord Commercial College, 1947-48. Vice president, Associated Enterprises Inc., Concord, 1970--. Young Republican National Committeewoman, N.H., 1960-64, assistant chairman, Republican State Committee, 1968-72, Republican National Committeewoman, 1972-80, executive committee, Republican National Committee, 1972-76, member, Defense Advisory Committee on Women in the Services, 1977-80, former director, Concord March of Dimes. Greek Orthodox. 82 Warren St., Concord.

Gerard John Zeiller

State, federal government official, retired. Brooklyn, N.Y., Dec. 24, 1914, Emil and Alice (Piel) Zeiller. Brooklyn Preparatory School, 1933, Univ. of Notre Dame, A.B., 1937. U.S. Army, 1942-46, 1st lt. Veterans Administration Center, White River Junction, Vt., executive assistant, physical medicine rehabilitation, 1950-53, organization and methods examiner, 1953-56, registrar, 1956-60; legislative assistant, Sen. Styles Bridges, 1960-61, executive assistant, Sen. Thomas Dodd, 1962-65, special assistant, Sen. Norris Cotton, 1965-69, commissioner, N.H. Department of Health and Welfare, 1971-73, special assistant, administrator of veterans affairs, Veterans Administration, Washington, D.C., 1973-75. Land development, real estate, 1975--, acting executive director, Alice Peck Day Memorial Hospital, Lebanon, 1978-79, trustee, 1979--, president, 1980-83; bailiff, Lebanon District Court, 1978--, bail commissioner, Hanover, 1981--. Betty (Kaiser), Dec. 20, 1943. Catholic. Poverty Ln., Box 616, West Lebanon.

Gerard John Zeiller

Charles Francis Zell

Charles Francis Zell

Chairman, Treasure Masters Corporation. Harrisburg, Pa., Sept. 7, 1914, Charles Sr. and Mary (Bitner) Zell. William Penn High School, Harrisburg, 1932, Lehigh Univ., B.S., 1938. U.S. Marine Corps, 1942-46, capt. Salesman, Rust Craft Publisher, 1938-42,46-51, divisional sales manager, 1951-58, vice president, sales, 1958-61; president, Treasure Masters Corp., Derry, 1961-83, chief executive officer, chairman, 1985--. Director, Indian Head National Bank, 1973--, Greater Derry Boys Club, 1972-76, president, Derry Rotary Club, 1975-76, executive board, Boy Scouts of America, Daniel Webster Council, 1973--, president, 1978-79; vocational board, Pinkerton Academy, 1975-79, Robert Frost Farmhouse Committee, 1974--, vice president, Forum on N.H.'s Future, 1978-80, district governor, Rotary, 1980-81. Timothy, Nov. 30, 1942, Barry, Nov. 27, 1946, Shirley, March 27, 1948. Helen (Eckstrom), April 29, 1967. St. ch., David Amenrud, Aug. 17, 1940, Brian Amenrud, Feb. 20, 1943. Protestant. Box 346, Derry.

Kenneth Frazier Zwicker

Assistant publisher, *Keene Sentinel*, retired. Brownville, Maine, Aug. 22, 1920, James and Mary (Bartlett) Zwicker. Brownville High School, 1937, Univ. of Maine-Orono, B.A., 1949. U.S. Marine Corps, 1941-45, sgt. Reporter, *Ellsworth* (Maine) *American*, 1949-51, city editor, managing editor, *Bangor* (Maine) *Evening and Sunday Commercial*, 1951-54, managing editor, *Ridgewood* (N.J.) *Herald News and Sunday News*, 1954-55, assistant publisher, *Keene Sentinel*, 1955-81. Granite State Award, Keene State College, 1972. Marilyn (Coy), Jan. 4, 1946. James, Dec. 4, 1946, Kurt, March 10, 1951, Liana, May 11, 1953, Susan, Sept. 20, 1954, Linda, June 23, 1956, Jennifer, Oct. 4, 1957. Unitarian. 99 Hastings Ave., Keene.

Index